FOR MY HUSBAND JOHN L. REZATTO

AND

IN MEMORY OF MY BROTHER J. B. (BENNY) GRAHAM

For Further Information on Mount Moriah Cemetery and Deadwood, see:

Library of Congress Number 89-084829

FENWYN PRESS
Rapid City, South Dakota 57701
12th Printing

TALES OF THE BLACK HILLS

By Helen Rezatto

Art by Rose Mary Goodson

ACKNOWLEDGMENTS

Gratefully, I acknowledge the assistance of many businesses, organizations and individuals. I wish to acknowledge the New York Times Company for their courtesy in allowing me to reprint my May, 1978, article, "The Black Hills: Where the Buffalo Roam in Custer Park." I thank the **Rapid City Journal** for permission to reprint "Legend of the Roses" by Richard B. Hughes; "Story of Black Hills Gold Jewelry" by Alice Gossage; and "Rapid City's Beginning" by John R. Brennan—all from **Holiday Greetings,** 1919-1920. My thanks to Marjorie Yates Price for permission to reprint "Legend of Sylvan Lake" and "Legend of Spearfish Creek," written by her late husband, S. Goodale Price.

Quotations from the following copyrighted works are used by permission of the publishers: **Black Elk Speaks** by John G. Neihardt, University of Nebraska Press, Simon and Schuster Pocket Books; **The Black Hills** or **Last Hunting Grounds of the Dakotahs** by Annie Tallent, Second Edition, The Brevet Press; and **The Jewel Cave Adventure** by Herb and Jan Conn, National Speliological Society.

I am indebted to innumerable people who contributed historical information and expertise and to those who helped in a variety of ways: Dr. Charles Thielen, Dr. Philip Bjork, Dr. Paul Gries and Professor Willard Roberts—all faculty members of the South Dakota School of Mines and Technology, Rapid City; Clara Lobdell, Mr. and Mrs. Trant McGillycuddy; Ruby Lee; Linda Hasselstrom; Harold Shunk; Don Schell; Bob Lee; Irma Klock; Virginia Driving Hawk Sneve; James Dunn; Mabel Brown; Katherine Twomey; Ron Bender; Al Gunther; Herman Red Elk; Marian Hersrud; Corlis Besselievre; Dorothy Hamm; Maxine Mader; Dorothy Ringsrud; Harvey Davis; Jim Gillihan; Sam DeCrory; James Kuehn; Joseph Gullion; Kelvin Van Nuys; Buck and Dorothy Shane; T. W. Westbrook; Herb and Jan Conn; Jeri Fahrni; Chuck and Marjorie McClain, Eileen Roggenthen; Inga D'Almeida; Cindy Reed; Mark Lamphere; Dave Strain; Helen Magee; Jessie Y. Sundstrom; Daryl and Irene Kennison; Earl Chace, and Jim Aplan. Thanks to my family for mixed blessings: Gordon, Arlyne, Gina, John T.; and Brian, Judy, Brett, and Justin—all Rezattos. Finally, I am grateful that adventurous Juanita Young did not desert me on top of Harney Peak when I got cramps in my legs.

I wish to thank the staff of these libraries for their cooperation: Dayton Canady and Bonnie Gardner, South Dakota Historical Resource Center, Pierre, SD; Carol Davis, Sturgis Public Library, Sturgis, SD; Leland D. Case Library for Western Historical Studies, Black Hills State College, Spearfish, SD; Jean Diggins, Reference Librarian, Rapid City Public Library, Rapid City, SD; Gretchen Olson, Crook County Library, Sundance, WY; Doris Williamson, Hot Springs Public Library, Hot Springs, SD; Mary Coffin, Custer County Library, Custer, SD; Thelma Sanito, Phoebe Apperson Hearst Free Library, Lead, SD; Pat Engebretson, Belle Fourche Public Library, Belle Fourche, SD; and again and again, thank you to Marjorie Pontius, Deadwood Carnegie Library and Centennial Archives, Deadwood, SD.

A 21-gun salute to Philip F. McCauley, Curator and Archivist, Devereaux Library, South Dakota School of Mines and Technology, Rapid City, SD, who generously gave invaluable guidance and expert direction to me in my search for suitable illustrations and hard-to-find sources for this book. I also appreciate the professional skills of Daniel Goodart, Photographer at the Media Center, South Dakota School of Mines and Technology, who made excellent copies of photographs and documents, some yellowed with age, from both the Fielder Collection and the Archives of the Devereaux Library.

I am amazed at accommodating Martha Behrendt and grateful beyond measure for her inexhaustible patience, trust and ingenuity as Curator of the Minnelusa Historical Museum, Rapid City, SD. I also acknowledge the assistance of the W. H. Over Museum, University of South Dakota, Vermillion, SD; the Yankton County Historical Museum, Yankton, SD; and the Adams Memorial Museum, Deadwood, SD.

I gladly pay homage to the generosity of those who donated photographs: South Dakota Tourism, Pierre, SD; Rapid City Chamber of Commerce; Deadwood Chamber of Commerce; **Sundance Times,** Sundance, WY; South Dakota Department of Game, Fish and Parks, Pierre, SD; Homestake Mining Company, Lead, SD; the Black Hills and Badlands Association, Sturgis, SD; Landstrom's Original Black Hills Gold Creations, Rapid City, SD; and the Bemidji Area Chamber of Commerce, Bemidji, MN. I also award kudos to the United States Forest Service, Custer, SD, for graciously answering many questions and for providing me with specialized information.

More than three cheers for generous individuals who loaned me photographs from their private collections: Jeri Fahrni, Edwald Hayes, Gloria and Warren Anderson, Helen Magee, Joseph Gullion, Kelvin Van Nuys, Dr. Leland Michael, Clara Lobdell, Linfred Schuttler, and Herb and Jan Conn. An extra cheer to Earl Chace, professional photographer, who made his vast photographic collection available to me.

I am happy, as always, to award plaudits to Rose Mary Goodson for her artwork for the cover and for her excellent map. What a delight it is to work with a creative artist.

Most of all, I am unceasingly grateful to my husband John L. Rezatto for his remarkable patience (usually), genuine interest in my writing projects, invaluable assistance with library research and researching trips. He climbed Bear Butte, explored ghost towns, and waited for me when he would rather have been golfing or reading or watching TV. When the deadline for this book loomed closer and closer, he came out of pleasurable retirement to take over unpleasant household chores, including cooking. Definitely, he is not a male chauvinist. As a result of his kitchen duty, he is well on his way to becoming a gourmet cook. I could never have completed this book without him. Thank you, John.

TABLE OF CONTENTS

PREFACE

When I was a young girl growing up in a prairie town in North Dakota, I enjoyed family vacations in the Black Hills, with my mother keeping us posted by reading aloud from **O'Harra's Handbook of the Black Hills.** How wonderful it was for a flatlander to be transported to a paradise of pine-forested mountains, rollicking creeks and ghost towns with gold dust shimmering in the clear air.

Now that I have lived in the Black Hills for seven years, I continue to be impressed with their scenic beauty, legends, and accessibility. An island oasis in a sea of grass, the Paha Sapa of the Sioux Indians, the new El Dorado of the gold-seekers, a geologist's paradise—yes, the Black Hills have been described in many ways. One oft-repeated observation is that they offer more variety than any area of comparable size in the world. I believe it.

Certainly, they offer more exciting history than one would expect in an area about 100 miles long and 50 miles wide. That history is both fascinating and contradictory, providing as many mazes to get lost in as do the caves that underlie the Black Hills. What a challenge it is to try to unravel and comprehend and communicate their past.

This collection of tales is not meant to be a formal history; perhaps it may be properly classified as an informal history of the Black Hills. Of course it is incomplete; it could easily be ten times as long.

Naturally, I have had to depend on the writings of professional and amateur historians, both white and Indian. Many accounts are often conflicting and mystifying; a case in point is the mystery and confusion surrounding the hanging of Lame Johnny, notorious horse thief, who allegedly robbed the Sidney-Deadwood stagecoach. Most of the primary sources about early days in the Black Hills were written by pioneers who didn't get around to writing their reminiscences until many years after the events they describe had taken place. All of these memoirs are interesting and informative although their reliability is often questionable.

The more I try to make sense out of history, the more convinced I become that "History is only a confused heap of facts," and that most

Black Hills history should be labeled "legend." A legend is generally defined as a story coming down from the past, especially one popularly taken as historical although not verifiable by historical record. Too numerous not to mention are the many versions of the lives of Wild Bill Hickok and Calamity Jane. Those two have become legends—and that's a fact.

Dependent on multiple sources from the past, I certainly cannot guarantee that my accounts are genuine history, the real thing at last. These are my own interpretations which I have tried to research and write from an honest and objective viewpoint. I make no claim to absolute authenticity.

I have used reprints of five uncopyrighted legends and a firsthand account of "Rapid City's Beginning" instead of rewriting them myself and tampering with the flavor of the originals. I have also retold many tales myself.

The careful reader will note that I have told her/him certain facts several times: Harney Peak is the highest peak east of the Rock Mountains; the Custer Expedition of 1874 officially discovered gold at French Creek in the southern Black Hills; the Laramie Treaty of 1868 has been the basis for long-lasting conflict between the whites and the Sioux Indians. The reason for this repetition is that I assume most readers will not read straight through all of these tales, each one complete in itself; therefore, the casual, now-and-then reader may need to be reminded from time to time of pertinent information which makes a particular account more meaningful.

In one way or another, I have been researching this book since I became a Black Hills pioneer of '76—1976. Even though I haven't found any "fairy gold," I have been rewarded in other ways. I have been amazed at the helpfulness and trust of librarians, museum curators, and friendly natives who freely loaned me their rare books and priceless photographs without even asking to see my driver's license or knowing how to pronounce my name. Very seldom did I ask a question without getting a good answer, even if it contradicted the last answer recorded in my notebook. I certainly had fun meeting many talkative Black Hillers, curious tourists, and lively ghosts along the historic trails.

This book includes a number of oft-told tales. Who would dare write a book without including Wild Bill Hickok and Calamity Jane and Poker Alice? However, to my knowledge, this is the first book that presents a wide variety of Black Hills tales under one cover. I have given prominence to several illustrious pioneers whom other regional writers have neglected: Dr. Valentine McGillycuddy, Alice Gossage, Dr. Cleophas O'Harra and others. Also included are many legends, both Indian and white, which have not received as much attention as I think they deserve.

Here, Dear Reader, for what I hope is your reading pleasure, is a potpourri of old favorites retold and of new subjects spiced with a mixture of fresh ingredients. These tales are presented by a captive tourist whose naturalization papers are being processed so I can become a bona fide Black Hills Pioneer.

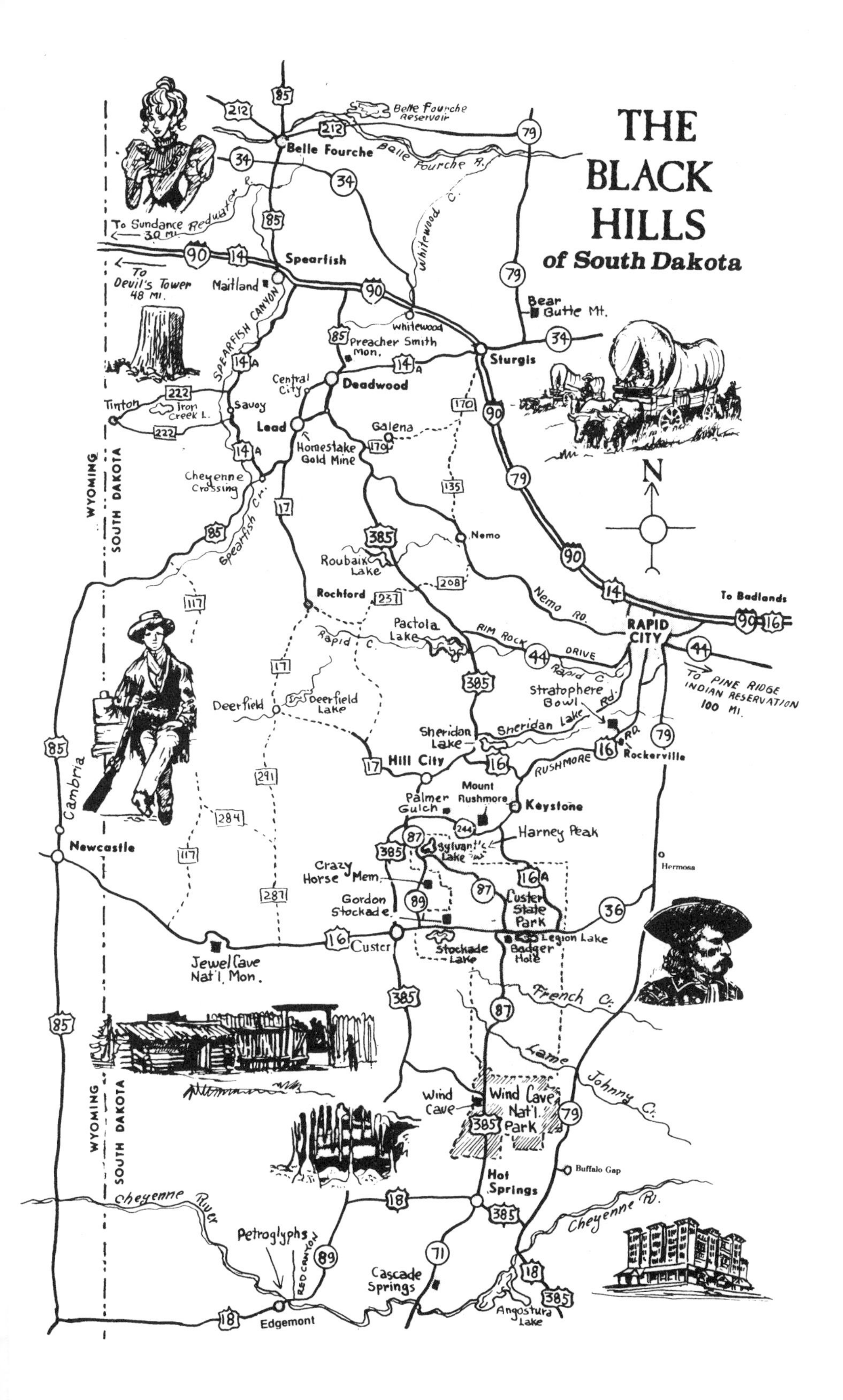
THE BLACK HILLS
of South Dakota
Belle Fourche Reservoir
Belle Fourche
Belle Fourche R.
Redwater R.
To Sundance 30 MI.
Spearfish
To Devil's Tower 48 MI.
Maitland
Whitewood C.
Whitewood
Bear Butte Mt.
Spearfish Canyon
Preacher Smith Mon.
Sturgis
Central City
Deadwood
Tinton
Iron Creek L.
Savoy
Lead
Homestake Gold Mine
Galena
Cheyenne Crossing
Spearfish Cr.
Nemo
Roubaix Lake
Rochford
Nemo Rd.
To Badlands
Rapid City
Pactola Lake
Rapid C.
Rim Rock Drive
To Pine Ridge Indian Reservation 100 MI.
Stratophere Bowl
Deerfield
Deerfield Lake
Sheridan Lake
Sheridan Lake Rd.
Rockerville
Hill City
Rushmore Rd.
Cambria
Mount Rushmore
Palmer Gulch
Keystone
Harney Peak
Sylvan Lake
Newcastle
Hermosa
Crazy Horse Mem.
Gordon Stockade
Custer State Park
Legion Lake
Custer
Stockade Lake
Badger Hole
Jewel Cave Nat'l. Mon.
French C.
Lame Johnny C.
Wind Cave
Wind Cave Nat'l. Park
Buffalo Gap
Hot Springs
Wyoming
South Dakota
Cheyenne River
Cheyenne R.
Petroglyphs
Red Canyon
Cascade Springs
Angostura Lake
Edgemont

I.
INDIAN LEGENDS

THE PAHA SAPA AND THE BLACK HILLS

Since the first Indian tribes migrated west of the Missouri River, the Black Hills have been the source of many legends and the basis for much Indian lore. One charming tale is that the Great Spirit had reserved the Paha Sapa with its glittering treasures and beautiful scenery as a temporary resting place for the spirits of departed warriors, thus preparing their eyes for the dazzling splendors of the Happy Hunting Ground. Then when confronted with the brilliance of paradise, the warriors would not be blinded, for they had already seen the Black Hills.

The Sioux Winter Count, a pictographic record of events in the nature of a calendar, shows the discovery of the Black Hills in 1776 and illustrated by a drawing of an Indian holding out a pine tree. By the process of association, the Sioux remembered that particular year because of one significant event: Chief Standing Bull had visited the Black Hills and brought back a pine tree.

An Indian holding a pine tree depicts the discovery of the Black Hills in 1776 by Chief Standing Bull who led a war party of Oglala Sioux into the region. He carried home with him a sample pine tree which his tribe had never seen before. This pictorial reminder of the year 1776 is on the winter count begun by American Horse. *Picture credit—Rose Mary Goodson.*

The Missouri River Count, an example of an Indian calendar, was painted on a prepared animal skin. The Count starts about 1790 after the Sioux discovered the Black Hills and does not show the Indian with the pine tree. At the Sioux Indian Museum in Rapid City, SD. *Photo credit —South Dakota State Historical Society.*

Before 1776, when Black Hills history began, Indian tribes who lived in and around the Black Hills were the Crows, Kiowas, and Cheyennes. When the possessive Sioux, moving westward, reached the area, they drove out other tribes; and today the Sioux still claim the Black Hills as their own.

The Sioux Indians (also called Dakota) named these mountains "Paha Sapa" meaning "hills that are black" because from a distance their pine-forested slopes look dark and somber. One Sioux belief was that the silhouette of the Hills resembled the figure of a reclining female from whose breasts flowed life-giving powers, an earth mother who held her Indian children protectively in her arms.

The Indians knew about gold in the Black Hills long before the white invaders did. The Indians used the gold-flecked stones as sacred objects to protect the wearers and bring them good luck, never to be traded. They could never understand why gold drove white men crazy.

Indians have always been fascinated with the natural phenomena of the region; they knew about the curative powers of the warm springs in the southern Hills. Each year tribes traveled great distances to treat their illnesses in the healing waters and to marvel at the ancient picture-painting on the rock walls in Red Canyon.

A petroglyph, presumably made by prehistoric man, in Red Canyon north of Edgemont, SD. This one has been named "Coronado's Map." Note the cross. Many petroglyphs decorate the walls of Red Canyon and Craven Canyon. *Photo credit—Joseph Gullion.*

The Indians loved and revered the beauty of the Hills: the pure water in the cool sparkling streams, the aged rocks, the whispering pines. They prayed to the sun, moon, stars, rocks and trees, thus communicating through nature with Wakan, the Great Spirit who ruled the world.

The Indians loved and revered the beauty of the Black Hills: the pure water in the cool sparkling streams, the aged rocks, the whispering pines. *Photo credit—Earl Chace.*

During the Moon of Changing Seasons the Indians thought the haze over the Hills was smoke from the Great Spirit's pipe of peace which puffed mistily when all was serene. To the Sioux, the sacred Paha Sapa were charged with mystery and supernatural power; they were a sacred shrine, a wilderness temple, an awesome sanctuary where spirits dwelt.

However, the Sioux did not actually live within the Hills—and the white man makes that assertion more often than the Indian does. Usually Indians camped within sight of the enchanted mountains in the sheltered and watered valleys around the edge of the Hills. They did most of their hunting in the wide-open plains and foothills where game was most plentiful. Occasionally, they ventured into the dense forests of the rock-bound Hills to cut lodge poles from the tall pines. But the Sioux never stayed long.

In the dark of night, even the rocks in the Hills turned into spirits who sang weird melodies. Hidden beneath the ground were crystal caves with grotesque formations, changeable winds, and echoing caverns. Many were the fearful noises that shrieked and thundered and howled.

Throughout the nineteenth century, the Indians, as well as many early white explorers, often described deep rumbling sounds in the Hills which frightened all who heard them. Naturally, the highest peaks were the home of the gods, particularly of the dreaded Thunder Bird, an enormous black bird with loud roaring wings and lightning flashing from his fierce yellow eyes. Another tale was that the sounds of the Thunder Bird's eggs hatching created the thunder.

From the highest peak named Harney, this supernatural bird with terrifying powers created violent storms, swooping down upon the Hills while shooting tongues of lightning, hurling thunderbolts, and whipping up violent winds blowing every which way. When very angry, the Thunder Bird yanked trees up by their roots, splintered their trunks with his lightning, often causing forest fires to rage endlessly.

The summit of Harney Peak. The Sioux believed that this highest mountain in their Paha Sapa was the home of the gods. The dreaded Thunder Bird lived here who created violent storms and flashed lightning from his fierce yellow eyes. *Photo credit—South Dakota Tourism and Rapid City Chamber of Commerce.*

Another interpretation of thunder storms was that the noise was caused by Evil People tramping around in the sky, and lightning was the fire arrows of the Evil One. Or perhaps a countless number of fluttering young birds caused the muffled sound of distant thunder. It was the Thunder Bird who gave the signal sound and the young mischievous birds repeated it by beating their wings, thus reverberating thunder from peak to peak and frightening all the mortals who heard it.

Legend has it that one peak was always on fire and could be seen from a great distance. A large column of smoke whirled from it, day after day. Indians thought the smoke to be the breathing of the giant white man who was buried alive beneath the mountain. The awful noises were the moans of that white giant whose fate was to be eternally crushed by rocks.

The Indians buried him there as punishment for being the first white man to invade the sacred land of the Sioux. In the winter he sometimes staggered forth from his mountain tomb, leaving tracks in the snow twenty feet in length. He was imprisoned on the mountain for all eternity as a warning to white men to leave the Indians in possession of their hunting grounds and the dwelling places of the spirits.

The white man has no ancient legends about the Black Hills, and most of his modern ones are about gold. However, modern scientists have agreed upon the theories of their origin.

The Black Hills, one of the world's oldest mountain ranges, existed long before the formation of the Alps, Himalayas, or the Rocky Mountains. Once at the bottom of an inland sea, the Black Hills region, in the distant Mesozaic age was the home of dinosaurs and other prehistoric monsters.

Millions of years ago, the bowels of the earth erupted and thrust upward the mountainous mass known today as the Black Hills. Countless centuries of geologic violence and erosion have created peaks, cliffs, and canyons, filling them with precious minerals; and nature has decorated them with pine forests.

This elliptical, dome-like area of 4,500 square miles, about 100 miles long and 50 miles wide, lies today in western South Dakota and eastern Wyoming. White people have often described these mysterious mountains as an island oasis rising in a sea of prairie grass.

"A geologist's paradise" is a popular name because the prehistoric upheaval turned everything upside down; now exposed on the topsy-turvy surface of the landscape are the deepest and oldest rocks and fossils. To the geologist, the rock strata encircling the Hills reveal the ancient story of the earth's formation.

Sometimes the ancient legends and the modern theories blend and support each other in a way pleasing to both races, red and white. Often, they do not.

The legend of the punished white man dramatizes the hereditary hatred of the Sioux Indians for the treaty-breaking encroachment of the white race in the Black Hills; their anger at the ruination of the ancestral hunting grounds surrounding the Hills; and their continuing protestations to the white take-over of their sacred Paha Sapa.

Today, in the latter part of the twentieth century, especially during the summer months, even white people have heard the Thunder Bird cursing and roaring to himself and the universe. Or could it be the punished white man groaning loudly in his mountain grave? These disturbing noises cannot be explained away as ordinary thunder, nor as mining explosions, nor as tourist cars rumbling along the highways.

Yes, legends in the Black Hills do live forever.

LEGEND OF THE RACE TRACK

The Race Track is the name both the Cheyennes and the Lakota Sioux gave to the red valley that encircles the Black Hills just inside the hogback ridges (or cuestas) that form a rampart around the entire Hills area. Here long ago in this natural pathway of reddish earth and rocks, the four-leggeds and the two-leggeds had a momentous race.

The Cheyennes believed that in ancient times the animals and people lived harmoniously together on earth until they started eating one another. The biggest problem over flesh-eating existed between man and the buffalo. The Great Spirit decided it would be helpful to have a race which would decide whether the buffalo should eat the people or the people, the buffalo.

Thus, the Great Spirit summoned all the creatures of the earth to assemble at a place east of the Black Hills on the race track. The starting point was near the area the white men later named Buffalo Gap.

The buffalo, bears, deer, antelope, wolves, mountain goats, coyotes, magpies, crows, hawks—all the four-legged animals and two-legged birds of the earth arrived to enter the race. The birds were racing on the side of the people. The Indians, who had so much at stake, did not race; they were watchers.

To prepare for the race, the animals and birds painted themselves with different colors. The meadow lark said: "I shall paint the moon on my breast." And it has been there ever since. The crow and the magpie blackened themselves with charcoal. The mountain goat decided on pure white. And so on—until each of the racers was painted decoratively.

The buffalo herd chose a buffalo cow named Slim Walking Woman to run for them. The buffalo lined up on one side; the rest of the animals on the other, with the birds hovering overhead. The Cheyennes offered a prayer for the two-leggeds to win. While they were all lining up, there was a deafening noise because each animal was making its own sound and each bird uttering its individual cry. There was much talking; almost everyone thought that the prancing, light-footed deer or the quick coyote would win.

A wolf and a coyote, howling in unison, gave the starting signal for the race to begin. The animals began to run at top speed on the race track and

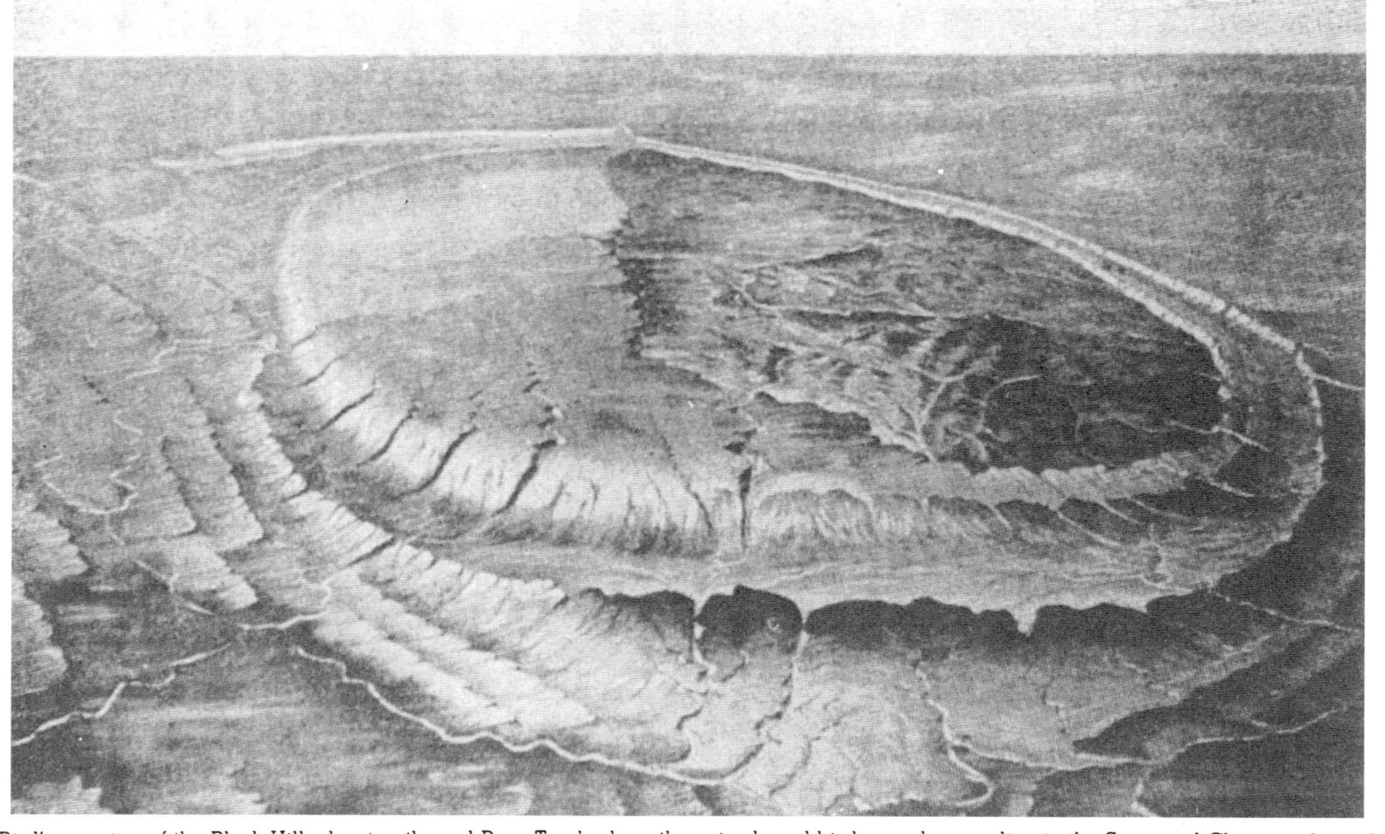

Bird's-eye view of the Black Hills showing the red Race Track where the animals and birds raced, according to the Sioux and Cheyenne legends. Drawn by Henry Newton after the exploration of the Black Hills by the Jenney-Newton Expedition of 1875. From the **Topographical and Geological Atlas of the Black Hills of Dakota**. *Photo credit—Fielder Collection, Devereaux Library, South Dakota School of Mines and Technology.*

In the Cheyenne legend of the momentous race between the two-leggeds and the four-leggeds, many of the participants thought that the prancing light-footed deer would win. *Photo credit—Rapid City Chamber of Commerce.*

the birds flew fast overhead. The Great Spirit had ordered that the racers must run or fly all around the race track, no matter how long it took.

At first Slim Walking Woman galloped ahead of the rest with a little bird flying close beside her. Although the other contestants were running and flying hard, they were far behind the first two. Then Slim Walking Woman began to tire and slowed to a walk even though the other buffalo were shouting encouragement to her. So much froth came from Slim Walking Woman's mouth that there are yet many places on the race track where the ground is white and frothy. The little bird's wings flapped slowly. The prancing deer and the quick coyote became so exhausted that their legs scarcely moved. Many animals bled from the mouth and nose, staining the earth in many places, and the ground is still red from their blood.

No one paid much attention to the lowly magpie, the slowest of birds. He was flying along steadily, conserving his strength.

Then the swift hawk, flying hard, passed the magpie, but at last the hawk too grew tired. One by one, the animals and birds dropped out of the race to rest, long before they reached the last lap.

Steadfastly, the magpie kept going; and when the end was in sight, he rose high in the air, then swooped down dramatically where the race had started. The magpie had won the race for the two-leggeds. The air was soon filled with joyful birds that fluttered and floated and soared in ecstasy, and these winged two-leggeds warbled and shrieked and cried, each singing his own song in honor of the magpie winning the race. And the two-legged Indians gave thanks to the Great Spirit.

When the animals straggled in from the race, they went sadly back to their homes. But each animal and bird was allowed to keep the same colorful decoration forever, the one with which he had painted himself.

The buffalo and the split-hoof animals slunk away, their heads hanging, because they knew they would never again be the equal of man. The

The Great Spirit of the Cheyennes decided to hold a race on the red Race Track surrounding the Black Hills which would decide whether the buffalo should eat the people or the people, the buffalo. *Photo credit—Paul Jones.*

Cheyennes from that time forward were entitled to eat the flesh of the buffalo. And when the Indians approached the buffalo with bows and arrows, the animals always tried to escape, knowing they would be killed for food, shelter, and clothing.

Never did the Cheyennes eat the magpie for he had won the race for the two-leggeds. Nor did they eat the swift hawk who had done his best.

The Great Spirit spoke in a voice of thunder to the magpie: "Because you were wise and had a plan, you were able to win the race for all your

The Great Spirit spoke in a voice of thunder to the magpie: "Because you were wise and had a plan, you were able to win the race for all your relatives, the two-leggeds of the air and of the ground." Never again did the Cheyennes eat the magpie. *Photo credit—Earl Chace.*

After the momentous race, the Cheyennes decided never again to eat the swift hawk because he had done his best to win the race for the two-leggeds. *Photo credit—Earl Chace.*

relatives, the two-leggeds of the air and of the ground. You shall from this time forward wear the rainbow in your tail as a sign of victory."

And to this day, the swooping magpie with the flashing rainbow tail is the special bird of the Black Hills.

****

Although the Lakota Sioux legend of the race track is similar to the Cheyenne version, it has some striking differences. It was not the Great Spirit but man himself who decided to settle the problem of whether buffalo should eat man or man, the buffalo, by having a race. All the animals and birds of the world were summoned to run and fly in the race on the prairie flatlands known as Island Hill, long before there was any uplift called the Black Hills. At this ancient time, huge animals roamed the earth and giant insects, large as eagles, clouded the air.

One of the purposes of the race was to divide up the animals, according to smell, into their logical species.

The excited animals and birds crowded the race track to begin. There were so many runners that the larger animals crushed and trampled the smaller ones who howled and squealed in pain. The birds screeched overhead to add to the din. All the contestants started the race by running as hard as they could. Soon the seething mass of animals, maddened with fatigue and hunger, circled the track like a hypnotized serpent chasing its tail. Clouds of dust from the pounding hooves rose into the air, choking and blinding the birds.

Before they could finish the race, a grotesque bulge began rising out of the earth. The ground groaned and shook and rumbled. Then the bulge exploded with a thunderous roar, and into the air spewed flames, smoke, and lava which fell upon the horrified racers and killed every single one. The Great Spirit, for an unknown reason, had brought about a curse, the Lakotas believed.

When the atmosphere cleared, lo and behold, there was a mountain of jagged rocks rising magnificently above the smoldering circle of dead animals and birds lying on the race track.

And that is how a violent upheaval created the Black Hills, according to Lakota legend. It was at this ancient time that the Lakota decided to call these magnificent mountains "Paha Sapa" or Black Hills.

Because the Great Spirit brought down a curse before the race was finished, the winners were not known. But at the time the grotesque bulge erupted, the magpie was ahead of the other birds; and the "Unkche Ghila," a dinosaur, whom no one living has ever seen, was far ahead of the animals.

This must be true for the mammoth bones of the dinosaur are still found protruding from the red earth of the race track or buried in the plains north and east of the Black Hills.

Bear Butte, the most historic place in the Black Hills, has been a landmark for man for over 4,000 years; first for many Indian tribes, and later for white explorers soon followed by military expeditions, wagon trains, and stagecoaches. *Photo credit—Deadwood Chamber of Commerce.*

THE MANY LEGENDS OF BEAR BUTTE

Bear Butte, the most historic place in the Black Hills, has been a landmark for man for over 4,000 years: first for many Indian tribes, and later for white explorers soon followed by military expeditions, wagon trains, and stagecoaches. With an elevation too high to be a butte, it is actually a mountain 4,425 feet high, rising 1,400 feet above the grassy plains; and located about six miles east of the Black Hills proper near the town of Sturgis and close to Fort Meade Veterans Adminstration Hospital, once a frontier military post.

Fort Meade, Dakota Territory was established in 1878 to protect settlers from the Indians. Shadowy Bear Butte six miles in the distance. *Photo credit—#1202. Grabill photo, 1888, South Dakota State Historical Society.*

Bear Butte has often been described as a sentinel because of its isolated location apart from the Black Hills range. Its scientific name is laccolith, a volcano that didn't quite make it to the eruption stage. Geologists believe that the eroded mountain with many of its slopes covered with talus debris is at least forty million years old. It is one of the most interesting laccoliths to study anywhere in the world because the volcanic core is visible on such a large scale.

Frequently described as a replica of the Black Hills in miniature, Bear Butte, although balding on its slopes, has a pine forest on its crown. There are also gushing springs, innumerable caves, craggy peaks, fossilized rocks, green valleys, and unusual plant life—the diverse scenic beauty similar to the Hills themselves.

Numerous are the explanations of how Bear Butte got its name, the most common being that it resembles a sleeping bear from either north or south and even from the east and southwest. Some imaginative viewers say the bear is sleeping on his belly; others say that he is lying on his back.

An oft-repeated legend describes how a huge bear sneaked into an Indian camp when all the braves were out hunting. He entered a tepee and grabbed a sleeping papoose in his mouth. The cries of the baby aroused all the mothers in the camp who ran screaming after the bear, hoping he would drop the child. But the swift bear climbed back up the steep mountainside and disappeared. Neither the bear nor the papoose was ever seen again. Thus, the lone mountain was christened Bear Butte. Indian mothers told this tragic tale over and over to their children to warn them of the many bears that lived in the region.

The Lakota Sioux believe that in ancient times a huge bear and a Unkche Ghila (a dinosaur) had a terrible battle which lasted for days. The monsters fought so fiercely that rivers of blood flowed into the valley. At last the dinosaur with his enormous claws and jagged teeth wounded the bear so severely that he crawled away to die. While the bear suffered his death agonies, the earth erupted and darkness descended. Fire and ashes spewed out of a volcano; water and mud spouted into the sky. Then as quickly as the chaos had begun, it ceased. The air became clear and calm again. The dying bear had disappeared; instead, there was a high mound, still smoldering and rumbling, reaching to the sky. Thus, Bear Butte became the burial place for the prehistoric bear who sleeps beneath its steep slopes, the outline of his body clearly visible.

Another story is that a momentous event occurred when a holy Sioux named Crazy Horse climbed Bear Butte to fast and pray for a vision. His prayer was answered: Wakantanka, the Great Spirit, appeared to him in the form of a bear. Because of the Indian's bravery in facing what looked like a ferocious animal, the Great Spirit promised to endow him with powers to overcome all obstacles and to vanquish all enemies.

Crazy Horse, who was then in his declining years and thought himself unworthy, asked humbly if he could bestow this wonderful spiritual gift on his promising young son Curly to accept as a sacred obligation to his people. The Great Spirit granted the father's request who later changed the name of his son to Crazy Horse.

From that time forward, the young Crazy Horse went into training to become the leader of his people, the Sioux. And because of the elder Crazy Horse's vision of the Great Spirit disguised as a bear, the mountain was called Bear Butte forevermore.

Whatever the true explanation of how this amazing mountain received its name, as early as 1835, the Sioux called it Mato Paha, meaning "Bear Mountain or Hill."

The Lakota believed that young couples who mated at Bear Butte were likely to be blessed with twins who alone possessed the secret to the phenomenon of reincarnation. Still haunted by echoes from old Indian camps on Bear Butte are the modern Lakota who hear sounds of children playing and of dogs barking. These echoes of long ago sadden the Indians.

Bear Butte has been the physical source and the mystical inspiration for many Indain legends and has had deep religious significance for several Indian tribes, especially the Cheyenne and the Lakota Sioux.

Even the Mandan Indians who lived in earth lodges on the Upper Missouri in what is now North Dakota had a flood myth in which the lone survivor of their tribe (inexplicably a white man) was able to moor his canoe and disembark safely on a "high mountain in the west," identified as Bear Butte by historians, both white and Indian. Consequently, for many years the Mandans made yearly pilgrimages to Bear Butte to make sacrifices of edged tools because it was these tools which had created the big canoe, their offering thus assuring the Mandans that no more floods would threaten to destroy their tribe.

However, it is the Cheyennes whose ancient religion, said to be two or three thousand years old, who have had the closest association with Bear Butte until the Teton Sioux eventually forced them out of the Bear Butte region.

The Cheyennes were there in the eighteenth century and Sweet Medicine became their prophet. He had grown up an orphan boy exiled from the tribe for committing a murder in self-defense. Eventually, a mysterious god on Bear Butte summoned Sweet Medicine into his cave and offered him the Four Sacred Arrows which became the most revered fetish of the Cheyennes. The god also presented Sweet Medicine with four commandments:

1. Thou shalt not kill.
2. Thou shalt not steal.
3. Thou shalt not commit adultery.
4. Thou shalt not marry your own relatives.

Then the god commanded Sweet Medicine and his wife to stay four more years on Bear Butte to receive instructions about this religion, after which he should then take his message to the Cheyennes who were becoming corrupt and needed guidance.

The Cheyenne religion is based on the number four: four sacred arrows; four commandments; four-day and four-night fasts with four men who hoped to receive visions and predictions of future life.

From Bear Butte came another Cheyenne artifact, the first shield for warfare, made from the shrunken neck hide of a buffalo with special protective powers for the wearer. Historians have credited the Cheyennes with the origin of the Sun Dance ritual of the Plains Indians and believe that the Sun Dance was first held at Bear Butte.

The Sacred Arrows with their eagle feathers, endowed with magical powers especially in battle, have been handed down from generation to generation. Still used in ceremonies, they are guarded by the Southern Cheyennes in Oklahoma along with the sacred buffalo cap with its two carved horns.

Presumably, only two white men have been permitted to see these sacred artifacts. The first was General George A. Custer on the Washita River in Kansas in 1868; and the second was the late Richard Williams of Sturgis, SD, director of the Visitor Center at Bear Butte, and a great friend of the modern Cheyennes.

Twice in 1945 and again in 1951, descendants of the old Cheyenne leaders returned to Bear Butte to pray for the end to World War II and later for the end of the Korean War.

The Cheyennes, in the 1980's, still come to Bear Butte every year to pray, to fast, and to participate in a vision quest ceremony in a sweat lodge.

The vision quest ceremony of the Cheyenne Indians begins in a sweat lodge made of willow or chokecherry branches which is then covered with blankets and canvas. The stones inside are heated to high temperatures; then water is poured on them. As steam fills the lodge, the worshipper usually prays for several hours while being purified for a four-day fast and prayer ceremony. In the 1980's the Cheyennes return yearly to Bear Butte for religious ceremonies. *Photo credit—South Dakota State Historical Society.*

Both the Cheyenne and the Sioux have complained that when the state of South Dakota began expanding the parking lots and requiring worshipers to register and limiting the time they could stay on the mountain, that their religious freedom was being threatened. Even today the Cheyennes consider Bear Butte as their sacred shrine, called Noavasse meaning "the Good Mountain."

The Sioux Indians, in their relentless movement westward, came to the Bear Butte area on the eastern side of the Black Hills probably a century after the Cheyennes, in about 1776, as recorded on the Winter Count. The Sioux subsequently fought many battles with the Cheyennes for the right to claim the sacred mountain as their own.

The Sioux had a ritual of placing rocks in the forks of trees on Bear Butte for a variety of reasons: to establish claims to the land; to offer prayers to the rocks; to make sacrifices for the dead, to mark the distances traveled; and to worship the phallus. Eventually, the branches have grown around these rocks which now appear to be part of the tree itself.

The Sioux, as had the Cheyennes before them, also held sun dances and scalp dances on Bear Butte's summit.

It was at Bear Butte, in 1857, that the most significant pow-wow of the Plains Indians took place. Known as the Grand Council of the Teton Sioux, this huge sprawling camp included the Seven Council Fires or tribes of the Sioux nation as well as the Cheyennes and other Plains Indians. Forgetting their own differences temporarily, the Indians congregated to strengthen their resistance against the white invaders of their territory. This was the occasion when young Crazy Horse vowed to his father that he would never give up fighting the whites.

The earliest recorded visit of white men to Bear Butte was that of the Verendrye brothers, French-Canadian explorers looking for the Northwest Passage. The Verendryes wintered near the butte in 1742 and probably climbed it. In recent years many people have searched for a lead plate on the mountain's summit, hoping the Verendryes might have left one there as they had on a Missouri river bluff near the present-day city of Pierre, South Dakota.

During the 1830's, many fur traders and mountain men rendezvoused at the distinctive mountain. The first of many scientific expeditions began in 1855 when the noted geologist, Dr. Ferdinand Hayden, became the first recorded white man to climb it.

Perhaps the most famous white man to climb Bear Butte (on his favorite horse Dandy) was General Custer. During the Black Hills Expedition of 1874, he and the 1,200-man expedition camped near the butte.

To this day, many Sioux Indians believe that Custer and his officers violated the sanctity of Bear Butte by climbing it and thus were doomed to die. And they did, two years later at the Little Big Horn. It was also bad

An enactment of the exploration of the Verendrye brothers who are believed to be the first white men to see Bear Butte. Although this picture shows the brothers burying a lead plate, no one has ever found it on Bear Butte. On the left far below is a river course. *Photo credit—South Dakota State Historical Society.*

medicine for Custer and his men to have their photographs taken at their camp with Bear Butte in the background. The Sioux have since pointed out that Illingworth, the official photographer for the expedition, committed suicide a few years later.

Visible for 100 miles, Bear Butte was a landmark and converging point for wagon trains from Fort Pierre and Bismarck in Dakota Territory, and from Sidney, Nebraska, all headed for Deadwood, the lively center of gold rush activity. Annie Tallent, the first white woman in the Black Hills, described in her history how Bear Butte looming in the distance guided the illegal Russell-Collins party invading the Black Hills in 1874, four months after the Custer Expedition had found gold.

From many vantage points on Bear Butte there are spectacular views of the Great Plains and of the Black Hills, especially from the summit where eagles soar. An old lookout point is Chimney Rock, a natural rock formation open at the top and bottom, from which the Indians sent smoke signals warning of an enemy's approach. The Indians often built mammoth fires on the mountain, and this is one reason there are not more forests on its sides.

Artifacts of prehistoric man, dating back 10,000 years, have been found at the Gant Site near Bear Butte. Archeologists have excavated a camp site and found implements used for hunting, butchering, and preparation of hides. Charcoal found in the hearth has been radio-carbon-dated at 2000 B.C.

Today, Bear Butte is a state park and a registered National Natural Landmark. The prehistoric laccolith is now a guide for the flights of jet airplanes. Many people have drunk from the perpetual springs where probably both Custer and Crazy Horse quenched their thirst—at different times.

Visitors of many races and religions have hiked the Summit and Ceremonial Trails of this sacred shrine of the Cheyenne and Sioux Indians. They also feel the spell of Bear Butte when reading the ancient "Sioux Prayer to the Four Winds":

"Great Spirit, I invoke the peace pipe in reverence and gratitude of Thy vast creation, of which I am a part. To the life-giving of Thy servant, the sun and all heavenly bodies, the blue sky, the great everlasting rocks, the magnificent mountains with their fragrant forests, pure streams, and the animal kingdom. We thank Thee for all these gifts."

Visitors used to ride burros to the summit of Bear Butte. Today many hikers ascend the winding trail to the top of the ancient mountain which is really a laccolith, a volcano that didn't quite make it to the eruption stage. *Photo credit—South Dakota State Historical Society.*

LEGEND OF SPEARFISH CREEK

By S. Goodale Price
(Adapted from *Pa-Ha-Sa-Pah, or the Black Hills of Dakota*
by Rev. Peter Rosen)

Long years before the white man came into the Black Hills, two orphan Indians, a brother and his sister, lived alone near the edge of the Hills on the bank of a beautiful stream. The boy was very small and as the years passed he failed to grow large as other chilren do. There had never been a dwarf before among the Sioux Indians and it was whispered among the tribes that the orphan boy was one of those little creatures who haunted the Hills, a Fairy.

Long ago an Indian girl saved her dwarf brother's life by spearing a fish who had swallowed him. Hence the name for beautiful Spearfish Creek which became a fisherman's paradise. *Photo credit —Deadwood Chamber of Commerce.*

One winter day the dwarf boy was playing with a ball along the shores of the stream. Suddenly the ball flew out over the smooth ice and to his surprise the dwarf boy found he could run after it as fast as the ball sped across the ice. The ball went a great distance out on the ice with the boy following until it stopped in the midst of four tall Indians lying on the ice spearing fish. One of the tall Indians seeing the little dwarf, was startled and cried out to his companions, "Hi! brothers, see what a little fellow is here." The

Reprinted from **The Black Hills—Land of Legend**
By S. Goodale Price

Roughlock Falls in Spearfish Canyon. The road to the falls used to be so steep that wagon-drivers had to brake their wheels by chaining them together (called rough-locking) to prevent the wagons from running into the horses. *Photo credit—South Dakota State Historical Society.*

three looked at the dwarf and then went back to their spearing fish. The little fellow thought, "They treat me with contempt because I am so small, but I will show them that I am powerful too."

Quickly picking up a large trout lying on the ice by one of the tall men, he flung his ball shoreward and with the trout in his arms he sped away at a great rate. The tall Indian looked toward his companions and said, "That

Spectacular 20-mile-long Spearfish Canyon now has a modern highway where the railroad tracks used to run beside the creek. *Photo credit—South Dakota State Historical Society.*

A pioneer's log cabin at Hell's Gate near the south entrance to Spearfish Canyon. Today, an unmarked trail leads down Jackass Gulch into Spearfish Canyon. *Photo credit—South Dakota State Historical Society.*

tiny dwarf has stolen my fish, what a shame.'' The dwarf boy took the fish to his sister and bade her cook it for him.

The next day the dwarf boy again flung his ball out on the ice and it rolled into one of the ice holes where the tall Indians were spearing fish. He followed the ball closely and said as he approached the men, ''Friend, hand me my ball.'' ''Indeed I will not,'' replied one of the tall Indians. The dwarf

In 1893, this narrow-gauge train used to stop on the trestle over Spearfish Falls to give the passengers a thrill. Eventually, the Homestake Mining Company diverted the water from the falls into a flume. *Photo credit—Centennial Archives, Deadwood.*

boy grasped the tall Indian by the arm, and broke it in two. He then sped toward his home with the tall Indians following him with loud cries of vengeance.

The dwarf boy ran swiftly to his lodge, which was a cave in a place of rocks, and entering he called to his sister to quickly bring him something to eat. She gave him his dish which was a large turtle shell and as the angry Indians dashed toward the doorway to his lodge the dwarf boy turned the turtle shell upside down and it immediately turned into a large round rock which rolled into the doorway completely closing it. The tall Indians beat upon the heavy rock with their clubs but could not crack it. At length they succeeded in making a small hole into which one of them peeked. The dwarf boy shot his arrow into the Indian's eye and the Indian dropped dead. The others not knowing what had befallen their brother also peeped into the hole and as they did so the dwarf shot them dead. After they were killed the dwarf boy told his sister to go out and see them. She opened the door but fearing they were not dead she turned back to her brother, who went out and hacked them into small pieces, saying, "Henceforth let no man be larger than you are now." So men became their present size.

The following spring the dwarf boy told his sister to make him a new set of arrows which she did, cautioning him not to shoot them into the stream. Disregarding her warning he purposely shot his arrow into the stream and waded in after it crying, "Ma-mis-quam-ge-gum-a, be-wan-wa-coos-zhe-shin," meaning, "You fish come and swallow me." Immediately a monster trout came and swallowed him. As the fish swallowed him he cried to his sister on shore, "Me-zush-ke-zim-ance." She wondered what that meant but thought it must mean an old moccasin, so she quickly tied an old moccasin to a rope, then tied the rope to a strong tree and flung the moccasin out into the stream.

The monster fish said to the dwarf boy, "What is that floating there?" The boy replied, "Go swallow it as quickly as you can." The fish darted toward the floating moccasin and quickly swallowed it. The dwarf boy laughed to himself and took hold of the rope and began to haul himself and the fish rapidly toward the shore, crying to his sister from inside the fish, "Make haste with your spear and release me." His sister did as he bade her, and soon made an opening large enough for her brother to get out.

When he was released, he told his sister to take the spear and cut the fish up and dry it as it would be food for many a day. Thus the beautiful Spearfish Creek derived its name, and so ends the legend.

DEVILS TOWER AND ITS LEGENDARY BEARS

Devils Tower, which some Indian tribes call "Mateo Tepee" meaning Grizzly Bear Lodge, resembles a giant tree stump rising about 1,200 feet above the Belle Fourche River, with an altitude of 5,117 feet above sea level. The majestic landmark dominates the region where the pine-forested foothills of the Black Hills merge with the grassy meadows of the Great Plains in northeastern Wyoming.

During centuries of erosion, the Belle Fourche River has worn away the softer rock on the tower to expose the mass of bare, hard rock underneath. Scientists are still puzzling about the origin of Devils Tower, but the most widely accepted geologic theory is that volcanic action created these extremely hard rocks when molten materials cooled and crystallized—about sixty million years ago. These igneous rocks form the striking polygonal columns on the tower's sides. In eons past, many columns have crashed around the base into huge broken pillars, some large as box cars. The tower is surrounded by tons of talus (rock debris).

A close-up shot of Devils Tower from the west side shows the tons of rock debris around the tower. At an unknown time polygonal columns crashed around the base, some large as box cars. *Photo credit—Grabill photo #3577, South Dakota State Historical Society.*

To explain the tower's origin, many Indian tribes have varying legends all featuring Mato—the bear. The Kiowa legend relates how numerous ferocious bears chased seven frightened little Indian girls. The bears were almost upon them when the girls jumped onto a low rock. One girl prayed, "Rock, have pity on us! Rock, save us!" Thereupon, the obliging Rock began to grow quickly upward, thus pushing the children higher and higher, out of reach of the bears. The girls were pushed up into the heavens where they are now preserved forever, for they were transformed into a group of seven twinkling sister stars, the Pleiades. And the Rock which was their salvation became Devils Tower where vertical scratches made by bear claws are still visible on its sides.

An artist's conception of a grizzly bear climbing Devils Tower to attack the Indians on top. A bear is the main character in many Indian legends about Devils Tower which some Indian tribes call "Mateo Tepee" meaning Grizzly Bear Lodge. *Photo credit*—**Rapid City Journal.**

The Cheyenne legend involves seven brothers who set out to rescue one of their wives from a bear that had carried her away to his cave. The youngest brother turned himself into a gopher and burrowed into the bear's den. The gopher, endowed with supernatural power, put the bear to sleep, then demonstrated to the woman how to crawl through the entrance. The bear awoke and soon led a horde of bears in a chase after the brothers and the fleeing woman.

When the bears were almost upon them, the youngest brother, now himself again, sang a song to the magic rock he always carried. The rock started growing and by the time he had finished singing, the rock was just as high as it is today. The Indians were spirited to safety on top of the magical rock. The seven brothers, from their vantage point, were able to kill all the bears with their bows and arrows—but not before the belligerent animals had left their claw marks on the sides of the rock. The resourceful youngest brother made a noise like a bald eagle. Four bald eagles swooped down. The Indians grasped the eagles' legs, and the birds carried them all safely to the ground from the top of Devils Tower.

A Sioux legend tells of two little Indian boys who were out hunting when they were chased by Mato, the bear. Exhausted, they collapsed on the ground, hoping the bear would not see them. Soon they felt a trembling underneath them, and the ground began rising toward the sky. They were carried along with the growing mountain of rock and found themselves on top of it. Thus, the Great Spirit saved the boys from the angry bear who clawed in vain at the mountain side, leaving gashes in the rock.

The Lakota Sioux add variety to the basic Sioux tale: instead of hungry bears chasing little boys, they are pursuing several little girls who were saved by clambering upon a fast-growing rock which raised them quickly skyward out of reach of the frustrated bears clawing at the sides. The little girls were afraid to open their eyes and look down from the top of their tall sanctuary until they heard the kind voice of Fallen Star instructing them to mount upon the backs of the large, beautiful birds she had sent to rescue them. Then an avalanche of both hard rocks and molten rocks poured down the sides of the new mountain and killed the giant bears. Their claw marks made the deep crevices on the sides of what became known as Mateo Tipilia meaning "Home of the Bears."

Interesting similarities among the Indian legends of various tribes are that in all cases, bears, which were numerous in the area, were motivating forces of evil while the friendly and helpful birds, who were two-leggeds like human beings, came to the aid of endangered Indians. In each legend the tower was created by growing with supernatural speed into a towering monolith with claw marks on its sides.

An intriguing point in the Lakota legend is the mention of molten rocks, which, at least in the minds of white people, is associated with the volcanic action that created Devils Tower at least sixty million years ago.

One wonders at what point in time the Indian story incorporated details supporting the volcanic theory of the creation of the Black Hills. Many Indian tribes have long marveled at the supernatural power of nature, but geologists did not present theories about the volcanic origin of Devils Tower until the late 1800's. However, the oral tradition of Indian story-tellers, with tales told and retold to countless generations, provided considerable freedom of interpretation. Did a twentieth century Indian story-teller add the molten rocks detail to embellish and modernize the basic legend?

White historians have been mystified that Devils Tower was not mentioned in the journals and reports of the earliest fur traders and explorers. The reason for this may be that even if their trails came fairly close to the tower, it was impossible to see it from every angle and direction. From the east, it is masked by the Bear Lodge Mountains (part of the Black Hills range); and from the west by the Missouri Buttes.

However, from certain vantage points, viewers can see Devils Tower from a distance up and down the westernmost north-south loop of the Belle Fourche River. A Kiowan historian, Isee-o, a soldier with General Hugh Scott in 1897, told the general, who was a student of Indian life, that he could see the tower from ninety miles away over a vista of three states from the high observation point in the Short Pine Hills in northwestern South Dakota, then look down the Little Missouri River below Saneville in southeastern Montana leading into the trough of the Belle Fourche River valley in northeastern Wyoming. Has anyone else found this long-range view?

The first explorer who wrote in his journal about Devils Tower was Henry Newton, the noted geologist with the Jenney-Newton U.S.

Henry Newton, the noted geologist with the Jenney-Newton U.S. Geological Survey exploring the Black Hills in 1875, was the first explorer to write about Devils Tower in his journal. Newton was wrong in assuming that this "object of wonder" was inaccessible to climbers. By 1983, over 12,000 climbers had made it to the top using 62 different routes. *Photo credit —South Dakota State Historical Society.*

Geological Survey, making a reconnaissance of the Black Hills in 1875. Newton wrote: "The tower's remarkable structure, its symmetry, and its prominence make it an unfailing object of wonder." The geologist also bemoaned the fact that "its summit is so entirely inaccessible that the energetic explorer, to whom the ascent of an ordinary difficult crag is but a pleasant pasttime, standing at its base could only look upward in despair of ever planting his feet on the top." Henry Newton was wrong about the permanence of that last observation.

Col. Richard Dodge, commanding the military escort for the Jenney-Newton expedition of 1875, is generally credited with giving the formation its white man's name of Devils Tower even though in his book, **The Black Hills,** published in 1876, he wrote that the Indians originally called it "Bad God's Tower." On the earliest maps of the region it was called Bear Lodge "Mateo Tepee." So, to the annoyance of many Indian tribes, the white man's name became "Devils Tower," a name without accurate historical precedent from the Indian viewpoint.

A momentous Fourth of July celebration was held at the tower in 1893. About a thousand people from considerable distances made the arduous trek in horse-drawn wagons and carriages to watch the well-publicized first ascent of the tower by William Rogers, an area rancher.

Before the actual public ascent, Rogers and Willard Ripley, another local rancher, had climbed the tower about two-thirds of the way, then constructed a 350-foot ladder to the summit by driving pegs into the cracks between the columns, then braced and fastened long wooden cross-strips. A dangerous undertaking. The two men also managed to haul a twelve-foot flagpole to the top on their treacherous trial climb combined with ladder-building.

Thus, the cheering crowd actually viewed Roger's second ascent made in about an hour and could, by craning their necks, see Rogers raise the Stars and Stripes on the flagpole. It was a thrilling experience for him and for the excited crowd. Up to that time, most people believed the tower was impossible to climb, including geologist and explorer Henry Newton.

Two years later on July 4, 1895, Mrs. Rogers, by using her husband's ladder for the final third of the ascent, became the first woman to climb Devils Tower. Since then, until about 1927, many climbers have used this ladder until its condition deteriorated. Scraps of the Rogers ladder are still visible today.

In 1906, climaxing the campaign of many people to insure the preservation and protection of the unusual formation, President Theodore Roosevelt signed a Congressional bill making Devils Tower the first national monument. Nobody knows for sure whether Teddy ever saw the tower on one of his western hunting trips. However, many westerners hoped the Cowboy President had a chance to admire it while taking a train trip in northeastern Wyoming which provided several glimpses of the imposing shaft.

The most sensational ascent—and descent—of the tower was performed by a parachutist named George Hopkins who parachuted from an airplane to the top of the tower in October, 1941, thus winning a $50 bet, even though he almost overshot his mark. During the landing he sprained his ankle, and not being a mountain climber, he didn't know how to get down, especially when two attempts by planes to drop him a care package of ropes and pulleys for his descent bounced over the side.

The weather turned bad and prevented several teams from going after him. Thus, the parachutist was marooned on the barren top for six days with only chipmunks, pack rats, and eagles for company. Planes successfully dropped food and blankets to him, and newspapers throughout the world published suggestions for his rescue. Finally, despite continuing wintry weather, an eight-man rescue team climbed up to bring him down. But he didn't have to be carried. He took a short course in rappeling (descending by using a rope), and by following expert instruction, he made it down the rock on his own power with over a hundred people watching. Hopkins commented, "I'd rather climb back up than face that crowd."

An aerial view of the top of Devils Tower where a parachutist landed in 1941. Although he won a $50 bet, a mountain rescue team had to climb up to show him how to get down by using a rope. *Photo credit—Centennial Archives, Deadwood.*

Devils Tower made its movie debut in "Close Encounters of the Third Kind," a science-fiction movie released in 1978. The tower was the site for the first meeting of earthlings and visitors from outer space. In the movie, special effects photography provided a landing strip near Devils Tower for space ships and their passengers. The movie attracted international attention and featured several spectacular shots of the tower taken from helicopters. During 1978, tourists at the monument increased twenty per cent. Perhaps many people wanted to see for themselves if Devils Tower was a real natural phenomenon or solely the creation of trick photography.

Today, by 1983, thousands of people have visited the monument through the years, and over 12,000 climbers, by following one of the sixty-two routes, have made it to the top with ropes, pitons, and sophisticated mountain-climbing techniques. There have been injuries and rescues but no deaths. The climbers swinging on their ropes provide free entertainment for the hikers who get dizzy looking up the columns while following the self-guiding nature trail around the tower.

Devils Tower has been described as the western sentinel of the Black Hills with Bear Butte the eastern sentinel. According to most geologists, both prehistoric formations are laccoliths—volcanoes that didn't quite make it to the eruption stage. Although the two laccoliths differ greatly in appearance, the legendary Indian origin of each is dominated by bears whose actions brought about the creation of the swiftly growing uplifts.

For the traveler coming from any direction—over the crest of a hill, or around a curve in the road, or from up or down the valley—the sight of the ancient tower rising in stunning isolation is a spine-tingling experience. The traveler can easily visualize a gargantuan bear clambering up the Mateo Tepee, leaving the marks of its claws forever; and paradoxically, one can also imagine a space ship landing on its flat top bringing curious visitors from another galaxy.

SUNDANCE MOUNTAIN AND THE SIOUX SUN DANCE

Sundance Mountain (5,800 feet) near the town of Sundance, Wyoming, on the western edge of the Black Hills, was once a summer rendezvous of the Sioux Indians who came here to hunt, to gather berries, and to hold sun dances. Some Sign Writers (Indian historians) believe that this was the original sun dance mountain of the Sioux nation.

One account from old twentieth century Sioux medicine men claimed that the first medicine man named Stretches Forth, over 800 years ago, gave the sun dance to the Sioux people.

History, whether Indian or white, inevitably contradicts itself.

According to the late Chauncy Yellowrobe, a Sioux Indian leader, the sun dance originated with the Blackfeet Indians who were worshippers of the sun. This legend of the dance's origin tells of an Indian maiden of the Blackfeet tribe who was told by the wisest medicine man that if she would marry the brave most pleasing to the sun, good fortune would befall both herself and the entire tribe.

Although the beautiful maiden had many suitors who traveled from

A snowy Sundance Mountain (5,800 feet) near the town of Sundance in northeastern Wyoming. Many Indian historians believe that this was the original sun dance mountain of the Sioux nation. The sun dance was not held in winter but during the Moon of Ripening Cherries (July). *Photo credit*—**Sundance Times**, *Sundance, WY.*

afar to woo her with ponies and all the riches they possessed, she rejected all their proposals.

At last, a young brave who had nothing to offer her except his love asked her to marry him. The maiden fell in love with him; but before she would consent to marriage, she said he must seek the sun's blessing on the union.

Willingly, the brave started out on his long and strenuous journey in search of the sun god. After many moons when he underwent severe trials and hardships, he finally reached the blazing presence of the sun. The sun blessed the ardent suitor and sent him happily on his way back to his beloved. When the maiden learned that the sun had given his blessing to this persistent young brave, she consented to marry him.

To celebrate the wedding, the Blackfeet Indians held a dance near a mountain. Many contests took place during this sun dance. The contestants tested their endurance by dancing all day facing the glaring sun until they were exhausted and dropped to the ground. They denied themselves food and water, and some pierced their flesh and bled in stoic agony.

Thus, according to the Blackfeet legend, this sun dance in honor of the marriage between the maiden and the determined young brave whom the sun had blessed became an annual ceremonial and a revered Indian custom.

Derived from diverse origins repeated for generations in the oral history of the red man, the Sun Dance of the Plains Indians with many variations became a pageant of mythical history, sacrifice, healing, thanksgiving, and ceremony with four days and nights of continuous dancing, usually followed by feasting and celebration. Because there are eighty different features of the Teton Sioux dance, including fourteen basic ones,

For the sun dance of the Teton Sioux the braves offered their flesh "so that the people might live." Medicine men pierced the breasts of the dancers with a sharp knife, inserted wooden pins through the slit, and tied buckskin thongs to the skewers. Then rawhide ropes were tied to the skewer and the other end was tied to the pole. *Photo credit—From Armstrong,* **The Early Empire Builders of the Great West**. *Fielder Collection, Devereaux Library, South Dakota School of Mines and Technology.*

there may be an infinite number of variations. Spiritual benefits for the whole tribe were insured by the ceremony, and a man might offer his flesh "so that the people might live."

According to Luther Standing Bear, hereditary chief of the Oglala tribe of the Sioux nation and author of **My People, the Sioux,** (1928) there was a great difference between the sun dances of the Sioux and the sun dances of other Indians. The sacrificial dance of the Sioux was a religious duty to perform every summer during the Moon of Ripening Cherries (July). Sometimes as many as thirty or forty braves prepared for the dance and often with a year's preparation in vision quests and other rituals. The women made elaborate feathered head-dresses and eagle-bone whistles which the men carried in their mouths while dancing.

The dancers blowing on eagle-bone whistles and wearing on their chests a rawhide replica of the sunflower, the only flower which follows the sun. In the old days, the dancers often wore buffalo robes with the hair on the outside and lavishly decorated. *Photo credit—Bell photo, C 163, South Dakota State Historical Society.*

Many complicated rituals were emphasized during the finding and the chopping down and the transporting of a cottonwood tree which the Indians carried to the place selected for the dance. They erected the stripped cottonwood pole with extreme care until they dropped it into a prepared hole.

The Sioux placed effigies of both buffalo and man on the cross-piece arranged on the topmost branches to insure plenty of buffalo meat and victory over the enemies.

The dancers in the old days wore buffalo robes with the hair outside and lavishly decorated. They also wore on their chest a rawhide replica of the sunflower, the only flower which follows the sun.

When the sun started to rise, the braves began dancing while facing the sun with both hands raised above their heads and the eagle-bone whistles in their mouths to blow on. All day long they danced in one position while staring at the sun until it set. The audience sang, chanted, and keened.

When a dancer fainted, the non-dancing warriors laid him on a sagebrush bed. If a young brave wanted to give himself as a living sacrifice, the medicine men would pierce his breast with a sharp knife and insert a wooden pin through the slit and tie a strong buckskin thong to the skewer.

Chief Luther Standing Bear explained: "From the pole two rawhide ropes were suspended and the candidate would now be lifted up so that he was hanging from his breasts, but the rope was long enough for his feet to remain on the ground. Although blood would be running from the knife incision, the candidate would try not to show any reaction to the intense pain."

Oglala Sioux performing the sun dance at Pine Ridge, SD, about 1950. In 1890, white leaders banned the sun dance, but today on many Indian reservations, Indians perform the sun dance which has an infinite number of variations. White visitors are frequently permitted. *Photo credit—South Dakota State Historical Society.*

Then the young brave would try to tear himself loose by leaning backward; and if he were unsuccessful, his friends and relatives would seize him around the waist while the dancer would throw himself backward until the skin came loose, and he was freed.

During this painful ordeal, the candidate fasted, taking no food and water; if he showed any pain or cried out, he was in disgrace. As soon as he freed himself from the torture, the virgins washed his wounds and dressed them with herbs. Often braves plunged into nearby streams or lakes to refresh themselves.

The sun dance actually means "Gazing at the Sun Suspended" and emphasized the importance of the vision quest, of power through self-sacrifices, and tests the four great virtues of the Teton Sioux: generosity, courage, integrity, and goodness. The sun dance was a tribal ritual between the people and the universe to propitiate the Great Spirit by personal sacrifice and to placate the evil spirits of the earth.

The white conquerors objected to the sun dance, presumably because they disliked the barbaric tortures; but in reality, they feared the uncontrollable frenzy and Indian patriotism stimulated by the hereditary dancing. The United States government outlawed the sun dance on reservations in 1890; but in the 1920's and 1930's, when freedom of religion was emphasized, many reservation Indians revived the sun dance ceremony and perform it yearly to this day.

Chief Eagle Feather from St. Francis, SD, dancing at Pine Ridge reservation in the 1960's. He is performing the Pull of Ignorance ritual by dragging around a buffalo skull attached to the rope fastened to the skin on his back. The flags on the tree-pole represent directions. *Photo credit—South Dakota State Historical Society.*

Legendary accounts of the sun dances held on Sundance Mountain in Wyoming, the "Temple of the Sioux," are often contradictory; some say the dances were held on top of this fairly flat-topped, long mountain with steep cliffs on its sides; others believe that the dances were held on a plateau at the base of the mountain. In all probability, both locations were used.

Still visible is a trail wide enough for the two-poled travois carrier up Sundance Mountain on the southwest side and a narrow foot trail up the steeper north side made long ago by Sioux Indians. They wanted to perform their sun dance as close as possible to the sun, the giver of much beneficence, both physical and spiritual.

LEGEND OF SYLVAN LAKE

By S. Goodale Price

Long, long ago, very far back before the white man's heavy boots disturbed the dim trails through the pine forests of the Black Hills—when only the soft buckskin moccasin of the Indian hunter trod lightly those mystic pathways through canyon and over mountainside, that far

Sylvan Lake (6,250 feet) in Custer State Park. When author S. Goodale Price sat on the rocks gazing into the waters, he was inspired to write this Indian-style legend of the "gem-like mountain lake." *Photo credit—Rapid City Chamber of Commerce.*

Reprinted from **The Black Hills—Land of Legend** by S. Goodale Price back—there lived an Indian tribe near one of the foothill streams. This tribe was known as the Sha-hi-ye-na or "Red Talkers."

In this tribe was a very wise medicine man called Bubo Siyuhk, the ghost of a mysterious owl, or Owl Man, as he was sometimes called. The Owl Man could not only foretell the future but also had communion with braves who had passed to the Happy Hunting Ground away back in the days when all Indian tribes lived only in deep caverns beneath the earth, and ventured forth only at night when the Sun God's sharp darts of light would not hurt their eyes.

The Owl Man was full of cunning and often talked with the lizards, snakes and turtles. He had many powerful charms and medicines and when his people wanted meat they would ask, "Wise Owl's ghost, where today do the buffalo feed?" The people said they needed meat against the coming of the long cold winter and the big snows.

The Owl Man bade them enter his lodge and sit in silence before his fire. Then taking his many-hued robe made from the skin of the White Deer, he carried it from his lodge and spread it on the grass by the stream. He then gathered a handful of bright pebbles from the stream bottom and intoning the Great Spirit to aid him, he spread the pebbles across the patterns and figures transcribed on the robe.

As a brown pebble rolled to rest on a blue cloud-like figure on the robe, it suddenly became a turtle which spoke as follows:

"Crafty Owl Man, lead your hunters many leagues up this very stream. When the sun is in the center of the heavens, you will come to a place where the waters fall from a ledge twelve times the height of your lodge poles. There will be a path opened up to you through the big rocks around the falls. Follow this path through the rock and it will lead you to the edge of a grassy valley lying under the shadow of a high peak whose rocks pierce the sky (thought to be Harney Peak). Do not go out into this valley but on its edge where the path through the rocks meet the grass, near where the stream falls over the ledge, place the skull of a white buffalo. On the skull let each hunter lay his best arrow; the last one must point directly toward the place where the North Wind comes from, the North Star."

The turtle as he said this turned back into a smooth brown pebble. The Owl Man then returned to the waiting braves where he repeated to them just what the turtle had told him.

There was much discussion as to its meaning and many were doubtful, but at last agreed to follow the instructions. On the day after, following many hours on the trail along the stream and just as the sun reached midheaven, the band arrived at the place among the high rocks where the water fell many feet from a ledge "twelve times the height of their lodge poles." In vain they searched for a way to go farther, but the solid canyon walls hemmed them in on all sides except the opening through which they had

Sylvan Lake, a man-made lake, is a lovely example of what man and nature can create when they cooperate intelligently. An unobtrusive dam keeps the water pooled in the deep natural basin formed from elephant's foot rocks. On the left is the old hotel which burned in 1935. *Photo credit—South Dakota State Historical Society.*

come. Tired and discouraged, they said to the Owl Man: "Are you trying to fool us? Why have you led us on this witless quest?"

The Owl Man implored them to be patient while he prepared his most potent medicine, the powdered root of the Black Oak, which was the funeral tree of his dead ancestors. Again he spread his robe and started to sprinkle some of this powerful charm across the pattern.

As the first flakes touched the robe, the sky suddenly became black as night, all light fled, heavy rumblings and crashes shook the earth, a huge arrow of fire sped across the sky from the high peak to the eastward and dashed itself into a thousand sparks against the big rock in front of them. The Indians fell to the ground in terror. Instantly, light and quietness returned and there before them was a passage cloven through the solid rock.

With fear and trembling they entered this passage and presently came out on the green meadow just as the turtle had said they would. By the edge of the rock through which their path led them they placed the buffalo skull and each hunter as he marched past placed his best arrow on it. As the last arrow was placed, pointing straight to the North Star, a fleecy cloud as large as the meadow settled slowly from the blue sky, and before their wondering eyes it dissolved itself into a silvery sheen of water. Where the green meadow had been there now appeared a gem-like mountain lake. Its surface was gently rippling in the breeze that came down off the peaks. As they stood amazed, down through the timber filed a splendid herd of fat buffalo who began to drink of the lake's clear waters.

The braves fitted arrows to their bows and the hunt began. Soon the winter's meat was killed. When the sun sent its last rays against the cliffs surrounding the lake, huge fires were built along its shores and the savory odor of roasting buffalo steaks filled the air.

All through the night there was great feasting and dancing and thanksgiving to the Great Spirit. The tall cliffs echoed to the shouts and laughter of the hunters. When morning came they returned down the stream heavily laden with meat and robes, their gifts from the Great Spirit.

It is said that on the Indians' return the following spring to the place of their hunt, the lake had disappeared, the grassy meadow again filled the valley at the cliff base. The path through the rock and the whitened pile of buffalo bones still remained and marked evidence of their experience, which was recounted from father to son, one tribe to another, generation after generation, until the present time when it came to the ears of white men, who with their energy and ability determined to once more capture a cloud in the meadow at the foot of Harney Peak. So after much hardship and expenditure of capital there was constructed the Sylvan Lake Dam which allowed the stream to form again that blue mountain lake, Sylvan Lake.

MINNEKAHTA AND HOT SPRINGS— A LEGENDARY BLEND

An old Indian legend, so ancient that no one knows from which tribe it came, relates the story of how a terrible epidemic afflicted all the Indian tribes of North America and threatened to wipe them all from the earth. None of the native medicines had any effect on this killing disease. Then one day a messenger arrived from the west with news of the marvelous springs which had been blessed by the Great Spirit.

This welcome messenger announced to all the tribes, one by one, that these warm waters would cure every disease known to Indians, including the one causing the fearful epidemic.

Soon, Indians from all over the country began migrating to this wondrous place in the southern Paha Sapa. Some tribes stayed to live in the foothills; others returned to their original homes but continued to make regular pilgrimages to the medicinal waters.

One of these visitors was a beautiful Indian princess who accompanied her family to the warm springs. She was in love with an Indian brave whom her father, a chief, did not consider worthy of her, and he ordered his daughter never to see her lover again. The broken-hearted princess ran from her father's lodge onto the highest cliff overlooking the warm springs and jumped to her instant death on the rocks below. This tragic maiden was Minnekahta whose name means "warm water." And this is how Minnekahta Springs acquired its name.

A Lakota legend tells of people with supernatural powers who lived underground in the recesses of the earth. They were dedicated to keeping perpetual fires burning to heat the waters that flowed upward into warm pools and streams on the earth's surface; that is why the flowers bloomed all year and the medicinal plants maintained their healing powers.

Minnekahta Falls at Hot Springs acquired its name because, according to an Indian legend, a broken-hearted Indian princess jumped to her death on these rocks. Minnekahta means "warm water." *Photo credit—Grabill photo 1889, South Dakota State Historical Society.*

Badger Clark, Poet Laureate of South Dakota, has written with perceptive humor about legends, both Indian and white. In his booklet, **When Hot Springs Was a Pup,** he relates an amusing tale about how the Indians "in dateless antiquity, tribe unknown," discovered the healing properties of the springs. An ailing and elderly squaw, suffering from agonizing pains in her legs, had to be carried in a buffalo hide by four warriors. They set her down beside a natural stone bathtub in the red rock. She touched the water with her hand, then eagerly rolled herself into it. The healing waters were so soothing and the pains in her legs vanished so quickly that she refused to get out, hurling bad language at those braves who tried to remove her from the hot tub. Finally, she laughed gaily and sprang out of the water completely cured. A happy squaw once again, she bustled about the camp cooking for her husband while singing an old war song and capering about like a young girl—to the amazement of the villagers.

If the springs could effect such miraculous cures, no wonder various Indian tribes claimed them for their own. Located in the southern hills where the elevations are much lower than around the Harney Peak area, the springs region was one place in the Hills where the Indians were not afraid to stay for long periods of time. The Cheyennes were in possession of the springs when the Sioux invaded the Black Hills country and tried to force the Cheyennes out. The two tribes fought over the Black Hills many times before they finally became allies.

One of their most fierce battles was for the possession of these magical springs in the red canyon. The battle took place on top of a mountain

Badger Clark, versatile author of **When Hot Springs Was A Pup.** He relates an amusing tale of how the Indians discovered the medicinal properties of the warm springs. *Photo credit—South Dakota State Historical Society.*

Col. W. J. Thornby claimed to be the first white man to discover the warm springs. On a tree trunk he blazed the words, "This is my spring, W. J. Thornby." A Black Hills Pioneer of 1877, Thornby was a State Senator, a U.S. assayer, and a Mason who helped lay out Mount Moriah cemetery, Deadwood. *Photo credit—South Dakota State Historical Society.*

overlooking the springs, now called Battle Mountain. The Sioux were victorious, but according to Badger Clark, the two warring tribes made a wise treaty after the battle, establishing the springs as neutral ground under a perpetual flag of truce. Thus, Indians from every tribe might come to bathe and continue to receive the blessings of the waters.

Another legend explains that the Sioux Indians, who called the watering place "the spring of healing waters," tried to keep its presence a well-guarded secret. Then one day a foolish warrior told a white man about the place. The white man promised the Indian a beautiful gray horse if the warrior would lead him there. Amazed and delighted at the warm water, the white man kept his promise and gladly gave the gray horse to the Indian. That night the Thunder Bird who lived on Harney Peak created a terrifying storm, hurling thunder bolts and lightning tongues throughout the Black Hills. Lightning struck and killed the beautiful gray horse that the foolish Indian had received for revealing the precious secret.

One of the first white men to discover the thermal springs was a Black Hills Pioneer of 1877, Col. W. J. Thornby, then a reporter for the **Deadwood Pioneer-Times.** In the spring of 1879, Col. Thornby and Professor Walter Jenney, the noted geologist who led the Jenney-Newton Expedition to the Black Hills in 1875, were taking a horseback ride exploring the southern Hills. They located the stream near the falls and followed it up the canyon to discover the source of the warm creek. Near the big spring where the Evans Plunge was later built, Thornby lopped off the top of a cedar sapling, then blazed the trunk with these words: "This is my spring, W. J. Thornby."

Some time later when the new owner visited what he thought was his property, two rough-looking squaw men announced that they were going to jump his claim and build themselves a log house on the spot. Right then and there, Thornby made the claim jumpers a gift of his right to the springs—with all good wishes. Thornby was much more interested in being remembered as the white discoverer of the springs than in possessing them. Thornby's greatest pleasure during his lifetime was telling in dramatic detail of his discovery—a memorable first.

The new white settlement, established in 1882, was at first named Minnekahta in honor of the tragic Indian maiden who had plunged to her death on the rocks. Not until 1886 was the name changed to Hot Springs.

Soon, the white settlers of Hot Springs began capitalizing on the commercial aspects of the healing waters, always said to be "blood-warm" which meant 98.6 degrees Fahrenheit. The town began to put on airs, advertising itself as a health resort and spa rivaling exclusive resorts in the east and in Europe. Soon health seekers began arriving, first by stagecoach and later by train "to take the waters," both by bathing and by drinking.

A 1901 brochure, published by the Hot Springs Commercial Club, advertised miraculous cures for a variety of diseases which the warm waters could cure: "comprising some ailments which often baffle the medical profession. Rheumatism in its varied forms, inflammatory, muscular, acute and chronic, yield to the effects of the baths and the copious drinking of the waters. Diseases of the kidneys and urinary organs, stomach troubles of all kinds, intestinal disorders, skin diseases, asthma, tuberculosis, paralysis, nervous prostration, liver complaint, gout, syphilis, chronic diarrhea, habitual constipation, and other kindred disorders, are here successfuly treated."

Today, the exaggerated curative powers of the springs are no longer touted—but the legend remains. The blood-warm waters in the Evans Plunge have cooled to ninety degrees. Still honored is the name of Fred Evans, a legend in his own right, and the master builder of Hot Springs who constructed both the first Plunge building and also the Evans Hotel, now a restored Historic Site.

In 1974, Hot Springs was fortunate to receive another gift from the earth when construction workers dug up the bones of mammoths in an ancient sinkhole. Mammoths were a type of elephant which roamed the Great Plains about 26,000 years ago. Today the Mammoth Site where digging continues for mammoth fossils has been designated a National Natural Landmark.

Although Hot Springs did not maintain its early reputation as a cure-all

A Chicago and Northwestern train leaving Hot Springs in 1897. Many health-seekers came by train "to take the waters." Promoters advertised the warm springs as having medicinal powers to cure a host of ailments and diseases. *Photo credit—Centennial Archives, Deadwood.*

resort for every ailment of the human body, visitors still enjoy dabbling their hands and feet in Hot Brook and Fall River whose waters never freeze, and bathers never tire of commenting on their sense of well-being after swimming in the Evans Plunge. As they have for years, the ducks and geese continue to enjoy year-around swimming in the warm waters of the streams.

Perhaps the Sioux were right in believing a powerful spirit dwelt in the warm springs to wash away pain and evil spirits. When the Sioux gave up the Black Hills, no wonder they were especially sad to lose Minnekahta.

The Evans Plunge in the early days of horse-drawn vehicles. Promoter Fred Evans built the first building in 1890. Today, the large warm-water swimming pool is enclosed in a modern structure. *Photo credit—South Dakota State Historical Society.*

II
WHITE MAN LEGENDS

TWO LEGENDS OF HOW PAUL BUNYAN CREATED THE BLACK HILLS

Paul Bunyan, America's favorite folk hero, started out as a mythical logger in French-Canada; then in one giant step, he strode across the Great Lakes and swaggered into the United States where in no time at all he became a rip-roaring legend, the super lumberjack who will live forever. He was the king-size logger of the North Woods stretching from Maine to, Washington (except for North Dakota which he and Babe, the Blue Ox, logged off in one month). No one can match the feats of Paul Bunyan, the personification of the glorified pioneer spirit; for his adventures have become the tallest tales, the biggest whoppers ever told about the American frontier.

This is the first version of how Paul Bunyan created the Black Hills:

Once there was a Mountain That Stood on Its Head in Dakota country. Instead of its peak being in the clouds, it was buried in the ground; and instead of the base of the mountain being at the bottom where it belonged, it was on top. And believe it or not—the trees grew upside down—an incredible sight. This topsy-turvy mountain was two miles high and 127 feet in circumference around the bottom which was on top. Defying nature, its slopes slanted outward instead of inward towards its summit. The whole thing resembled an ice cream cone.

This mixed-up mountain presented quite a problem to Paul Bunyan because he wanted to finish logging off Dakota. Busy Paul had many jobs lined up and he needed a good foreman. He decided to hire Hels Helsen, the Big Swede and Bull of the Woods, to log this crazy mountain.

Hels Helsen, whose ambition was to outshine Paul as the champion lumberjack, went ahead without getting instructions from the boss on how to proceed. A bad mistake. Hels crawled under the slope of the mountain,

Paul Bunyan and Babe, the Blue Ox. One legend says that the giant lumberjack accidentally created the Black Hills from the Mountain That Stood On Its Head. Another legend relates that after Babe died, Paul piled rocks and shoveled dirt on the carcass and eventually the Black Hills were created out of this mound. *Photo credit—Bemidji Area Chamber of Commerce, Bemidji, MN.*

thinking he could log upside-down trees as easily as he had logged right-side-up trees in Sweden. Hels urged the lumberjacks to follow him and to hang onto the cables that he had stretched between trees. Soon the loggers got dizzy from walking upside down with their heads pointing toward the ground. They complained that sawdust and blood and pine needles were getting into their eyes, noses, and mouths, but the worst thing was that their snus boxes kept falling out of their pockets.

The loggers didn't like hanging upside down and they said so. They quit work and scrambled off the slopes and ran back to their bunks to rest. Hels Helsen was both furious and frustrated. He couldn't beat Paul Bunyan without brave, hard-working loggers.

Hels tramped through the logging camp until he found Paul Bunyan who was resting between jobs by snapping pine trees in two with his bare hands.

"Yumping Yehosofat," said the Big Swede and Bull of the Woods to Paul, "I tank I give up and go to anudder camp, Meester Bunywan. Dese loggers ain't monkeys to hang oopside down. Besides, dey got no tails."

Paul Bunyan was disgusted with Hels who hadn't waited for instructions, but he had already figured out how to solve the problem. Paul yelled at the men resting in their bunks from hanging upside down, "Roll out, you dang-blasted loggers, I'll show you how to log upside-down timber."

While everyone in camp watched, baiting their breath lumberjack style, Paul got out his best double-barreled, gold-butted shotgun, studded with diamonds, and slung it over his shoulder. The lumberjacks, even though they should have known better, were astonished that Paul could carry such a heavy weapon. (Later he used the barrels for smokestacks in one of his sawmills.) In his belt, long as the Red River of the North, he packed cartridges loaded with dynamite and filled with shells of hollowed-out cedar logs, capped with sheet iron. Then he was ready.

Paul Bunyan took aim at the Mountain Standing on Its Head and fired his mighty gun which roared and thundered. Exploding sheets of steel ripped and sawed into the upside-down forest, slicing trees off at the base and dropping them head first onto the ground.

It took Paul not quite eleven and one-half hours of firing his shotgun to clear out all the timber; but by nightfall, the job was done and prickly piles of pine trees covered the prairie.

Now Hels Helsen, the Big Swede and Bull of the Woods, became angry and jealous. Paul Bunyan had done the impossible again. So the next morning Hels climbed backwards up the mountain sloping outward to the top and began tearing up the tallest pine trees with his bare hands.

When Paul saw Hels, his foreman, using this primitive method of clearing timber, he was enraged. Paul gave a tremendous leap to the mountain's flat top two miles in the air, caught hold of the edge with his gigantic hands and pulled his hefty body onto the platter-shaped top.

Then Paul stood up. When Paul rose to his full height, he would have been taller than Harney Peak—if Harney Peak had been made yet. The two giants charged at each other furiously; their bellowing and roaring could be heard as far north as the forests surrounding the Lake of the Woods on the Canadian-Minnesota border.

The loggers in the camp heard all the commotion too. They were so terrified at this battle of the goliaths that they crawled into their bunks again and covered up their heads to shut out the sounds of bone-crunching, arm-twisting, blood-gushing, head-pounding, eye-gouging, ear-biting, knee-cracking, butt-kicking—with every five minutes the sound of pine trees crashing to the ground. The earth shook and trembled and heaved. It must have been an earthquake. Jagged pieces of the mountain's flat edge broke off and smashed into the logging camp. Then a tremendous convulsion overturned the bunk houses and threw the loggers out on their backsides. The rest of the night all was quiet.

At dawn, Paul Bunyan strode into camp, carrrying a limp Hels Helsen on his shoulder as easily as if his trophy were a grizzly bear. The victor, not even puffing, dumped Hels Helsen on the ground and shouted, "Are you going to be a good foreman now?"

Opening one black eye, Hels Helsen, the Big Swede and Bull of the Woods, croaked, "Aye tank I behave now, Meester Boss."

The loggers, while sighing with relief, gazed in astonishment at what wasn't there. The wonderful upside-down mountain had disappeared. The battle of the behemoths had demolished it, had smashed it to pieces with their trampling and wrestling and brawling. After that knock-down, drag-out fight, all that was left when the dust cleared was a cluster of dusty, blood-stained mounds called the Black Hills—with nary a tree growing. And that's how Paul Bunyan accidentally created the Black Hills from scratch. Thank goodness the Black Hills improved—a century at a time.

There's another version of how Paul Bunyan created the Black Hills with the help of his pet, Babe, the Blue Ox. This story of creation is both marvelous and sad in its way.

Babe, as everyone knows, measured forty-two ax handles between the eyes with room for a plug of tobacco in between. Babe was so big that every time the hundred blacksmiths shod her, the Finns and Scandinavians had to open up a new iron mine near Lake Superior. Babe was so strong that she could haul a whole section of timber behind her at one time.

Babe worked hard and she had a healthy appetite. Every day she ate four tons of oats but only two and a half tons of hay with a wagon-load of turnips for dessert. After her meals, it took two men to pick baling wire out of her teeth. When Babe had worked especially hard, Paul gave her an eighty-pound lump of sugar—as he had after she helped him dig Puget Sound.

No matter how many calories she consumed, Babe was always hungry. One fateful day she got a whiff of pancakes cooking on Paul's huge griddle in the bunk-house kitchen. Now this griddle was so large that nine small black boys greased it by skating over it with hams strapped to their feet. Babe sniffed that delicious lumberjack flapjack until she had to do something. The cooks were out to lunch, so cow-like, she bull-dozed her way into the kitchen. There were 400 pancakes sizzling on the griddle and Babe gulped every one; then she took another bite and down went the sizzling griddle, followed by the red-hot, cast-iron stove. Her stomach growled.

Babe coughed and bellowed and gargled. With her tail straight up, she took off toward South Dakota with Paul chasing her. Even though Paul took giant strides, he couldn't catch the galloping ox who was bawling in anguish. By the time Paul caught up, Babe had collapsed on the ground, the crash heard as far north as Hudson Bay. Her four legs and one tail stuck straight up in the air with her toes curled. It was obvious that she had died of heartburn.

Paul Bunyan cried and cried over his pet's demise, but there weren't any handy buckets around to catch his grief. So many tears flowed and gushed and poured from his eyes that they formed the Missouri River.

There were enough tears left over to create the Belle Fourche River and the Cheyenne River whose courses act as boundaries for the area where Babe had died, while also serving as tributaries for the Missouri River.

At last, wiping away rivers of tears, Paul wondered what to do with the body. He decided that even for him it was too much work to dig a grave for his mammoth pet whose stomach was loaded with 400 pancakes, a sizzling griddle, and a red-hot, cast-iron stove. He believed it would work just as well to pile rocks and shovel dirt on the smoking carcass until it was completely covered. So that's what Paul did. Because he was burdened with sorrow, he was slow, and it took him all sixty minutes of a long, sad hour to give Babe a decent burial.

Centuries passed solemnly by. Grass and pine trees began to sprout on Babe's private cemetery, a real attention-getter humping above the plains. The burial plot was roughly rectangular in shape and approximately 100 miles long and 50 miles wide. When it rained, the peaks on top grew taller, and the rivulets ran down the sloping sides forming beautiful canyons and valleys. After two and a half centuries had passed, birds, deer, chipmunks, and other creatures came to investigate the hump. They liked what they found and decided to stay and live on the lush green heights.

However, the birds and the animals reported a startling observation to Paul when he was on a routine century pilgrimage to Babe's final resting place and eons before Paul himself went to that big logging camp in the sky. The revelation was this: that from a distance the dark green pine trees covering Babe's mountainous grave looked black.

So that's how Paul Bunyan created the Black Hills—by accident again.

THE THOEN STONE

The white men's tale of the Thoen Stone and gold-seekers in the Black Hills in 1834 is a wonderful example of a legend, which is defined as a story coming down the past, especially one popularly taken as historical although not verifiable by historical record.

The legend surfaced one March day in 1887 in the form of a slab of sandstone about twelve inches square and two and a half inches thick, with writing on both sides. A stone mason named Louis Thoen unearthed it on Lookout Mountain near Spearfish at the northern edge of the Black Hills. Thoen was building a house at the foot of Lookout Mountain and was engaged in digging up stones and hauling them to the site of this house. That is how he made the discovery of the unusual stone, he said.

Thoen detected writing in script scrawled on both sides of the slab with these words:

"Came to these Hills in 1833, seven of us, De Lacompte, Ezra Kind, G. W. Wood, T. Brown, R. Kent, W. King, Indian Crow. All dead but me,

Lookout Mountain near Spearfish, SD, where Louis Thoen claimed he found the stone with writing on both sides. The stagecoach is the Spearfish-Deadwood U.S. mail coach in 1910. *Photo credit—Linfred Schuttler.*

Ezra Kind. Killed by Ind beyond the high hill Got our gold June 1834." (one side)

"Got all the gold we could carry. Our ponys all got by indians. Have lost my gun and nothing to eat and indians hunting me." (obverse side)

If the tragic drama writ in stone is to be believed, then this proves that prospectors in 1834 found gold in the Black Hills long before the Gold Rush of 1874-1879. Although many researchers have tried to prove the authenticity of the evidence, none has been successful.

Many questions have been asked: Why wasn't it possible that Louis Thoen, a stone mason accustomed to working with stone, could have created a huge historical hoax? Why couldn't Thoen have carved the message with a hunting knife as easily as an unlucky character named Ezra Kind could while presumably hiding from the Indians on Lookout Mountain in 1834?

At the time of the intriguing discovery, Thoen requested that a John Cashner, a respected businessman of Spearfish, take charge of the controversial stone. Cashner made a thorough investigation. He pointed out that the penmanship and vocabulary were typical of a literate person in the 1830's. Many people came forward to testify that Louis Thoen was a conservative man, thoroughly honest and unimaginative, and that it was not in his nature to be a practical joker, especially about anything as serious as gold.

But there was no proof one way or another whether Ezra Kind or Louis Thoen had carved the message.

The believers in the Kind authorship pointed out that the slab had been concealed under a large flat rock in a crevice ten or twelve feet below the level of the surrounding ground and near two large oak trees for markers. They also emphasized that the ground near the discovery was overgrown with vegetation and packed with ancient dirt, as though nothing had been disturbed for at least forty-two years.

On one side of the Thoen Stone the writing says: "Got all the gold we could carry our ponys all got by indians have lost my gun and nothing to eat and indians hunting me." This controversial evidence of gold-seekers in the Black Hills in 1834 is displayed in the Adams Museum, Deadwood. *Photo credit—South Dakota State Historical Society.*

But, argued the non-believers, no one was with Thoen when he uncovered the stone.

If Ezra Kind had actually survived after he scratched his message, what became of him? If Ezra Kind had escaped from the Indians, or had not perished from starvation and had actually made it to an outpost of civilization, he might have changed the course of history.

In 1834, if Ezra Kind had been an exhausted but exultant prospector lugging all the gold he could carry into a fort or a fur-trading post, and yelling "Gold from the Black Hills!" imagine the excitement. He would probably have started a gold rush to the New Eldorado much earlier than it actually began in 1874. It might have been named the "Ezra Kind Gold Rush." And if it had occurred in 1834, it would have beaten the California Gold Rush of 1849 by fifteen years. Little things like a heavy bag of gold have often affected western expansion in the United States.

In 1887, newspapers throughout the country published accounts of the discovery of the Thoen Stone. As a consequence of the publicity, many readers responded with information about the people whose names appeared on the stone.

Cashner, the informal investigator, received a letter, since lost, from a nephew of T. Brown stating that Brown had left Missouri in 1832-1833 with a man named Kent and was never heard of again. Another man wrote Cashner that Kent was his uncle who had disappeared in the 1830's with an adventurer named Kind. A surviving Kind relative also wrote a plausible explanation which added credibility to the existence of the seven men listed on the controversial stone.

Author Frank Thompson of Spearfish devoted years to researching all aspects of the Thoen Stone and tracking down all leads related to the survivors of the famous seven. He wrote an earnest, interesting book entitled **The Thoen Stone,** but try as he might, was unable to prove the reality of the Kind party.

An Indian story which some historians believe refers to Ezra Kind, was allegedly repeated by aging braves on the Pine Ridge Reservation. A band of Indian hunters noticed a muddy stream in the foothills of the Black Hills. Thinking that beavers must be stirring up the usually clear water, the eager hunters followed the creek upstream where they were surprised and angered to find a party of whites gold-panning and digging the sandy banks, thus muddying the waters. Reportedly, the Indians killed all the whites but one who escaped. Later they took over the pile of gold and were able to sell it to the Hudson Bay Company for $18,000 in merchandise.

Certainly, there is plenty of evidence that prospectors were digging into the Black Hills for many years before Horatio Ross of the Custer Expedition of 1874 found gold. The Russell-Collins Party of late 1874 found old sluice boxes, a decaying log cabin, and a grave marked 1846.

An early pioneer in the Spearfish area found rusty camping utensils cached on Lookout Mountain, not far from where Louis Thoen said he found his stone.

In 1878, two years after gold was discovered in Deadwood Gulch, the **Deadwood Telegraph-Herald** published this feature:

"Every few months the miner or the adventurous prospector brings to light fresh evidence of early mining operations in the Hills . . . Mining implements have been unearthed many feet below the surface of a spot where no mine workings were known to have existed. An iron chain was found imbedded in a large tree where it had probably hung for many years."

Without a doubt, many gold-seekers preceded Custer long before 1874. But whether Ezra Kind and his comrades were among the early prospectors cannot be definitely established.

History buffs may view the Thoen Stone at the Adams Museum in Deadwood. Is it genuine or isn't it?

FAIRY GOLD

"Fairy Gold" is the name given to buried treasure in the Black Hills which was hidden either by its rightful owners or by road agents (stagecoach robbers), or is simply inaccessible. Often in the rugged mountain wilderness, those in possession of the heavy gold, whether legal owners or thieves, were in a hurry. And if they were lugging gold nuggets or gold bullion by foot or on horseback or in a wagon, were frequently in danger, and had to get rid of their treasure pronto. Hence the caching of gold was necessary for a quick getaway.

Sometimes those who buried the treasure under a certain rock pile or under a distinctive tree stump forgot to memorize the landmarks; and, when they returned for their loot were unable to find it. In some cases, owners of the gold died before they could return to the cache.

So thousands of dollars of fairy gold is alleged to be hiding somewhere in the Black Hills just waiting for a lucky scavenger to unearth it. Many gold-seekers have dug up the countryside and torn up floors and fireplaces in deserted log cabins with little success being reported. Perhaps there is a pot of gold at the end of the rainbow.

Sometimes the golden dream comes true—especially by serendipity—when the finder isn't actively looking for treasure. There's the tall tale of the hunter who, while drinking from a creek, noticed a rusty knife sticking out of the sand. He began to dig at the spot with his own hunting knife and found a buried tin can packed with gold dust worth about $6,000.

Fairy Gold legends abound in the Black Hills. A tangled lot they are, full of contradictions, exaggeration, murders, harrowing adventures, and perhaps now and then a dash of truth.

Many searchers for "fairy gold" have torn up floors and fireplaces in deserted log cabins with little success being reported. Perhaps finders want to be keepers and do not report their good fortune. *Photo credit—South Dakota Tourism.*

An oft-repeated tale is about a party of miners from New York state in 1876 who found gold in the Big Horn Mountains of Wyoming worth $160,000, weighing exactly 286 pounds, which they were transporting with difficulty on horseback. Somewhere east of the Belle Fourche river, just beyond the northern edge of the Black Hills in Butte County, Crazy Horse and his warriors threatened to attack the group. Quickly, they buried their heavy gold and galloped off, riding for their lives. Later when they returned to recover their treasure, they couldn't find it. The cache has been described as a day's ride from Deadwood and is said to be located in an unusual terrain "where the waters run in four directions."

A classic case of fairy gold when the stolen treasure had to be gotten rid of quickly is the Canyon Springs robbery in September, 1878. This was the only successful robbery of the Deadwood treasure coach on the Cheyenne-Deadwood trail. Canyon Springs was a stagecoach relay station just across the Wyoming line, about forty miles south of Deadwood.

When the stage stopped at Canyon Springs, the road agents overpowered the station tender and ambushed the stage. After the shooting was over, there were dead and wounded on both sides. The robbers broke the chains and smashed open the iron treasure box, supposedly impregnable for at least twenty-four hours. The four survivors loaded the heavy loot, an estimated $100,000 to $250,000 of gold from the Homestake Mine, into a rickety wagon, taking one of their wounded and leaving behind the body of Big Nose George. Somewhere on the escape route through the mountainous wilderness, the wagon broke down; the robbers had to hide the gold bricks in a hurry and flee for their lives.

Eventually, lawmen found two gold bars with the Homestake stamp on display in a bank in Iowa. Whether or not all of the gold was recovered has been argued about for over a century. The plateau area around Canyon Springs and Four Corners, Wyoming, has been thoroughly searched, no stone left unturned. But which way did the road agents escape in their wagon? Some say over the Hills to the east toward the Fort Pierre trail; others claim it was southeast to Custer City; or was it southwest toward Cheyenne? Searchers should check out all the possible hiding places in the foothills too.

Gale Hill, a shotgun guard on the treasure coach when it was robbed at Canyon Springs, WY. He was wounded in the fight with the road agents and died several years later of his injuries. Legend says robbers hid much of the gold but searchers have never reported finding it. *Photo credit—South Dakota State Historical Society.*

The illegal Russell-Collins (or Gordon Party) which included Annie Tallent, the first white woman in the Black Hills, wintered near the present site of Custer in 1874-1875 before they were run out by the United States military. The party was supposed to have buried $45,000 in gold coins, gold dust, and nuggets somewhere near the Gordon Stockade east of Custer. Why no one returned for the loot is a good question. Even when the Stockade was being rebuilt, none of the workmen uncovered anything exciting. Maybe the gold is at the bottom of Stockade Lake, a man-made lake.

In Red Canyon north of Edgemont and south of Custer occurred one of the worst massacres in the Black Hills. The Metz family, in 1876, had just sold their bakery in Custer City and were on their way home to Fort Laramie, Wyoming. The group stopped their wagon for lunch in Red Can-

Stockade Lake near Custer in the area where members of the illegal Russell-Collins or Gordon Party wintered in 1874-1875. They were reported to have buried $45,000 in gold near the Gordon Stockade. Could their gold be at the bottom of Stockade Lake, a man-made lake? *Photo credit—South Dakota State Historical Society.*

yon, a dangerous portion of the Cheyenne-Deadwood trail where Indian attacks often occurred. Here Joseph Metz, Mrs. Metz, the wagon driver, and a black servant were ambushed and killed.

When the next stagecoach came along, its driver and passengers found a ghastly scene of bodies scalped and mutilated with dismembered limbs strewn over the bloody trail which was littered with ransacked trunks and smashed boxes. Although the Metz murders were usually blamed on Indians, there was some evidence that the atrocities may have been committed by a band of white renegades, headed by Persimmon Bill, an infamous outlaw.

Many pioneers believed that the Metzes had time to hide their $5,000 in gold before the attack and that the attackers never found it. Several years later, a sheep-herder in Red Canyon found a rusty tin can full of nuggets valued at several hundred dollars. But where is the rest of the $5,000?

Somewhere in the wilds of Castle Creek four German miners working a claim were killed by a roving band of Indians. Then—the legend goes—the Indians buried their victims along with their gold nuggets in a lush meadow overlooking Castle Creek. Because they were presumably overcome with remorse or religious superstition, these remarkable Indians, behaving in an uncharacteristic fashion, blazed four crosses on four big pine trees to mark the graves. Although prospectors later worked this mining claim again, no one was able to locate any pine trees with blazed crosses somewhere near what is now the Deerfield Reservoir.

"Knights of the road"—as the road agents were sometimes called—held up the Deadwood-Sidney treasure coach in July, 1877, about four miles south of Battle Creek on the eastern edge of the Black Hills. The bandits were able to rip open the strong box packed with $200,000 in gold bullion. They also stripped the terrified passengers of their money and jewelry. One woman hid her diamonds in the long coils of her hair. The suspected band was known to have its "Robbers' Roost" in the foothills of the Hat Creek area south of Ardmore, South Dakota, on the present South Dakota-Nebraska line. In recent years there have been many hikers carrying metal detectors, maps, and old letters looking for this buried treasure. No one has reported finding anything valuable. Maybe finders want to be keepers and do not broadcast their good fortune.

Legends of ghosts and trolls and underwater gold haunt the old Holy Terror mine whose buildings still dominate the skyline at old Keystone. A hard-drinking Englishman, named Rocky Mountain Franklin, made a big strike in 1894; he named his glorious discovery in honor of his nagging wife—the Holy Terror. Franklin sold his claim to a mining company, and the Holy Terror became a world-famous gold producer with more legends and anecdotes spicing up its history than any mine in the Black Hills. The weekly take was said to range anywhere from $10,000 to $70,000 per week. Many stockholders got rich.

True to its name, the Holy Terror was a dangerous mine. Through the years of its operation, numerous miners were killed by gas explosions and other accidents. A disastrous fire in the early 1900's caused the building to collapse and killed an uncounted number of miners whose bodies were not

The Holy Terror Mine in old Keystone about 1900. This world-famous gold-producer was a dangerous mine where many miners were killed by fires and gas explosions. Underground flooding forced its closing in 1903. Legend says that amphibious trolls have chained the rich gold ore in impregnable treasure chests on the watery bottom. *Photo credit—Edwald Hayes.*

recovered until thirty years later. Ruinous flooding in its subterranean workings closed the mine for good in the early part of the twentieth century.

Mining experts, both professional and amateur, believe there is still plenty of high-grade ore under water, more than ever found its way to the top. The Holy Terror was always plagued by dishonest miners hiding gold ore in their boot tops and dinner pails. Although there have been many plans to reopen the mine, they have all ended in failure.

Many observers are convinced that there really are trolls, both trouble-making and amphibious, living in the watery depths of the Holy Terror. Reportedly, the trolls have locked up the rich gold ore in absolutely impregnable treasure chests chained to the rocky bottom. Rumor has it that the trolls are determined to guard their cache until Doomsday.

Several versions of the following tale still circulate in the Black Hills around campfires and blazing fireplaces, wherever legends are remembered. An early prospector in Rapid Canyon was shot and wounded by Indians but managed to crawl with his bag of gold into a limestone cave to die in peace. Somewhere along his arduous crawl, he was able to drop a message, later found, saying he planned to cache gold nuggets in a particular cave. He wrote that hereby and forever after he willed his gold to be divided among all impoverished miners.

Through the years, searchers have found many limestone caves, one or two skeletons in a cave, but no mouldering bag of imperishable gold. The message with the last will and testament has of course been lost for years. Nor have any impoverished miners reported receiving their inheritance from this dying philanthropist—not even one gold nugget.

So, dear reader, in your quest for buried treasure in the Black Hills, be sure to check rusty, half-buried tin cans, the rock that looks out of place, pine trees with crosses blazed on their trunks, gloomy limestone caves, tumble-down log cabins, and abandoned underwater mines. May lucky you strike it rich with fairy gold.

LEGEND OF THE ROSES

By Richard B. Hughes

The wild rose (Rosa Carolina) grows in great profusion throughout the Black Hills. It is found on the banks of every stream, in every grassy park and on every mountainside, attaining a depth of coloring that is denied the rose of the plains. The Legend of the Roses first was published in the **Deadwood Pioneer** in 1878 by John M. Whitten, then city editor, into whose hands the manuscript had fallen by accident. A controversy as to the

---

Reprinted from **Holiday Greetings** (1919-1920)
By Richard B. Hughes

authorship arose, which finally was settled by crediting it to F. C. Graham, a Deadwood attorney, since deceased. It is probable that no copy of a paper containing the legend is now in existence, as the entire files of the **Pioneer** were burned in the Deadwood fire of September, 1879. The present writer has attempted to reproduce it from memory, but realizes his inability to do it justice, for as originally written and published, it was a gem.

****

The wild rose grows in great profusion throughout the Black Hills. Legend says that a wild rose blooms wherever the ashes of a white man killed by Indians have found a resting place. *Photo credit—Earl Chace.*

Long, long ago, when the oldest man now living had not yet been born, there came from the Land of the Morning Sun a band of white men in search of gold. For many moons they had traveled by day through dense forests and over wide prairies, and by night their campfire shone upon the streams. At last from a high place they beheld before them the Valley of the Beautiful River, while beyond the peaks of the Paha Sapa glistened in the sun. Then were their hearts glad, for this was the land of their desire.

Descending to the valley they found a village of red men. But no smoke arose from the lodges; no children played about the doors. From all sides came sounds of mourning, for the people had been stricken by a deadly sickness. Many already had died, while of those who yet lived, none were able to gather fuel to keep the fires burning. Famine, too, was there, for though there were buffalo on all the hills, no warrior had strength to draw the bow string that his woman and children might have food.

Now were the hearts of the white men melted with pity. They gathered and heaped high the fuel for the teepee fires, and hunted the buffalo until every want for food was supplied. But better than all, there was among the pale faces a great medicine man. So powerful was his medicine to cure that those who received it at once felt the stagnant blood leap in their veins. This man ministered to the sick by night and by day, until all who were yet alive at his coming stood upon their feet strong and well. Then the white men went upon their way to the land of gold, and the red men gave thanks to the Great Spirit who had sent them help in their time of need.

But there was one among the red men whose heart was bad. The medicine man whose medicine was of no avail against the sickness was filled with anger because that of the white man was more powerful. He whispered in the ears of his people that if the pale faces were allowed to go back to the Land of the Morning Sun with gold they would return in numbers so great that the red men would be driven from their hunting grounds, and the buffalo and elk and deer and antelope would be destroyed. Thus he wrought upon their fears until they sought out the camp of the white men where they delved in the earth and labored in the streams of the mountains. In the early light of the morning while the white men slept they came upon them with tomahawk and knife, until not one was left living, and built fires that consumed the bodies of the dead to ashes, that no trace of them might remain.

Then was the Great Spirit angered. His voice was heard in thunder tones in the gorges; clouds blacker than the darkest night rolled over the mountain tops, and from them came lightnings, blasting and withering all they touched. The winds arose, and catching up the ashes of the white men, carried them upon their wings far and wide.

The red men, now knowing that their work had been evil, fled from the wrath of the Great Spirit; fled from the mountains to the plains. To them henceforth were forbidden the delights of Paha Sapa. Never more might the Indian hunter pursue the elk or deer in their fastnesses; never again build his campfire in the beautiful parks or trap the beaver along the streams. To the place of the sinking of the waters he might go, but no farther. (The rock formations near the foothills were broken by the upheaval of the hills so that many of the streams find a subterranean outlet toward the plains.) Thus the Paha Sapa became to the red man a land of dread.

The wrath of the Great Spirit having been appeased, He caused His Rains to fall upon the earth, and wherever the ashes of the pale faces had found a resting place sprang up and blossomed in beauty the wild rose.

Richard B. Hughes, author of "Legend of the Roses," was the first reporter in the Black Hills. Later he became editor of the **Rapid City Journal**. When he was an old man with hands crippled with rheumatism, he wrote **Pioneer Years in the Black Hills**. *Photo credit—Minnelusa Historical Museum, Rapid City.*

THE LEGEND OF OLD SCATTERGOLD

By Gustav Gottlieb Wenzlaff

The Black Hills may be counted among the most beautiful mountains in the West. They rise high and rugged into the air. Dark evergreens cover mountainside and valley, except where the ruthless axe or fire has felled or consumed the ancient trees. Bright mountain streams rush through valleys and canyons. Perpendicular crags pierce the sky, and around their heads clouds lower and gleam in the evening light.

But the Black Hills are chiefly valued for the gold that they conceal. Here gold in abundance has been found in valleys and streambeds; and gold is still found in abundance in the rocks of the mountains.

Hikers still search the streams of the Black Hills in hopes that Old Scattergold had left gold nuggets sparkling in the clear waters. *Photo credit—Rapid City Chamber of Commerce.*

According to the story, there was once a time when the Black Hills existed in all their beauty, but without gold.

It was in the days when the radiant rainbow spanning the mountain peaks was prized above the luster of silver and gold, that a fair maiden lived with her people in these mountains. She helped her mother in grinding the corn, preparing the food, and tanning the skins. Although thus occupied, and not getting far from home, she nevertheless knew much of these mountains, which she loved. It was to her a joy to watch the morning light upon

---

Reprinted from **Sketches and Legends of the West**
By Gustav Gottlieb Wenzlaff

the lofty peaks, or the storm clouds dashing against the rocks and pines, and the lightning crashing hither and thither, or the timid deer grazing in the glen.

This maiden had a lover, and he loved not only the maiden, but also the things that she loved of nature. He was good and brave.

"Maiden," said he, "how rich I am and happy in these Hills. The sky, the cliffs, the pines, the birds, and the flowers are all ours."

"Young man," said she, "all this is not only ours, but also belongs to whosoever looks. The brooks and birds sing for all who listen. The trees murmur for all ears."

Now, it happened that a stranger came among these people, and he saw the maiden, and was pleased with her looks.

"I must win her for myself," said he. Yet the maiden would not look at him. But the strange young man had gold without limit. This he now brought in large leather bags and poured it on robes spread on the ground.

"This is valuable," he said. "In the distant world this metal will procure whatever the heart desires."

The people looked and marveled at the gleaming gold. The pile grew bigger and bigger, until it was a mountain itself.

"How rich and powerful the stranger is!" they exclaimed. "Maiden, listen to his voice!"

"I am rich without gold," she quietly replied.

"What have you?" asked some.

"I have yonder rainbow bending over these beautiful Hills."

They laughed at the girl, because they had so long looked at the mountain of gold, and listened to the stories of its power, that the rainbow had lost its beauty for them.

"Then I have the sky gleaming each morning and each evening in the purest yellow, red, and purple," she continued. "And I have you, my friends."

They laughed scornfully, and said, "Fool of a girl! What can you do with rainbows and bright skies? Choose the young man with the mountain of gold, and we all shall be rich and happy for all time to come. Choose him or we'll drive you out!"

"Give me until the new sun comes," answered the maiden.

To this they consented.

Now the maiden quietly went up the forest where twilight reigned even when the sun was highest.

"Must I renounce my beautiful Hills and my people, and be untrue to my heart?" she cried. "My rainbow spanning these peaks is dearer to me than a mountain of gold higher than the rainbow's arch. I shall remain true to my heart and my love."

She heard a moan and a roar among the ancient pines; then they creaked and crashed. It became so dark that she could not see the trunks of the trees. She groped her way to a huge granite block with overhanging sides. Then lightning flashed and roared, and a flood of water rushed through the forest.

Below, the mountain of gold was washed and scattered and driven and melted into the imperishable rocks. The people themselves were terrorized, and they crept away in whatever sheltered places they could find. In their fright, above the din of the storm and the roar of thunder, which re-echoed and multiplied between the mountain walls, they believed that they heard something shout, "I'm Scattergold! I'm Scattergold, the friend of the faithful maiden!"

After the storm and agitation had subsided, the people came out of their hiding places and said, "Let the maiden love the rainbow and the colored sky over Hills, and we shall love with her. But the stranger may take his gold and go."

When they looked for the stranger, they failed to find him—he was gone, as was the heap of gold.

In later years, whenever a child found a nugget of gold in a pebbly brook, he said, "Old Scattergold left it here."

The Open Cut in Lead, SD, from which the Homestake Mining Company has removed millions of dollars of gold ore. Was Old Scattergold responsible for leaving so much gold in what was once a solid mountain? The Open Cut is the location of the original Homestake Claim. *Photo credit—Rapid City Chamber of Commerce.*

THE STORY OF BLACK HILLS GOLD JEWELRY

By Alice Gossage

Black Hills gold jewelry is always admired by people coming to the Hills, and many times the question is asked about the origin of the design. The pattern consists of grape leaves and grapes and the leaves are always in two colors, red and green, which are obtained by using two alloys. Gold is alloyed with copper to produce the red color and with silver to produce the green. The same general design is carried out in nearly all articles such as stick pins, brooches, hair pins, cuff-links, beauty pins, bracelets and rings. Black Hills gold jewelry is now sent to practically every state in the union and even to Europe. A matter of fact story is to the effect that J. B. LeBeau brought the pattern with him from California in 1876, but a much prettier story came to the ears of the writer several years ago, which, as near as can be remembered, is as follows:

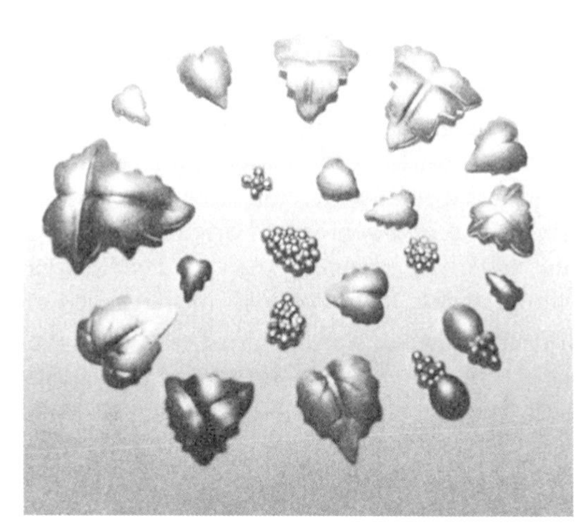

Because of this legend, the traditional design of Black Hills Gold Jewelry consists of grapes and grape leaves, always in light shades of red and green. *Photo credit—Landstrom's Original Black Hills Gold Creations.*

Away back in the early days a couple of young men were making their way to the famed Eldorado, the Black Hills. They had started from Fort Pierre with a freight outfit, but in some way had gotten lost from the outfit while hunting. They had managed to get back to the wagon trail only to find that the outfit had gone on. At one point they found a small piece of bacon and a loaf of dry sour-dough bread, which one of the kind-hearted freighters had left by the side of the road in the hope that the lost men would find it. This appeased their hunger for a day, and they forged ahead. But there was nothing else for them to eat. They came to a small stream and drank their fill, but that was the last of either water or food for nearly two days. They crept on, the awful fear of starvation staring them in the face. Finally

---

Reprinted from **Holiday Greetings** (1919-1920)
By Alice Gossage

they saw ahead of them what they hoped might be trees, and, if so, they knew there would be a stream. After hours of painful tramping they realized that they had not been deceived. Trees were ahead of them. They were so weak through lack of food and drink that they could only drag themselves along, and they also feared that Indians might be lurking in the shade of the trees which seemed to be their only salvation.

At last they reached the friendly trees, thankful for shade and hoping for water. Hope spurred them on, but to no avail. If there was a stream it was some distance on. When about to give up and resign themselves to their fate one of the young men espied a low-hanging grape vine upon which were several bunches of luscious, ripe grapes. Their lives were saved, for the grapes were both food and drink. After eating enough to partly appease their hunger, they crept by the side of a fallen tree covered with weeds and vines, where they would be hidden from Indians, should they happen to be thereabouts, and went to sleep. When they awakened they found more of the grapes, and much refreshed, started on their way.

They learned later that the place of their salvation was the Cheyenne River, near Frank Cottle's ranch. Much to their delight another freight outfit came along, and upon hearing their story, gave them something to eat, and let them work their way into Deadwood, where one of the young men, who was a jeweler, a short time later found work in a jewelry shop. Being something of a genius and original at that, he experimented at times when not otherwise engaged, and one day showed his employer the result of his work, saying, "The originals of that saved my life on my way to the Hills."

The jeweler was delighted with what was placed in his hands. It was a gold ring embellished with grapes and grape leaves, in colors as are to be seen now on the beautiful jewelry, the pride of all Black Hillers, and the prized souvenirs of visitors to this section. So popular did the conceit of the young man's brain become that all his time was given to making the articles that have since become known the world over.

Alice Gossage, pioneer Rapid City newspaper woman. She wrote many colorful historical tales for the **Rapid City Journal**. She and her husband Joseph were publishers of the **Journal** for many years and also published **Holiday Greetings** from which this legend is reprinted. *Photo credit —From Carl Leedy, Fielder Collection, Devereaux Library, South Dakota School of Mines and Technology.*

III.

HISTORIC DRAMA

THE CUSTER EXPEDITION OF 1874

"It was a strange sight to glance back at the advancing columns of cavalry and behold the men with beautiful bouquets in their hands while the headgear of the horses was decorated with wreaths of flowers, fit to crown a Queen of May. . . . I named this Floral Valley."

So wrote General George A. Custer in July, 1874, in his official report describing his expedition to the Black Hills. He and his soldiers were delighted to discover that as they traveled closer to the dark and serpentine ridges humping abruptly out of the tawny plains, this magical range was transformed into the blue-green of pine-forested mountains, an oasis of sparkling water, painted canyons, and flower-bedecked valleys.

Custer's official military report actually became the first publicity brochure advertising the attractions of the Black Hills where B.C. still means "Before Custer."

B.C., no one knew much about the Black Hills even though various expeditions had made some limited explorations, especially the Warren Expedition of 1857.

The Custer Expedition of 1874 was organized at Fort Abraham Lincoln, on the Missouri River across from Bismarck, in northern Dakota Territory; and the home post of Custer's famed Seventh Cavalry. The Expedition was in direct violation of the Laramie Treaty of 1868 which made the Black Hills off limits to all whites for whatever purposes without express permission from the Sioux, the acknowledged landowners of this coveted region, the sacred Paha Sapa of the Sioux Indians.

Despite the words of the treaty which states: "The United States desires peace, and its honor is hereby pledged to keep it," the United States government, responding to continuing pressure to open up the Black Hills to white

The Custer Expedition of 1874 was organized at Fort Abraham Lincoln in northern Dakota Territory, the home of Custer's famed Seventh Cavalry. Photographer Illingworth took many excellent pictures for stereoptic views which he developed in his traveling darkroom wagon by the wet-plate process. *Photo credit—Illingworth, South Dakota State Historical Society.*

settlement, was determined to find out whether persistent rumors of gold in the Black Hills were true. The government also wanted to find a suitable location for a military fort whose establishment would keep the Indians under control—just in case.

Thus, the United States government, under President Ulysses Grant and his controversial Indian policy, commissioned Custer, the flamboyant "boy general" of Civil War fame to explore this relatively unknown region.

General George Armstrong Custer. The United States government commissioned Custer to explore the Black Hills to discover whether rumors of gold were true and to find a suitable location for a military fort. The Expedition was in direct violation of the Laramie Treaty of 1868 which made the Black Hills off-limits to whites. *Photo credit—South Dakota State Historical Society.*

The Custer Expedition, said to be the best equipped reconnaissance to be sent on a mission "outside the states," consisted of 1,200 men including ten companies of the Seventh Cavalry, two companies of infantry, and an engineering detachment. Teams of six mules pulled 100 wagons and three Gatling guns (machine gun cannons). There were over 2,000 animals including mules, horses, beef cattle, and Custer's Irish wolfhounds.

A galaxy of scientists and experts accompanied the Expedition, including an engineer and map-maker, a naturalist, a botanist, two geologists, two practical miners, and a photographer whose excellent examples of the old wet-plate process are preserved.

Five newspaper correspondents came along, and they sent back via Indian scouts colorful dispatches of their travels, recording their reactions to the plains and the Black Hills country, to military life, to the violation of the Laramie Treaty of 1868, to the gold prospects, and to the personality of Custer, the commanding officer. Through the wide newspaper coverage, they influenced readers not only "outside the states" in Bismarck, Dakota Territory, but also "back East" in St. Paul, Chicago and New York.

Two of Custer's younger brothers were with him, Lt. Col. Tom Custer, an experienced cavalry officer; and Boston Custer, a greenhorn on the frontier, who was listed as a civilian forage master.

"I don't know what Tom and I would do without Boston to tease," wrote Custer to his wife Elizabeth, nicknamed Libbie. The two practical jokers tricked Boston with mirages, sent him on impossible errands, pretended to lose him in the wilderness, and shot from ambush over the bewildered boy's head.

There was one lone woman, Sarah Campbell (called Aunt Sally by the men), a colored cook for the sutler. She therefore earned the distinction of being the first non-Indian woman to visit the Black Hills.

A Custer innovation on a reconnaissance expedition was the military band, its sixteen members, all enlisted men, carrying their instruments and riding on matched white horses. Felix Vinatieri of Yankton, the capital of Dakota Territory, was the band leader and official bugler; during the journey he became inspired to compose "The Black Hills Polka." When the command with guidons flying paraded out of Fort Abraham Lincoln, the band played "Garry Owen," the regimental battle song, and then the sentimental tune "The Girl I Left Behind Me," as the tearful wives waved good-bye to their soldiers.

It was an impressive cavalcade—whether for war or for peace.

Buckskin-clad General Custer wearing a wide-brimmed grey felt hat, his red kerchief bright as a battle flag, and riding his prancing thoroughbred horse Dandy, led the way. Riding beside him was Lt. Col. Fred Grant, the President's son and a special aide to Custer. The General was flanked by his favorite white guide, Charley Reynolds, and by his most trusted Indian

scout, Bloody Knife, an Arikara Indian. There were about 100 additional scouts, guides, and interpreters—mostly fantastically dressed Indians.

Felix Vinatieri of Yankton, Dakota Territory. Born in Italy in 1834, he became Custer's popular bandmaster. Band music frequently echoed in the wilderness during the Custer Expedition, to the delight of the soldiers. *Photo credit—Photo by S. J. Morrow, 1882, Yankton County Historical Society.*

(Custer, Reynolds, and Bloody Knife, in addition to Tom and Boston Custer—a total of 294 members of the Seventh Cavalry—would all be killed two years later at the Battle of the Little Big Horn in Montana Territory.)

Up front trotted the matched white horses of the popular musicmakers, followed by covered wagons loaded with supplies and pulled by mule teams, arranged in four columns in the middle with columns of cavalry on either side; the infantry, the beef herd, herdsmen, blacksmiths, and three Gatling guns brought up the rear.

The Expedition, marching in colorful pageantry out of Fort Lincoln on July 2, 1874, wound slowly in a southwesterly direction into the valley of the Little Missouri River in what is now western North and South Dakota, cut through the corner of Montana Territory, down into eastern Wyoming, to approach the Black Hills from the Wyoming side.

On the twentieth night of the march, they camped near Inyan Kara, the highest Black Hill in Wyoming (elevation 6,870 feet), twelve miles south of the present-day town of Sundance, Wyoming. Custer and several officers climbed Inyan Kara where Custer left his autograph on top, "Custer—'74"—and still visible.

Two soldiers died in this Wyoming camp, one of dysentery, and one from a gunshot wound in a fight with another soldier. Both men were buried with full military honors near Inyan Kara.

Custer broke into the main range of the Black Hills near Inyan Kara by following a tributary of Spring Creek, and this was the beautiful park-like area Custer named "Floral Valley," where the horses waded belly-deep in flowers and the happy riders decorated the bridles of the horses with posies. A correspondent for the **New York Tribune** called the valley, "An Eden in the Clouds."

The enclosed graves of Custer's two soldiers who died when the Expedition camped near here. Inyan Kara mountain, WY, in the background. Custer and several officers climbed Inyan Kara where Custer left his autograph on top, still visible. *Photo credit —Fielder Collection, Devereaux Library, South Dakota School of Mines and Technology.*

After crossing the hot windy plains and badlands, fighting dust and grasshoppers, and drinking alkali water, the troopers were overjoyed to quaff the cold water of the mountain streams, to bathe themselves, and to wash their clothes—all the while enjoying the fresh calm air, the magnificent scenery, and the musical entertainment.

"A String of Pearls," the Expedition's wagon train in Castle Creek valley. Photographer Illingworth must have been a mountain climber to find vantage points for his cumbersome camera and tripod. *Photo credit—Illingworth, South Dakota State Historical Society.*

The band celebrated this entrance into paradise by getting off their horses and scrambling up on a ledge to serenade the group with the old favorite, "Garry Owen," followed by "The Mocking Bird," "Artist's Life," "The Blue Danube," and arias from the opera "Il Trovatore," the notes echoing from peak to peak, and undoubtedly startling the ears of any Indians within hearing distance. To the members of the Expedition, it was like music in the park back home. Hardened Indian fighters, both they and their horses decked out in garlands of flowers, had never enjoyed themselves so much "out in the field."

Professor A. B. Donaldson, the botanist and St. Paul newspaper correspondent, wrote: "The music of the band was weird and fascinating. It seemed to come from genii, concealed in the graves and caves of the mountain's side and fancy suggests the haunt of muses. No wonder the Indians have strange superstitions in regard to such fairy dells, and think them the bones of departed spirits."

This lyrical correspondent, sounding more like a poet than a scientist, described the spectacular sunset, the deepening purple twilight, and then the stars coming out one by one. He concluded the record of his first impressions with a paean: "The band played, and thus mingled with earthly and heavenly music, terrestrial beauty and celestial glory, the first day ends and the first night is ushered in to the strangers among the Black Hills."

After Donaldson's readers in Minnesota absorbed his glowing reports, they must have been ready to leave pronto for the Black Hills—even before gold was discovered.

Throughout the journey, frequently tedious and arduous, the popular band played many impromptu concerts, often to ease the tensions and monotony when the mule teams got stuck or bridges had to be built or wagons lowered with ropes into gulches. The band music drowned out the profanity and yelling of the mule-whackers cracking their long black whips at the poor mules struggling to pull the wagons out of a disaster area. The strains of "The Blue Danube" often soothed both man and beast on the Expedition.

At last, the long train of wagons, men, and animals, reached French Creek just east of where the town of Custer is now, and the Expedition camped in "Permanent Camp" there for five days. The men, who thought the area rivaled the beauty of Floral Valley called it "Custer Gulch" and later Custer named it "Golden Valley" for a reason.

Typically, the first thing Custer had to do was to climb Harney Peak (elevation 7,242 feet), obviously to all eyes the highest peak in the Black Hills, and known today as the highest mountain between the Rocky Mountains and the Atlantic Ocean.

Accompanied by several officers and a cavalry escort, Custer set out early the morning of August 2nd to ascend Harney. Leading their horses

Custer's permanent camp at French Creek (Golden Valley) in the southern Hills, located between the present town of Custer and Custer State Park. Here is where the group discovered gold. *Photo credit—Illingworth, South Dakota State Historical Society.*

more than riding them, the men had rough going through the steep trackless wilderness of dense forests, deep canyons, fallen trees. By late afternoon, they had made it almost to the top where they were stopped by high granite walls reaching to the sky. Even Custer had to admit they could not reach the actual summit without ladders. The men had to be satisfied to write their names on a note which was then jammed into a copper shell and driven into a fissure in the rock walls.

But all agreed they were rewarded for their strenuous climb by the stunning panoramic views in every direction: Bear Butte, the lodestar of the Expedition, was silhouetted to the northeast; the spires of the Badlands to the east; and far below were the grey pinnacles Custer named Organ Pipes (later changed to Needles).

Col. William Ludlow, the chief engineer, suggested names for two high peaks in the distance: Terry Peak for General Alfred Terry, commander of the Department of Dakota; and Custer Peak for their leader.

After drinking a toast with cold coffee from their canteens to General William Harney, the veteran Indian fighter for whom the peak was named, the men and their horses started their difficult and dangerous descent at twilight. By nightfall, they were greatly relieved to see a huge bonfire in the distance which guided them in the darkness. Their worried comrades at the French Creek camp had built the signal fire. The exhausted explorers reached camp by one a.m., all hoping they were the first white men to climb Harney—almost to the summit.

By the end of July, the Expedition was burning with gold fever. The two miners, Horatio Ross and William McKay, had been gold-panning the streams ever since entering the Black Hills and had found some particles of gold here and there. Then on French Creek in the southern Hills in the last days of July, the two experienced prospectors found more and more dust and specks and even nuggets of gold in loose diggings yielding ten cents a pan. The miners sank a hole in the gravel bar beside the creek, and the prospects looked glittering.

Gold! That was the cry that stimulated everyone to try prospecting, including Aunt Sally, the Negro cook and the only woman on the Expedition. The hopefuls used whatever tools were handy: shovels, picks, tin dishes, bowie knives. Both experienced and inexperienced miners were excited; they examined the gold particles, which were scientifically tested and even tasted and found to be genuine "pay dirt." The group established a Custer Park Mining Company and filed their illegal claims. According to tradition, the first strike was always called "Discovery" to honor the one who found it, in this case Horatio Ross, whose name shines forevermore in Black Hills history.

Custer, in his military reported dated August 2nd, wrote ecstatically about the scenery, the spectacular views, the delicious wild berries, and the luxuriant grazing for the horses and beef herd. Not until the end of his report did he casually mention that gold had been discovered in several locations.

In a later and more detailed dispatch, Custer said that miners reported finding gold "among the roots of the grass," but he warned that no conclusions should be reached "until all the facts were in."

But first the world should hear the news.

And General Custer was prepared. He knew how to spread the news in the quickest way possible—with Charley Reynolds as courier, the bravest scout in all the west. Taking five companies of cavalry, Custer escorted Reynolds forty-five miles southwest to the Cheyenne River at the edge of the Black Hills. From there Reynolds, declining more protection, set off alone in the heart of Indian country for Fort Laramie, Wyoming, and the nearest telegraph.

Riding during the night with his horse's shoes on backwards to confound the Indians, Reynolds hid and slept during the day. The scout made it in four days to the telegraph where Custer's dispatches of gold discoveries in the Black Hills were flashed over the wires.

The nation, still recovering from the Panic of 1873, was ready for some good news; and the adventurous went wild, especially when the five correspondents released their gold discovery features, some with many exaggerations, which their newspapers quickly publicized from coast to coast.

The Chicago Inter-Ocean carried banner headlines on its front page:

GOLD!
THE LAND OF PROMISE
STIRRING NEWS FROM THE BLACK HILLS
THE GLITTERING TREASURE FOUND AT LAST
A BELT OF GOLD TERRITORY THIRTY MILES WIDE
THE PRECIOUS DUST FOUND IN THE GRASS
UNDER THE HORSES' FEET

No wonder people began packing for the Black Hills—Treaty or no Treaty!

After five days of gold frenzy on French Creek, the Expedition was ready to start for home. Enroute through the Nahant area, Custer shot a grizzly bear with the help of Col. Ludlow, Bloody Knife, and Custer's orderly; and the hunters had their picture taken by Illingworth, the official photographer for the Expedition.

"I have reached the hunter's highest round of fame . . . I have killed my grizzly," Custer wrote his beautiful wife Libbie.

Writing his Libbie, whom he addressed as "My Darling Sunbeam" or "My Darling Bunkey" or "Dear Little Durl," used up some of Custer's boundless energy. When "out in the field," Custer's letters to his wife averaged 30 to 40 handwritten pages, describing the scenery, the explorations along the way, how he was keeping his promise not to hunt far ahead

General Custer shot this grizzly bear near Nahant during the Expedition of 1874. He is flanked by Bloody Knife, his favorite Indian scout, and by two soldiers. *Photo credit—Illingworth, South Dakota State Historical Society.*

Elizabeth "Libbie" Custer, the General's beautiful wife. While exploring the Black Hills, Custer wrote long descriptive letters to "My Darling Sunbeam." After Custer's death at 37 at the Little Big Horn, Libbie spent her remaining years glorifying her husband's memory, writing three books about their life together. She died at age 91. *Photo credit—South Dakota State Historical Society.*

of the wagon train, his skill in trail-blazing—in addition to his inexhaustible love for her. Reputed to be absolutely indefatigable, Custer wrote these newsy epistles after he finished his military reports even though he had ordered reveille at 2:45 a.m. on the Black Hills tour.

During the sixty days of the reconnaissance, Indian scouts on their fleet ponies carried mail four times back to Fort Lincoln, their saddle-bags marked "Black Hills Express." The Expedition correspondence included Custer's long letters to Libbie, his military dispatches, and the reports from the five newspaper reporters.

From the French Creek area, the Expedition went north nearly to Custer Peak until they hit Box Elder Creek and followed it past the present village of Nemo. Custer called the area "Paradise Valley." He finally found a good pass out of the Hills for the wagon train, near the present site of Black Hawk, where the ruts are still visible.

At Bear Butte, six miles east of the Black Hills range, the Expedition camped two nights. Custer and several officers on horseback climbed the historic and isolated mountain which General Phil Sheridan had mentioned in his orders to Custer as a well-known point of reference for the exploration.

Bear Butte in 1874. The Sioux believed Custer and his officers were doomed because they climbed this sacred mountain and the photographer was cursed for photographing it. Custer and his command died two years later and eventually Illingworth committed suicide. *Photo credit—Illingworth, South Dakota State Historical Society.*

(Afterwards, the Sioux Indians claimed that because Custer had climbed their sacred Mato Paha, he was condemned to an early death; and two years later Crazy Horse and Sitting Bull fulfilled the Bear Butte curse at the Little Big Horn.)

Reluctantly leaving the Black Hills, the Expedition started off across the arid plains in a roundabout loop of exploration to Fort Lincoln. From many miles distant, the sentinels on the high bluffs behind the fort saw the cavalcade and clouds of dust approaching one day earlier than expected. Soon the garrison was agog with excitement; and on August 30th, 1874, by the time the sunburned and bedraggled men rode in with the band playing "Garry Owen," flags flying, the crowd was laughing, crying, and cheering.

Libbie Custer, in her book **Boots and Saddles,** recalled that on that memorable day she was simply wild with joy and impulsively ran out to meet her hero who leaped from his horse and bounded toward her on his long cavalry legs. When the General kissed Libbie, who momentarily fainted in his arms but quickly recovered, the men cheered and tossed their campaign hats in the air. It was great to be home!

From the Black Hills, Custer had brought his wife a keg of delicious mountain water. Other souvenirs included elk horns, specimens of gold and mica, pressed flowers, fossil shells, snake rattles, and petrified wood. Always the jokester, he also presented Libbie with a menagerie of live animals, including rattlesnakes and horned toads.

The significance of the Expedition was far-reaching. It had traveled 883 miles, not counting the side trips, on a 60-day journey and had had no confrontation with hostile Indians; for the soldiers had met only friendly ones. From an unknown region, it brought back valuable maps, photographs, and scientific information about the geology and geography, the mineral resources, the flora and fauna.

Custer and his team of scientists and miners proved that the rumors of gold in the Black Hills were true. From the white point of view, the Expedition was a smashing success and another example of the proverbial Custer luck.

True, the well-published gold discoveries were mainly responsible for the Black Hills Gold Rush of 1874-1879, the last frenzied stampede for gold in the Wild West. Then the United States government had to decide how to cope with the illegal invasion of Indian territory and subsequent white settlement of the Black Hills.

From the Indian point of view, the summer march of the "Yellow Hair" was a violation of the Laramie Treaty of 1868 and contributed to the growing anger and belligerence of the Plains Indians, to their disillusionment with promises and broken treaties. The hated trail became known as the "Thieves' Road" and influenced events leading up to the Battle of the Little Big Horn two years later, in June, 1876.

War clouds began to gather. The sacred Paha Sapa of the Sioux Indians were doomed—and so was Custer.

GOLD STARTED IT ALL!

GOLD! That was the banner headline in newspapers coast to coast publicizing Custer's enthusiastic account of his Black Hills Expedition in 1874 which had discovered gold at French Creek in the southern Black Hills.

By the latter part of 1874, the Black Hills Gold Rush began in secrecy when the covered wagons of the illegal Russell-Collins or Gordon Party invaded the Black Hills. During the winter snows, the men built the Gordon stockade on French Creek near the Custer diggings. However, before they struck it rich, the United States Army, trying to uphold its orders to keep out the whites, escorted them all back to Fort Laramie, Wyoming, where they were released without punishment.

Throughout 1875, other gold-seekers broke into the Hills while evading the army. Finally the government gave up trying to stop the gold rush. It didn't matter to the hordes converging on the Black Hills that the Laramie Treaty of 1868 guaranteed the Black Hills to the Sioux Indians who could not read the words of the ambiguous treaty.

People welcomed the excitement of gold discoveries in the Black Hills. Everone rejoiced at a chance to get rich. Who cared about treaties and Indian rights?

Soon experienced miners, would-be miners, visionaries, doctors, lawyers, gamblers, adventurers, prostitutes, and at least one minister of the gospel—all the floating population of the west—and undoubtedly many respectable gold-seekers from all over the country began studying maps and requesting information about the quickest route to the new El Dorado.

By the spring of 1876, miners had found a considerable amount of loose gold in the Deadwood-Lead area which turned out to be the richest placer deposits in the world. Then Deadwood, without even trying, became the rip-roaring capital of the gold rush.

Deadwood in 1877, not 1876 as labeled. Liquor dealer John Treber whose name is on the sign did not arrive until 1877. Deadwood soon became the rip-roaring capital of the gold rush because of rich placer deposits in the locality. Logs cover the placer mine on Deadwood's main street. *Photo credit—South Dakota State Historical Society.*

The newspapers in towns nearest the Hills, all about 200 miles or so from the gold activity, rivaled each other with extravagant claims about the quickest and safest route to the wealth awaiting the opportunists. These excited towns were Sioux City, IA; Yankton, Dakota Territory; Bismarck, Dakota Territory; Cheyenne, WY; and Sidney, NE.

Rawhide Buttes stage station was an important stop on the Cheyenne-Black Hills trail where the horses were changed; weary travelers stretched their legs; ate frugal meals of hardtack, pork and beans, coffee; and used the outhouses. Rawhide Buttes was so named because the Indians skinned alive a foolish white man who had fired into an Indian camp. *Photo credit—Wyoming State Archives, Museums and Historical Department.*

Gold-hunters came by rail to both Bismarck and Yankton in Dakota Territory; to Sidney, NE; and to Cheyenne, WY. They had to travel the last lap by stagecoach or wagon train unless they rode horseback or walked.

Supply boats steamed up the Missouri river to loading docks at Fort Pierre, Dakota Territory, where big Fred Evans and other freighters took over and unloaded the supplies from the boats onto the white-topped wagons. Then oxen and mules began pulling these heavily-loaded wagon trains through the prairie grasslands to bring merchandise of all kinds to the Black Hills. The rutted wagon trails are still visible in many places.

Scene on the Missouri River, Pierre, SD, 1915. Before the railroads came in 1886, tons of freight came by steamboats to Fort Pierre docks where the merchandise was loaded onto wagons for the 15-day trek to the Black Hills. *Photo credit—South Dakota State Historical Society.*

On the trails from Fort Pierre, from Bismarck, from Cheyenne, and from Sidney the wagon trains brought an enormous volume of mining equipment, furniture, beer, flour, sugar, coffee, portable saw mills, and even a wagonload of cats to Deadwood where all the trails converged. In Deadwood Gulch, the wagons had to be lowered into the gulch by ropes, pulleys, and chains. Of course, the wagon trains delivered supplies to other settlements too. At Custer City, the main street had been built especially wide to allow an eight-yoke bull train to turn around without going around the block.

Main street of Custer with a parade in progress, 1889. The pioneers had made wide streets to enable an eight-yoke bull train to turn around without going around the block. *Photo credit —Jessie Y. Sundstrom.*

Many pilgrims, as the newspapers called the gold-hunters, paid a small fee to walk beside the caravan which was so packed with supplies that there was no room for passengers. Pioneers traveled together for protection from hostile Indians and the hostile elements; there were deep and wide rivers to cross, hot winds and blizzards to battle, and loneliness and fear to conquer.

Always making a grand entrance into town were the stagecoaches with their horses galloping the last mile to unload the weary but exhilerated travelers. Often these newcomers were disappointed because they didn't find gold nuggets lying on the muddy, stinking streets of the gold camps. A Deadwood newspaper in 1877 reported that in one day 300 disillusioned fortune-hunters boarded stagecoaches to return to Sidney, NE.

George Hearst bought the Homestake claim for $70,000 from the Manuel brothers in 1877, and thus began the Homestake Mining Company. Hearst, a United States Senator and mining engineer founded the Hearst fortune. *Photo credit—South Dakota State Historical Society.*

Homestake Mine in Lead, SD, the largest gold-producing mine in the western hemisphere. The large brick tower in the upper center is the hoisting plant for the Yates Shaft. Cross-section of the mine in the lower photo shows how Homestake's shafts and tunnels follow the ore body under Lead. *Photo credit—Homestake Mining Photos, South Dakota Tourism.*

In April, 1876, the Manuel brothers, who were experienced miners, discovered a rich quartz vein of hard rock ore from which they took out $5,000 in gold the first summer. In 1877, they delightedly sold their rich claim to George Hearst of California for $70,000. Thus began the Homestake Mining Company of Lead, SD, which became the largest gold-producer in the western hemisphere and one of the world's largest from which millions in gold have been mined. Had they known the future, the Manuel brothers might not have thought $70,000 was such a good price for their claim.

In 1878, the treasure coaches began carrying bullion from the Homestake to the nearest railroads at Cheyenne, WY, and Sidney, NE.

Pouring gold into bricks at the Homestake Assay Office about 1920. In the stagecoach days when gold bricks weighed about 200 pounds each, it took a foolhardy, strong road agent to rob the treasure coach and get away with the heavy gold. *Photo credit—Centennial Archives, Deadwood.*

Soon stagecoach robberies became an important fund-raiser for a few successful road agents; those who were captured with or without the loot were often hanged until dead from a handy tree.

Wells-Fargo Express. Deadwood Treasure Wagon and guards with $250,000 in gold bullion from the Homestake Mine. The strong box was supposed to be impregnable for at least 24 hours. The Canyon Springs robbery was the only successful hold-up of the treasure coach. *Photo credit —Grabill photo, 1890, South Dakota State Historical Society.*

One wonders if as late as 1876 whether there were any Indians alive who remembered the words of missionary Father Peter DeSmet. During the 1850's he had reportedly warned the Indians around the Black Hills never to show the glittery rocks to whites because just the sight of gold drove white men crazy. But DeSmet's warning was to no avail: Custer had later shown off the gold and the newspapers did the rest.

The Black Hills Gold Rush was unstoppable, at least by the United States Government whose vacillating and hypocritcal Indian policies brought about endless troubles with the red man lasting to this day. Congress officially declared the Black Hills open to settlement in February, 1877. According to historian Watson Parker, author of **Gold in the Black Hills,** the gold rush ended with the devastating Deadwood fire on September 26, 1879.

After the terrible Deadwood fire which almost destroyed the entire business district, a plucky Deadwood rebuilt with bricks and stones to replace the tents, log cabins, and flimsy wooden structures.

Devastation after the Deadwood fire on September 26, 1879. Only one life was lost from the fire which started in a bakery. By this date, the gold rush was over. Deadwood rebuilt with bricks and with determination to become a stable community instead of a lawless gold camp. *Photo credit—Centennial Archives, Deadwood.*

Individual mines, especially the mighty Homestake, took over the expensive business of extracting gold from the hard quartz while the rewards from placer mining began to diminish for the gold-panners and sluice-box operators. The twin cities of Deadwood and Lead, as well as other settlements in the Black Hills, began to develop into stable communities with schools, churches, and regular systems of transportation and communication.

The pioneers of the gold rush years from 1874-1879 never forgot the glorious thrills, the hardships, and heartaches of the gold rush which was the motivating force magnetizing the white civilization to the Black Hills. Such is the power of gold.

RAPID CITY'S BEGINNING

As Told by One of the Original Locators, John R. Brennan
Introduction by Richard B. Hughes, editor of the **Rapid City Journal:**

When in 1915 the first number of "Holiday Greetings" was issued, the compilers were fortunate in securing for its pages the story of the location of the site of Rapid City, written by two of the men who had taken part in that important event. Those men were Major John R. Brennan and Samuel Scott. Since that time both have died. Others might write the story, but from the pen of no other could it come possessed of the heart-interest that attaches to it as told by those, the last of the pioneers who drove the stakes or stood guard against hostile Indians on that February day in '76. Hence it is here reproduced as by them written. Our beautiful little city is a monument to those men and their companions. We are thankful for the example of their unfaltering faith and their high courage. As makers of the history of the west, their names will be handed down to posterity while summer clouds shall wrap old Harney's brow and Black Hills waters run toward the sea.

Richard B. Hughes

John R. Brennan, a founder of Rapid City, held many firsts: he conducted the first miners' meeting in the Hills; was elected first president of Rapid City city council; was appointed first postmaster of Rapid; was appointed first Pennington county superintendent of schools; and built the first Rapid hotel in a one-room log cabin. *Photo credit—Minnelusa Historical Museum, Rapid City.*

Reprinted from **Holiday Greetings,** (1919-1920)
By Richard B. Hughes and John R. Brennan

Excerpts from John R. Brennan's Report

I had the honor to be one of a small party who on the 20th day of February, 1876, came from the mountains to Rapid Valley, arriving at a point about four miles west of the present site of Rapid City and camping at what is known as the Cleghorn Springs.

Within the next few days after our arrival we explored Rapid Valley for twenty miles east, also the Box Elder, Spring Creek and other valleys in this immediate section of the country. We held a meeting or two and decided to lay out a town site, and the natural advantages for a town of this particular spot appealed to us and on the 25th day of February, 1876, we paced off a mile square and with a pocket compass and tape line surveyed six blocks in the center of the mile square. The center of the six blocks is now the square of Fifth and Rapid streets.

After this work was done we had a drawing for the lots comprising the six blocks.

A meeting was called, our town site was christened Rapid City, and a board of trustees elected for purpose of administering the affairs of the town.

Committees were selected to go out among new arrivals and make an effort to induce prospective merchants and others to locate in the new town, to look out for the most practical and best places to open up wagon roads leading to and from the future metropolis of the Black Hills—Rapid City.

We began to hustle, do business and make history. It was learned a man from Bismarck was on his way to the Hills with a saw mill. He was waylaid thirty or forty miles north of here and induced to bring his mill here and locate same on Rapid River about three miles above the big springs. This insured us for a time rough lumber for building. About the only inducements we had to offer for new enterprises were an excellent townsite, good water and plenty of it, good climate and town lots. We were long on town lots and could afford to be liberal.

Considerable activity was displayed for a few months. Wagon roads to different parts of the Hills were opened up, one to Sheridan, Hill City, Custer, one to Pactola (known at that time as Camp Crook) and to Rochford, also a road to Deadwood after that town was established, April, 1876.

Because of the government's blockading the roads leading to the Black Hills from different points—Sidney, Cheyenne, Fort Pierre, and Bismarck—and because of Indian attacks, thousands of people became discouraged. Many quit the country and many lost their lives from Indian raids. Here at Rapid City we were compelled to fight them at least twice a week all through the month of August, some of our people being wounded or killed nearly every day.

About August 23 we had a population of some 200 people, and the

24th, four of one party—Patterson, Pendleton, Erquart and Jones—were killed in a fight with the Indians just west of town. A majority of our people became tired of the struggle and pulled out for the Missouri River. Early on the morning of the 25th we borrowed a team and wagon to bring in the bodies of those killed the evening before. We gathered up the bodies and brought them back to town. When the wagon train started for Pierre, most of our population went with it.

On the afternoon of the 25th, and after the freight train had left, those of us who remained met and called the roll; it was found that the population had dwindled to nineteen men and one woman. We had the bodies of the four who were killed to bury. Rough boxes were made, the bodies placed therein, names of the persons written on the lids of the boxes, or coffins, and then they were taken across to the plateau north of the river (North Rapid) and buried in one large grave.

After returning from another burial duty, a meeting was called and the question was discussed as to whether we would give up the fight and follow those who had gone the day before or remain. I am pleased to say it was decided to remain, and the next day we began the construction of a block house for use in standing off the Indians. This building was completed as quickly as possible. It was a two-story affair thirty feet square, built out of heavy logs hewn on two sides and was located on the square of Fifth and Rapid streets.

The block house was the first building erected in Rapid City, 1876, for protection from frequent Indian attacks. Hangman's Hill and Cowboy Hill in background. Located on square of 5th and Rapid streets. *Photo credit—From S. Goodale Price, Fielder Collection, Devereaux Library, South Dakota School of Mines and Technology.*

From this time on for a month or more we had the time of our lives. Indians were in evidence every day. All had to do a stint at standing guard every night and do some fighting during the day. Provisions were scarce, also ammunition. We were prevented from going out of town to secure game or other food. Finally a small party arrived from the Missouri with the welcome news that the government had withdrawn the troops and the blockade was raised.

We took on new life and began to grow again in population. Placer mining was the only industry in the Hills in 1876. No paying mines of this class having been discovered in this immediate neighborhood, we were somewhat handicapped. Rival towns sprang up at different points in the Hills and naturally they did their best to divert travel from each other, and it seemed they all had it in for Rapid City. We were dubbed the Hay Camp, and later on the Gypsum Camp, etc.

Haying in Rapid City where Halley Park and Minnelusa Museum now stand. Other towns dubbed Rapid City the "Hay Camp" because wagon trains enroute to the gold camps in the northern Hills stopped here to buy hay for their animals. *Photo credit—Minnelusa Historical Museum, Rapid City.*

We induced the Sidney Stage Company to abandon their route through the Hills and come via Rapid City. All freight from the Union Pacific to the Hills was turned this way. A little later the Pierre stage line came this way. Rapid City's postoffice was established April 18, 1877. Mail for all the towns and camps south, west, and east in this section was handled from here.

From that time on Rapid City kept going to the front. What was accomplished at that time to establish a solid business and commercial foundation and future prominence required the hardest kind of work on the part of the founders. Fortunately there were very few deadheads among the population. They were made of the material that does things; were hustling and boosting on very little capital. The term "knocker" was not coined at that time, and if we had any of that class of individuals among us they were

Rapid City in 1881. No trees in sight except on foothills in background. No identification on photo. Can anyone identify exactly which hills these are and locate this part of Rapid City? *Photo credit—Minnelusa Historical Museum, Rapid City.*

Watching the Indian war dance in Rapid City, corner of Main and 6th streets, 1893. The moving Indians are blurred because of early photographic equipment. *Photo credit—From Carl Leedy, Fielder Collection, Devereaux Library, South Dakota School of Mines and Technology.*

Rapid City between 7th and 8th streets on Main, 1896. What is the wooden structure from where the picture was taken? *Photo credit—From Carl Leedy, Fielder Collection, Devereaux Library, South Dakota School of Mines and Technology.*

First log cabin built in Rapid City, 1876. Now in Halley Park. *Photo credit—Rapid City Chamber of Commerce.*

The Sidney Stage in the Flormann Block, Rapid City, 1880. John Brennan was instrumental in persuading the Sidney, NE, stage to stop at Rapid; and he became its stage agent. He is also credited with convincing the Fremont, Elkhorn, and Missouri Valley Railroad to enter the Hills through Rapid. *Photo credit—South Dakota State Historical Society.*

not very much in evidence. Rapid City has never had much use for a knocker.

From a hay camp the town has advanced to the position of railroad metropolis of the Black Hills. The same natural advantages that induced the pioneers to locate here and establish a town at this point are still in evidence on every hand. You are fully equipped now to handle and develop these resources; and with the same quality of push and energy as was displayed by our citizens in the past, Rapid City should be the leading city of the richest three hundred miles square on earth. I raise Marvin Hughitt two hundred miles.

Of those who helped establish the town of Rapid City few are left; many of them have passed over the Great Divide. I know of but one, Samuel Scott, of Custer, besides myself, of the original locators, who is now a resident of the Hills. There may be others, but I do not know of their whereabouts. Of those who joined us a month or two later and was here all through the trying time during the summer of '76 and stood up to the rack manfully through all our trials and troubles, was Howard Worth, a resident of Rapid City today. (Mr. Worth has also gone over the Great Divide.)

AUTHOR'S NOTE: John R. Brennan, an Irish immigrant, had many firsts to his credit:
Conducted first miner's meeting ever held in the Black Hills.
Was elected first president of city council in Rapid City.
Was appointed first postmaster of Rapid City in 1877.
Built the first hotel in Rapid City, a one-room log cabin.
Became first president of First National Bank.
Was appointed first county superintendent of schools.

He helped locate the first wagon road from Pierre and was a guide for first wagon train to enter the Hills over that road. He was fire chief of Rapid City, President of the board of trustees at the South Dakota School of Mines. He was agent at Pine Ridge Reservation from 1900-1914. He built both American and Harney hotels.

He married Jennie Leedy who also became a prominent civic leader, founding both the Baptist Church and the YWCA.

John Brennan died in 1919 at age 72. Jennie Brennan died in 1950 at age 89.

CHINESE FUNERALS IN DEADWOOD

The Chinese funeral was a picturesque ceremony in early Deadwood and well-attended not only by the Chinese but also by the curious whites who never ceased to marvel at the bizarre and joyous processions to Mount Moriah cemetery.

The first public funeral for a Chinese was that of Yung Set in September, 1878, which was described in detail in the **Black Hills Daily Times.** As long as Chinatown existed in Deadwood until well after the turn of the century, the whites were close observers of Chinese burial customs.

This Chinese funeral in Deadwood was for a man named High Lee, 1891. Curious whites were permitted to observe the colorful Oriental ceremonies. Note the tea pot, serving dishes, and joss sticks. *Photo credit—Grabill photo, 1891. #3618, South Dakota State Historical Society.*

The funeral procession began in Chinatown in lower Deadwood where first a gong had sounded in the Chinese church called a Joss House to signify that death had occurred.

A horse-drawn wagon bearing the corpse in a cloth coffin led the funeral procession, often followed by a brass band with drums, tom-toms, and cymbals. The Chinese mourners dressed in white robes with white streamers floating from their hats. Some carried joss sticks which were lighted and scented. Every Chinese mourner wore a pink ribbon around his left arm, and some carried gorgeous banners with Chinese inscriptions.

While the noisy procession wound its way upward to Mount Moriah cemetery, the man sitting beside the driver of the hearse scattered hundreds of small pieces of colored paper which had tiny holes punched in them. The purpose of these papers was to detain the devil who must try to pass through each small hole before he could do any damage to the spirit of the deceased. Thus, this ritual gained sufficient time for relatives and friends to bury the dead and save him from the devil.

At the gravesite, the ceremonial costumes, banners and paper were piled up for a bonfire. The coffin was lowered into the grave to the accompaniment of firecrackers being set off. All of these rituals were designed to appease the gods during the flight of the soul of the departed to paradise, the Flowery Kingdom.

Then the mourners poured whiskey and rice on the ground, set quantities of roast pig, cooked chicken and geese around the grave, and passed sugar cakes to all those assembled. Part of the meat was eaten by the funeral party and part of it was left in the cemetery. Apparently, the Chinese were never happier than when celebrating a death.

Many elderly Deadwood citizens can still recall how they as children hid behind rocks and tombstones in Mount Moriah during the burial ceremonies; then when the funeral party had left, they sneaked out to sample the delicious picnic left by the Chinese.

An oft-told tale of Deadwood lore is that an impertinent white man asked the Chinese when the dead would rise to eat the feast left as provisions for their journey to paradise. The Chinese replied, "Just as soon as the 'Melican man comes up to smell his flowers."

During the 1880's, various population estimates placed the number of Chinese in Deadwood at between 250 and 500. The frugal Chinese worked for low wages in the mines and charged cheap prices in their cafes and laundries. Many anti-Chinese meetings were held because of the competition from the Chinese in the labor market. **The Black Hills Journal** of Rapid City, in a 1878 editorial, wrote: "The people of the Hills should take time by the forelock and the Chinese by the queue, and save their country and its hard-working miners from inevitable ruin by flinging these nasty beasts on the other side of Jordan."

The Wing Tsue Wong family. A successful merchant popular with whites, Wing Tsue was a prominent leader in Deadwood's Chinatown. A child of Wing Tsue's was buried in the Chinese section of Mount Moriah in 1895. According to the Record Book of the Deadwood Cemetery Association, Wing Tsue paid for many burial lots for Chinese people. *Photo credit—Centennial Archives, Deadwood.*

Black Hillers were antagonistic toward many Chinese ways, including smoking opium and running brothels in competition with their white brothers. Chinatown was accused of having many stenches that incense and opium could not mask. However, the Congregational Church in Deadwood conducted a school where the Chinese were taught to read, write and speak English.

One of the most sensational murders in early Deadwood, where a murder a day was not uncommon, was that of Yellow Doll, a beautiful Chinese prostitute, whose body was hacked to bits. The mystery of her death was never solved. Chinese officials handled the tragedy with great secrecy and never revealed her burial place. This gory legend is recalled every year when little white girls vie to be chosen to play the part of the murdered Yellow Doll in the "Days of '76" parade.

According to the often illegible and incomplete records in the Record Book of the Deadwood Cemetery Association, there were about sixty Chinese buried in Mount Moriah.

Just how many Chinese are still buried there is a disputed question among Deadwood historians. About twenty removals have been recorded. The Chinese had a clause in their labor contracts that after about seven years, their bones were to be shipped back to China in zinc-lined boxes. Many Chinese undoubtedly did not have reliable employers or relatives with sufficient funds to follow these instructions. The Chinese had a superstition that if their remains were not buried in the sacred soil of China, the spirit of the departed would remain forever a wanderer.

The Chinese cemetery is on a steep hillside in Mount Moriah, and there is no accurate way of determining how many Chinese are still buried there. No wooden markers with Chinese inscriptions remain. At last, vandals and the weather have destroyed all of them.

The colorful and controversial Chinatown of Deadwood's early years has long ago disappeared, but many pioneers nostalgically recall the Oriental contributions to the Deadwood mystique. Visitors can find many reminders in the Adams Museum in Deadwood and perhaps detect the odor of incense still wafting over the slopes of Mount Moriah cemetery.

The Chinese section of Mount Moriah cemetery about 1904. The larger structure was for burning ceremonial papers and incense. The smaller oven was for roasting pigs and other food in preparation for the elaborate burial ceremonies. These ovens have disappeared. Vandals and weather have destroyed all of the wooden markers with Chinese inscriptions. *Photo credit—Centennial Archives, Deadwood.*

HANGMAN'S HILL IN RAPID CITY

A. J. Allen
Age 35 years

Louis Curry
Age 29 years

Jas. Hall
Age 19 years

Horse Thieves Beware

Here lie the bodies of Allen, Curry, and Hall.
Like other horse thieves they had their rise, decline and fall;
On yon pine tree they hung till dead,
And here they found a lonely bed.
Then be a little cautious how you gobble horses up,
For every horse you pick up here, adds sorrow to your cup;

We're bound to stop this business, or hang you to a man,
For we've hemp and hands enough in town to swing the whole
damn clan.

This poetic epitaph scrawled on a pine board was erected over the triple grave of three alleged horse thieves. They were lynched and hanged in Rapid City on June 21, 1887, for stealing horses from the Salisbury-Gilmer Stage Company's barn in Crook City.

Many yarn-spinners of this old horror tale claim that Jas. (Kid) Hall, the nineteen-year-old, was innocent; and that he was simply a hitchhiker who rode in with the two thieves on a borrowed stolen horse.

A sheriff's posse caught the three of them napping on Cowboy Hill, then locked up the trio in a granary barn in Rapid City. Kid Hall protested his innocence so vehemently and flung so many obscenities and insults to the mothers of the sheriff and his deputies that he infuriated his captors.

On that exciting day when officials of the Salisbury-Gilmer Stage Company identified the stolen horses as belonging to them, they celebrated by ordering free drinks for the grateful crowds in the saloons.

During the evening Judge Robert Burleigh conducted a hearing, listened to a lot of evidence which he gave to the grand jury. No written record was kept of the proceedings, and no verdict was ever announced. Afterwards, there was much disagreement as to what went on.

A posed photograph—not the actual scene of the hanging of three alleged horse thieves in June, 1877, on what became known as Hangman's Hill on Skyline Drive above Rapid City. *Photo credit—Minnelusa Historical Museum, Rapid City.*

At midnight, a group of masked men broke into the temporary jail and dragged the prisoners up the hill. They tied the three men to horses which were then led under the branches of a pine tree. The mobsters tied the ropes fast around their necks and to branches overhead. Then the horses took off, leaving the victims hanging.

Kid Hall died yelling and insisting on his innocence. For years, many repentant Rapid Citians who had been drowning their questions in free drinks said they were haunted forever by Kid Hall's death screams. The midnight hangings divided the citizens of Rapid City into two warring factions.

The next morning the Judge turned coroner, and in the presence of about fifty interested parties, conducted an inquest on the three limp bodies. He determined that the knots had been poorly tied leaving the trio with their toes touching the ground; and therefore that instead of dying from broken necks as horse thieves were supposed to do, the three had died from strangulation.

Ever after, the worst epithet you could hurl at a Rapid Citian was "strangler." Oh yes, the judge also concluded that the accused thieves were "hanged at midnight by unknown parties." There was considerable evidence that Kid Hall was innocent—but he was certainly guilty of having a big mouth.

This gnarled tree embedded in cement on Hangman's Hill may or may not be the original tree where the infamous necktie party was held. This example of frontier justice haunted Rapid City for many years. *Photo credit—Rapid City Chamber of Commerce.*

A gnarled, dead tree, embedded in cement, still stands on Hangman's Hill on Skyline Drive above Rapid City. Many insist that it is not **the** historic pine tree—only an innocent bystander to the tragedy. However, it commemorates the first necktie party conducted by vigilantes in Rapid City.

GHOST TOWNS

Adventurous motorists, bikers, or hikers, equipped with maps, guide-books, and even a compass, can easily find a ghost town or an abandoned mine in the Black Hills. The explorers should leave the main highways, and then by traveling up hill and down dale, be willing to follow gravel roads, rutted dirt trails, and footpaths overgrown with wild roses and kinnikinnick ground cover leading into clearings among the tall pines.

Rockerville has preserved much of its past. Adventurous motorists, bikers or hikers, equipped with maps, guide-books, and even a compass can easily find a ghost town or an abandoned mine in the Black Hills. *Photo credit—South Dakota Tourism.*

At the end of the rough woodsy trails and occasionally beside a good road, they will discover clusters of tumble-down buildings, moldering railroad ties, crumbling stone foundations, and mine shafts, yawning dangerously. Even if there are no whispering ghosts floating above the melancholy ruins, the perceptive observer can sense the life and activities of by-gone days, and the photographer can preserve the fading outlines of the legend.

NOTE:
Books used as sources for information about ghost towns are these:
The Black Hills or Last Hunting Grounds of the Dakotahs by Annie D. Tallent
The Black Hills and Their Incredible Characters by Robert Casey
Black Hills Ghost Towns by Watson Parker and Hugh K. Lambert
Yesterday's Gold Camps and Mines by Irma H. Klock
A Guide to Black Hills Ghost Mines by Mildred Fielder.

Even if there are no whispering ghosts floating above the melancholy ruins, the perceptive observer can sense the life and activities of by-gone days, and the photographer can preserve the fading outlines of the legend. *Photo credit—South Dakota Tourism.*

Sometimes, so-called ghost towns are not completely deserted but are populated by several families who live in the decrepit houses surrounded by a collection of rusty old cars and machinery. Or in the forgotten settlement, many have built handsome new homes connected with a tangle of wires and hook-ups to modern civilization.

The Black Hills area is dotted with ghost towns with varying populations: some are completely abandoned and others have human inhabitants with post offices combined with general stores. Usually they were founded in the early days because gold or silver or other minerals were discovered here. Occasionally, villages sprang up because they had hopes of becoming a popular resort or a thriving trade center on the railroad.

The village of Sheridan lies twenty feet below the surface of Sheridan Lake, the largest lake in the Black Hills and created by a dam in 1938. Today scuba divers visit the watery ghost town which was the first county seat of Pennington County. *Photo credit—South Dakota State Historical Society.*

Then disaster struck and wiped out the golden dream: the mines no longer produced; the money ran out; the railroad went the other way; and the investment schemes for grandiose development collapsed.

Soon the people moved away, often in such a hurry to find another livelihood, another home, that according to one legend, they left their houses almost intact with the tables set and the rocking chair creaking with ghostly vibrations. Disheartened mine owners abandoned countless mines, leaving thousands of dollars worth of machinery and equipment as a playground for the squirrels and chipmunks.

Roubaix on the Nemo Road in Lawrence County. Only a few houses remain of the old mining community with stores, homes, saloons, barber shop, school, and even a small hospital. *Photo credit—South Dakota State Historical Society.*

Terraville, located between Central City and Lead, was a busy center of mining activity in 1910. The stamp mills of the Homestake Mining Company were built in the gulch and the miners' houses on the steep hillsides. Open Cut in the background. *Photo credit—Centennial Archives, Deadwood.*

Rochford

All roads lead to Rochford. At least it seems that way to travelers noting the many road signs throughout the central and northern Black Hills which give the mileage to this pretty little mountain hamlet on swift Rapid Creek.

A beguiling blend of old and new, Rochford has a combination general store, post office and liquor store with a gas station across the street. The same genial couple run all these businesses while freely dispensing local news for the regulars and giving directions to the visitors searching for lively ghosts.

Two false-fronted buildings dominate what is left of the old business section: the Irish Gulch Dance Hall is now a modernized hunting lodge, and Moonshine Gulch is a beer and sandwich parlor during the summer months.

The attractive log, non-denominational church is a well-attended "little church in the vale" in warm weather.

The old schoolhouse burned down or it would surely be an historic spot because Annie Tallent, the beloved first white woman to enter the Hills illegally, used to teach school there.

Famous Annie Tallent, the first white woman in the Black Hills, taught in the Rochford school, 1881-1883. Both her house and the school burned to the ground. *Photo credit—Centennial Archives, Deadwood.*

Still standing is the Standby Mill, built in 1879 and 1880 by George Riley Beardshear and Van Dorn brothers, with all the original mill machinery and equipment freighted in by ox team on the Bismarck-Deadwood trail.

The mill was powered by a water wheel which furnished enough power to run three crushers, sixty stamps, and an air compressor to provide com-

The Standby Mill at Rochford. During the winter of 1982-'83 the heavy snows caused part of the roof to cave in. *Photo credit—Fielder Collection, Devereaux Library, South Dakota School of Mines and Technology.*

pressed air for the drills in the mine. Water for the water wheel came from Rapid Creek and flowed about three miles in a wooden flume into a head box over 100 feet above the water wheel.

The Standby Mill is a much-photographed landmark. Most of the machinery and much of the original building has been stolen. According to George T. Beardshear, grandson of the builder, the Homestake Mining Company of Lead, SD, leased the property in 1979, and is conducting extensive explorations in the mine area.

The founder of Rochford, Richard B. Hughes, author of **Pioneer Years in the Black Hills,** really got around the Hills he knew so well, both on horseback and by foot. In 1876, Hughes and two companions, William Van Fleet and M. E. Rochford, were hunting deer when they found fine specimens of gold-bearing quartz on Montezuma Hill. They also found gold in Rapid Creek. In 1877, Hughes returned to the promising area, laid out the town site, built the first log cabin, and named the new settlement "Rochford" in honor of his hunting companion. M. E. Rochford became a county commissioner after Rochford finally decided it must be in Pennington County instead of in Lawrence County.

By 1878, Rochford was a full-fledged gold camp with about 500 settlers and 300 log cabins. Many stores sported canopies over the wooden sidewalks. At first Rochford could not boast of a hotel, or gambling dens, or even one murder. Despite these handicaps, Rochford boomed and provided enough excitement with crowds of prospectors, promoters, and swindlers who knew all the tricks to convince investors to buy their get-rich-quick schemes. Promoters for the Balkan mine tried salting their claims with chopped-up gold coins until a sharp-eyed victim noticed the words "E Pluribus Unum" on one of the fake nuggets.

A small army of claim jumpers bumped into each other stumbling over the forest of stakes while trying to avoid falling into the prospect holes, numerous as prairie dog tunnels in the Rochford diggings.

Two prospectors posted this sign:

> We, the undersigned, knowing our racket, take up this tree. We claim 1,500 feet upwards and a radius of 300 feet from branches to spread and the first son-of-a-bitch who disturbs our stakes is liable to be cannibalized immediately thereafter.
>
> Signed, C. B. Strong and A.B. Striker
> from Montany

Today, the claim-jumping controversies are all in the past. About 25 people live right in the village. Many beautiful homes are perched on the surrounding mountain-tops, accessible only by scary roads which often turn out to be real cliff-hangers.

A few miles up the good road toward Lead is Nahant, an uninhabited ghost town except for one house beside the railroad track. The crumbling stone foundations scattered about do not tell the story of the time when 500 people lived here before the McLaughlin saw mill burned in 1909.

The 1880 train from Hill City, an authentic steam locomotive, often makes autumn runs to Rochford to give passengers a view of the fall colors in the Black Hills. *Photo credit—Rapid City Chamber of Commerce.*

Nahant's claim to lasting fame is that General George Custer shot a grizzly bear near here during his Black Hills Expedition of 1874. The General along with other hunters had his picture taken with the bear displayed over a rock. Road construction work later buried the historic rock.

In the fall, the Rochford area is a paradise for hunters of deer and wild turkeys. No one has reported any recent sightings of the descendants of huge mountain lions that used to frighten the pioneers by blocking the

Huge mountain lions used to frighten the pioneers by blocking the wilderness trails. Today, mountain lions still prowl the Rochford area and raid ranch corrals. *Photo credit—Paul Jones.*

wilderness paths. However, after a rendezvous in Rochford, modern hunters have reported hearing ghostly howls on moonlit nights, but no one has been able to decide whether the eerie sounds are made by mountain lions or by the ghosts of frustrated claim jumpers.

Carbonate

Carbonate is the ghost town populated entirely by ghosts of the past hovering over a beautiful isolated mountain-top not far from the rim of Spearfish Canyon and situated near Little Crow Peak.

James Ridpath, an amateur horticulturalist and a contractor who could not read or write, moved there in 1880. His first project was to plant an apple orchard which still exists. Then he began prospecting and found high-grade silver ore in solid rocks. After he had staked out his silver mine and publicized his discoveries, a wild stampede began from Central City with prospectors galloping up the trail on recently purchased horses and mules. Outfitters soon ran out of picks, shovels, and gold pans to equip the excited stampeders.

At first, Ridpath called his silver mine the West Virginia, then Virginia, and finally Carbonate. It became the silver camp rivaling Galena on Bear Butte Creek.

Despite the difficulties of getting up there from Deadwood, Spearfish, and Central City, by 1884, there were hundreds of people and hundreds of mining locations staked out in the new settlement mushrooming on the broad meadow high in the forested Black Hills. During Carbonate's zenith, the population was said to have reached 2,000.

Carbonate had everything a booming mining camp should have: countless saloons, three boarding houses which fed hundreds of miners, three Chinese laundries, a bank, a newspaper, a school, a bakery with an earthen oven, a Sunday School, and three red light districts.

Carbonate was a lively place and the echoes of its activities must have reverberated from Little Crow Peak to Spearfish Peak. When one miner imported a respectable English lady for his wife, the town celebrated with a big dance. There were baseball games and hunting contests to see who could shoot the most fool hens (grouse). A kilt-wearing McDonald played the bag pipe. A popular little bachelor named Raspberry Brown made more money selling raspberries than he did prospecting. Two wagons of a mule train from Montana were upset. A ten-horse team hauled up a boiler without breaking down. Four daily coaches from Deadwood jounced in, charging two bucks for a round trip on the rugged forest trails which became impassable after a rain.

The pride and glory of Carbonate was its hotel, the William Hugginson Black Hills Hotel, advertised as the largest in the territory, three stories high with sixty-three rooms, an elegant saloon, and a huge ballroom.

A ten-horse team from Lead hauling a boiler up the twisting trails to Carbonate Camp high in the Hills. *Photo credit—From Homestake Library, Fielder Collection, Devereaux Library, South Dakota School of Mines and Technology.*

The largest and most productive mine was the celebrated Iron Hill whose presidents were illustrious leaders like millionaire Harris Franklin from Deadwood; and Seth Bullock, the first sheriff of Deadwood. Between 1885 and 1891, the Iron Hill produced $667,000 in silver, gold and lead. As late as 1930, the Iron Hill was still producing.

Harris Franklin, a poor Jewish immigrant who became a multi-millionaire in Deadwood, was president of the Iron Hill Mining Company in 1887. Between 1885 and 1891, the Iron Hill produced $667,000 in silver, gold and lead. *Photo credit—Centennial Archives, Deadwood.*

Other big mines were the Spanish R, the Seabury-Calkins, and the Union Hill from which a miner dug out a bar of pure silver. During the boom when Carbonate had sixteen mine whistles blowing daily while the miners were bringing out loads of precious ore to the smelter in Rubicon Gulch, it was enough to upset the equilibrium of experienced old prospectors and conservative stockholders, let alone the impressionable tenderfeet, all of whom flocked to Carbonate.

Skeleton of Seabury-Calkins headframe, Carbonate Camp 1955. By 1964, nothing was left of this structure except piles of timbers. *Photo credit —Fielder Collection, Devereaux, Library, South Dakota School of Mines and Technology.*

There was even a mine named for Black Nell, a notorious madam in Deadwood who later operated brothels in Rapid City. In 1982, a history buff showed an author a treasured item: Black Nell's scrapbook. But the owner would not allow it to be shown to the public; it was full of photographs of young men who had patronized Black Nell's establishments in the Black Hills. What if someone recognized those innoncent young faces?

Carbonate had disasters too: fires and floods and accidents in the mines; diphtheria and scarlet fever epidemics; Indian scares when the women and children hid in the mine shafts; arsenic fumes from the smelter killing the cats and causing respiratory problems for the humans.

Before the versatile Carbonate mines petered out, hard-working miners had extracted five million dollars in silver alone.

Today, seven miles northwest of Central City, Carbonate ghosts are difficult to reach whether from Central City via Maitland or from Trojan or from the Maurice turnoff in Spearfish Canyon. Jeeps can manage the rutted trails. So can determined hikers make it while wondering how in blazes the drivers, horses and wagons managed in the old days.

At the Carbonate site with its magnificent views, explorers will find a pine-sheltered cemetery overgrown with wild roses and tansy with many small graves of children who died in the diphtheria epidemic. Throughout a large area, wanderers will discover sunken foundations, a scattering of tumble-down shacks, rusting machinery, rotting timbers, dangerous shafts. A pleasant surprise is Ridpath's apple orchard, its descendants still blooming although over a century old.

Perhaps visitors while trying to imagine what it was really like to live here during the Carbonate boom may be startled by the recurrent sounds of an axe chopping wood in a steady rhythm—but no woodchopper in sight.

According to Irma Klock, author and an experienced ghost-hunter, the axe is swung by a ghost of a Swedish woodchopper, Nils Swenson, who hanged himself in 1884. Through the years many listeners have shivered at the sounds of his axe echoing through the Carbonate wilderness. And they still do.

The Cleopatra Mill on Squaw Creek a few miles from Carbonate Camp, as it looked in 1954. The gold-processing mill constructed of huge timbers, bricks, and stonework was at the bottom of a steep mountain. *Photo credit—From Fred Mosley, Fielder Collection, Devereaux Library, South Dakota School of Mines and Technology.*

Tinton

Tinton, as the name implies, was a tin-mining community which was founded in 1876 by a Civil War veteran named Capt. Edgar St. John who lived here through all its booms and busts until he died in 1928.

Tinton is the best-preserved of the ghost towns in the Black Hills and has the greatest number of buildings still standing. Located near the Wyoming border southwest of Spearfish and not far from the Cement Ridge Lookout in Wyoming, Tinton is in remote wilderness country. Its present owners discourage visiting without permission, perhaps because vandals and looters have already done severe damage to the historic settlement.

The headframe of the Dakota Tin & Gold Company, Tinton, when it was being rebuilt in 1935. Tinton is the best-preserved of the ghost towns in the Black Hills and has the largest number of buildings still standing. Its present owners discourage visiting without permission. *Photo credit—From W. O. Fillmore, Fielder Collection, Devereaux Library, South Dakota School of Mines and Technology.*

In 1879, a group of Deadwood miners who wanted to discourage blacks from settling there perpetrated a hoax by recommending that the Negro prospectors take off over the hills west to Tinton where gold nuggets lay thick as pine cones. The racist joke misfired: the blacks had the last laugh because as it turned out, they very efficiently were able to sluice out quantities of gold. According to reports, four of them took out a fortune in gold on burros and quickly left the country, avoiding Deadwood on their way out of the new El Dorado, and thus losing none of their fortune in Deadwood's gambling dens and clip joints. Ever since, this spot east of Tinton has been called Nigger Hill, and miners have taken out over a million dollars in gold, not counting the four Negroes and their take.

In 1882, Cornish miners found tin in what is called the Spearfish lode and began shipping it to England. In 1888, the American Tin Company sold 500,000 shares on the New York Stock Exchange for two dollars each.

Through the years, a number of companies have controlled the destinies of Tinton, but the American Tin Company was the largest and most influential. By 1890, when the tin lodes were all staked out, a prospector discovered a rich lode of tin on nearby Potato Gulch, where many years later Potato Creek Johnny found the celebrated nugget. In 1893, Nigger Hill tin was displayed at the World's Fair in Chicago.

Tinton, said to be located in one of the most beautiful areas of the Hills and in the magic region where the most gold nuggets have been found, went through a series of ups and downs with consequent changes in living conditions for the miners. If the mines didn't produce profitably, the mines would close, then open again a few years later under different management.

In 1903, Tinton was an attractive company town with a post office, a bank, a newspaper office, boarding houses, numerous company buildings, and houses—all built in a circle around Roosevelt Park named in honor of Kermit Roosevelt, TR's son who had visited here.

In 1927, a promoter named John Blank took over managing the Black Hills Tin Company. He ordered the old mill torn down and built a new 300-ton tin mill that he claimed was the largest in the world. Blank installed electricity and running water pumped from a spring. He built a gymnasium

This wrecked building is all that remains of a gymnasium which had a stage, dressing rooms, theater, basketball court. Built for the mining families by the Black Hills Tin Company in 1927. *Photo credit—South Dakota State Historical Society.*

where dances were held every Saturday night. He even put in a tennis court.

Irma Klock, author of **Yesterday's Gold Camps and Mines** explained how the first giant diesel to generate electricity got up the winding road from Iron Creek to Tinton. Eleven teams of horses produced the animal power, with seven teams in front to pull and four teams in the rear hitched to a push pole to move the heavy wagon with its tremendous load. The wagon tongue was hitched only to the first teams so that the big wagon could swing wide like a modern semi to negotiate a sharp turn at the curves. In several spots, the men had to brace the narrow road with rocks and corduroy the road with logs to support the straining horses and the weighty load. That's how electricity came to Tinton, and the project cost the company $500 for transporting the diesel the last three miles up the winding road.

In addition to tin and gold, in 1928, the company began to mine minerals with strange names and a mixture of colors: columbite (black), tantalum (grey), tantalite (reddish-brown), spodumene (pink or lilac), and amblygonite (whitish-green). But there were still not enough minerals to process to keep the mill operating at a profit. The Black Hills Tin Company closed in 1929. Another company opened Tinton again in 1935 and closed down in 1938.

During the 1930's, people continued to live there and work in the mines when they were operating. As late as 1939, the citizens were reported to occasionally pay for their groceries with gold nuggets.

During World War II the tin, gold, amblygonite, and spodumene mines opened again. Rumor has it that a mysterious blend of minerals from Tinton was used to produce the atom bomb in Tennessee.

In 1953, the big mill burned down, as had many mills before it. Then a sawmill commenced operations in Tinton for a time. Even today prospectors are reported to be working placers near Potato Creek and Bear Creek.

Surprisingly, Tinton looks like a livable village today with well-defined streets lined with the post office, numerous houses covered with tar paper, stores, and small sheds. In the area are the shaft house, the reservoir, and the mill.

When this writer visited Tinton in 1978, the doors to many houses were wide open, as though even unexpected guests were welcome. In the empty living rooms, sparkling fireplaces were made, not of tin, but of a shiny, multi-colored substance resembling mica. Embedded in the decorative base surrounding the fireplace opening were pieces that looked like tiny gold nuggets and odd-shaped metallic fragments of exotic hues, perhaps from the minerals with unpronouncable names.

The houses looked as though the inhabitants had left only last year and that the ghosts had not yet settled in. However, in the cemetery many observers have reported seeing glowing phosphorescent lights hovering over the graves of miners who had died violent deaths.

Cambria

Cambria, Wyoming, was the location of the biggest coal mine in the Black Hills. A man named Frank Mondell found coal in an almost inaccessible spot in Coal Creek Canyon and later became manager of the entire operation. The Burlington Missouri Railroad ran a spur to the site north of Newcastle, WY, the West Gate to the Black Hills, and a wide-open cowboy and mining town. The Kilpatrick Brothers and Collins construction firm built the town of Cambria for the contract labor imported from Greece, Italy and Yugoslavia.

Cambria, WY, the biggest coal mine in the Black Hills, mined over 13,000,000 tons of high grade bituminous coal from 1887 until 1928. The houses for the miners imported from southern Europe were built along the sides of the canyon. Today, only a few skeletal houses, a weigh station and coke ovens remain. *Photo credit—Anna Miller Museum, Newcastle, Wyoming.*

The contractors built rows of look-alike houses stacked up and down the gulch with lodge halls for both Protestants and Catholics, a three-story hotel, an opera house, three churches, and a commissary building which sold quality merchandise at reasonable prices. Built on the west rim of the canyon, the school opened in 1889 with 365 steps for children to climb.

The history of Cambria, like most Black Hills history, is often contradictory. One source states that the railroad company enforced prohibition and would not permit liquor of any kind to be sold in Cambria; another source claims that no liquor was sold in Cambria because the Kilpatrick brothers promised their mother not to allow it; a third source says that beer wagons from Newcastle delivered beer to the edge of town and sold it to the thirsty miners.

Surprisingly, all sources agree that there was extensive bootlegging but disagree on whether it was hard liquor or beer which caused the brawls, highjackings and at least one murder. Whether the murder was followed by a lynching is another disputed point.

One fact that is agreed upon which had nothing to do with the bootlegging is that it was a sad day in 1917 when an overloaded train went out of control and rammed into a drug store killing the druggist and injuring five men.

By 1904, the coal mine employed 350 men of many nationalities, and the population was about 1400. For 41 years Cambria prospered as a mining community. The mines produced thirteen million tons of high-grade bituminous coal used by railroads and by smelters throughout the Black Hills. The Homestake Mining Company discovered gold and silver when they purchased Cambria coke. The Homestake paid the company a bonus for the gold and silver content.

The late Robert Casey, author of **The Black Hills and Their Incredible Characters**, was a colorful spinner of yarns. Over thirty years ago when he wrote his book, he related the story of Cambria; and since then, many writers and researchers have repeated his version of what happened when the Cambria mines were closed.

According to Casey, in 1928, when the vein of bituminous coal began to pinch out to a narrow streak, the company posted a notice that the mine would continue to operate until a certain day and that if the coal supplies didn't improve, the mine would close and the municipality of Cambria would dissolve. The miners, who of course knew better than anyone that the coal supplies were decreasing, didn't want to believe it. Then at noon on the specified day, with men, women, and children holding their breaths and praying, the mine whistle blew in quick short blasts, the signal for disaster. Men whose faces were covered with coal dust filed out of the shaft for the last shift. Soon the families moved in a trance-like procession to their homes. The tellers in the bank closed their accounts and threw their pens like darts into the wall and quit working right that minute.

Before the last man came out of the doomed mine, the populace was on its way out in model-T Fords, wagons, buggies. By midnight the town was empty.

Six years later, in 1934, author Casey reported that when he made the arduous two-mile walk over the hill to Cambria, the ghost town looked as though people were still living there. The houses were open; the tables were set with dishes; scraps of food stuck to the frying pans on the stove; cards lay face down on the tables in the pool halls, clothes flapped in the wind on the clothes lines, and the rocking chairs on the porches were still creaking. A coffin lay across the sidewalk. The water sprinkler for the hotel grounds had been left on until the reservoir ran dry.

Certainly Casey's account of the sudden demise of Cambria is a dramatic story and sounds like good material for a movie script.

But it's not true, declares Mabel Brown of Newcastle, WY. Mrs. Brown is an author, historian, director of the Anna Miller Museum, and editor of **Bits and Pieces,** a magazine of eastern Wyoming history.

Mrs. Brown has interviewed many of the miners who lost their jobs when the Cambria coal mines closed in 1928, including the man who blew the final whistle. But it did not happen the way Casey told it. Her research indicates that the miners had plenty of notice that the mine would be closing; in fact, most of them had already left town before the last day. The populace did not desert Cambria all in one mass exodus with food left in pans on the stoves and the hotel lawn sprinkler running until the reservoir ran dry.

Mrs. Brown concludes: "I have always enjoyed reading Casey's entertaining stories about the Black Hills, but I do object to his taking excessive literary license with Cambria history."

So runs the course of history—seldom smoothly—and often lurching from one side of the ledger to the other.

Five miles north of Newcastle is a set of handsome buildings that resemble a medieval town, the Flying V Ranch, built as a memorial to the officials and miners of the Cambria Coal Company with two swimming pools, one with hot salt water and one with cold fresh water. In recent years the complex has been used as a resort. At present it it privately owned.

Just beyond the Flying V buildings on US 85 is an old trail leading to what is left of Cambria. In the early 30's Cambria was razed but was not completely dismantled until World War II. Of course, the vandals got there

The Flying V Guest Ranch five miles north of Newcastle, WY, built as a memorial to the miners and Cambria officials had two swimming pools, hot salt water and cold fresh water. Today it is privately owned. *Photo credit—From Carl Leedy, Fielder Collection, Devereaux Library, South Dakota School of Mines and Technology.*

early. Several skeletal houses are standing; the weigh station and coke ovens are still there but not much else. Cambria looks like a ghost town.

According to imaginative Robert Casey, many observers reported seeing ghosts with lanterns streaking along the road from Cambria to Newcastle. Were these ghosts of miners who lost their jobs, whether unexpectedly or not? Or were they the ghosts of bootleggers searching for their contacts? Who can say for sure? Cambria ghosts are a mystifying throng.

Rockerville

Rockerville is a rebuilt ghost town with false-fronted buildings, wooden sidewalks and relics of the boom years just off the four-lane highway to Mount Rushmore.

Rockerville has a colorful history. In 1876, a miner named William Keller and his burros were taking a shortcut from Sheridan (now covered by a lake) when a blizzard struck. Keller made camp to wait out the storm; then he began to prospect a little and discovered the first gold in that locality. Because his snowy bed turned out to be right on top of a gold mine, the fabulous gold rush to Rockerville began.

Within eighteen months after Keller's luck, Rockerville had a population variously estimated at 500, or 1,500 or 2,000; at any rate, it was much larger than Rapid City, the hay camp ten miles east.

In the magical style of gold camps, Rockerville soon had a dozen or more saloons, a brewery, a bank, a billiard hall, several outfitting stores, a

McNoun Hotel in Rockerville during the gold boom when there were a dozen saloons, a brewery, a bank, outfitting stores, a newspaper, cafes, and dives where the roulette wheels never stopped spinning. *Photo credit—Gloria and Warren Anderson.*

baseball team, a lecture lyceum, a glee club with lady vocalists, a weekly newspaper, and several cafes, the most popular being the Delmonico. Gambling dens kept roulette wheels spinning day and night.

Captain Jack Crawford, the poet-scout, made his headquarters at Rockerville during the boom, and the town was often called "Captain Jack's Dry Diggins." There is still a Captain Jack's Gulch.

The trouble with Rockerville was that it had no water supply to run the sluices. A placer miner had to use his precious water over and over again in a primitive arrangement called a rocker to shake down the gold from the dirt and stones. During a rain storm the miners ran outside to utilize the water for finding gold in the mud.

Then in 1880 a miracle was wrought. Mainly with eastern capital, the Black Hills Placer Mining Company was founded and raised $300,000 for an engineering marvel designed to rescue the Rockerville diggings from its water problems. By using hundreds of men for doing hand labor without machines, the company built a flume seventeen miles long to carry the water down hill from a dam at Sheridan. It was an immense wooden structure made of planks tied together with timber every four feet and high trestles with two of them being eighty feet high. Bull trains from Fort Pierre hauled in keg after keg of square-sided nails and twleve miles of hydraulic pipe. At last, the flume was completed and twisted and turned over mountains and gorges to bring the surging water from Sheridan to Rockerville.

Men posed in front of the Rockerville Flume, a 17-mile-long structure bringing water from Sheridan to Rockerville where gold was more plentiful than water. Built in 1880 with hand labor, the flume eventually sprung big leaks which rags and horse manure could not plug. *Photo credit—Gloria and Warren Anderson.*

After a few months of success and prosperity in Rockerville, the flume began to fall apart and rot, springing big leaks. No matter how hard he worked, the official leak-stopper equipped with rags and buckets of horse manure could not stop up all the leaks. When the water dwindled to a trickle, people began moving away from the disaster area leaving rows and rows of empty log cabins and businesses which quickly took on a dejected appearance with their sagging doors and broken windows.

A journalist named Ambrose Beirce was the manager of the flume project, which was actually a remarkable engineering feat. He later became a noted writer of excellent but depressing short stories in which his heroes were always victimized by unpredictable and disastrous fates.

Beirce also wrote **The Devil's Dictionary** which included these definitions: "Love—a temporary insanity curable by marriage." and "Inventor—a person who makes an ingenious arrangement of wheels, levers and springs, and believes it civilization."

Beirce's experience with the failed Rockerville flume undoubtedly disheartened him. After struggling to get recognition for his writing, he disappeared during a revolution in Mexico and presumably died there an embittered man, partly because he failed to be successful with his "ingenious arrangement" of the Rockerville flume.

Although placer miners were supposed to have washed out over half a million dollars with their slow rockers (hence the name "Rockerville") be-

Hydraulic mining in Rockerville, 1889. Washing away gravel and dirt from gold deposits. Not a rocker in sight. Crude wooden rockers enabled the miners to use precious water several times to shake down the gold from the dirt and gravel. *Photo credit—Minnelusa Historical Museum, Rapid City.*

tween 1876-1879, optimistic promoters in the boom days claimed there was at least two billion dollars in gold in the area just waiting for miners with a reliable water supply to extract it from the ground.

Today, modern promoters do their best to take in tourist cash. Several eating establishments and business places are located on the boardwalk. The gold mine with fragments of the flume visible here and there along the route is still there as are a log cabin and the original schoolhouse. Ascension Street, running north and south, turned out to be appropriately named because it leads to the Stratosphere Bowl where the first successful balloon flights into space were made in the 1930's.

Sometimes people hear the ghosts of yesterday frantically working their noisy rockers. But the resurrected ghost town is not as populous or roaring as it used to be in the hey-day of the gold camp.

Galena

Galena, a ghost town about six miles southeast of Deadwood, as the magpie flies, is in a deep forested gulch along Bear Butte Creek and was once a busy silver-mining town. The word "galena" means lead ore and that's where the silver was found.

In 1877-1878, Galena had a sawmill, a smelter, a narrow-gauge passenger train, four stores, three butcher shops, wet and dry drinking establishments. There was also an opera house which burned, following the tradition of most opera houses in the Black Hills.

Pioneers reported that mountain lions sometimes stalked into town, and on one memorable occasion a hungry lion kept a frightened man locked all night in his privy.

Galena's biggest promoter was Colonel J. H. Davey who arrived in 1880, took over the Florence mine and began mining silver, taking out $75,000 in three years. He built the first completely equipped silver-smelting plant in the Hills and also an elegant sixteen-room house which was a center of social life for the community.

Davey became involved in litigation over whether he had the right to follow the horizontal drift of a ledge beyond the boundaries of his mine. The sixteen-year dispute in the courts favored the plaintiff who said Davey had no right to infringe on the adjacent claim, and in a significant, far-reaching decision, the courts agreed. When the case went to the supreme court of Dakota Territory, Davey settled in an out-of-court compromise. Then Davey closed his mines and pulled out of Galena for new enterprises in the far west.

Although Galena had several more boom periods, the mining industries never fully recovered from Davey's leaving the country.

A bird's-eye view of Galena silver mining camp in 1890. In 1877-1878, Galena had a saw mill, a smelter, a narrow-gauge passenger train, four stores, three butcher shops, wet and dry drinking establishments, and an opera house which burned. *Photo credit—#3567 Grabill photo, South Dakota State Historical Society.*

Today, within a two-mile radius of Galena are an amazing number of glory holes, tunnels, shafts, and collapsed timbers of many mines and claims, both silver and gold, including the Florence, the Sitting Bull, the Hoodoo, the El Refugio, the General Custer, the Red Cloud, the Golden Crest, the Gilt Edge Maid, and the Oro Fino.

Several of the original buildings are still standing: the log cabin which belonged to Thomas Walsh who became a millionaire after he left Galena; the schoolhouse with the bell tower built in 1882; and the assay office, which now houses the ghost town's only business, an art gallery owned by a local artist and named "Inga D's Little Gallery in the Hills." In 1983, Galena has a population of sixteen and a number of attractive residences.

The Sitting Bull tunnel, Galena, in 1954. Now closed. Many ghost-hunters have been injured exploring old tunnels and mine shafts. *Photo credit—Fielder Collection, Devereaux Library, South Dakota School of Mines and Technology.*

Galena's most famous resident was Sarah Campbell (Aunt Sally), the black cook for the Custer Expedition of 1874 and the first non-Indian woman to enter the Black Hills. Pipe-smoking Aunt Sally spent her last years in Galena where she was a popular midwife and cook. She is buried in beautiful Vinegar Hill cemetery in Galena. For years, her grave was tended by Fred Borsch and Seth Galvin, two sons of pioneer parents who had liked and admired her.

Aunt Sally Campbell's grave and marker in Vinegar Hill cemetery, Galena, SD. Marker erected by Seth Galvin and Fred Borsch, Galena pioneers. "She Ventured With the Vanguard of Civilization." *Photo credit—Fielder Collection, Devereaux Library, South Dakota School of Mines and Technology.*

Fred Borsch III, whose parents had managed an early boarding house, was born and raised in Galena and became its most prominent citizen. In 1947, he acquired a pet coyote named Tootsie who was eventually designated the state animal of South Dakota. During the day Tootsie roamed the hills hunting and howling, just as a coyote should; at night, she always returned to sleep quietly on Borsch's bed. Tootsie was an honored guest for twelve years at the "Days of '76" parade in Deadwood riding on a float with her master.

Fred Borsch and Tootsie, his pet coyote, who became South Dakota's official state animal. For twelve years Tootsie rode with her master in the "Days of '76" parade in Deadwood. *Photo credit—L. L. Cook Company, Milwaukee, Jeri Fahrni Collection.*

Borsch, who was reputed to own all the mining claims in Galena, lived in a beautiful log cabin overlooking the declining silver camp. He loved to show visitors his artifacts and historical materials, including the original mahogany bar from the Gem Theater in Deadwood, a pair of Potato Creek Johnny's tiny boots, and Seth Galvin's handwritten memoirs. Borsch, a pioneer pilot in early South Dakota aviation, proudly claimed to have helped push Lindbergh's "Spirit of St. Louis" out of the hangar before Lindy's memorable Atlantic flight.

To the end of his days, Fred Borsch talked wistfully of building a helicopter pad on his property and of the future when Galena would again become a booming silver-mining community.

Fred Borsch died in 1981 at age 81. According to his written request, the song, "Toot-Toot-Tootsie—Goodbye" was sung at his funeral where he did not want friends to mourn his passing. Instead, he had suggested that the mourners enjoy themselves visiting about the good old days in the Northern Hills. Paul Harvey, a national radio announcer, devoted an entire program to reporting the life and death of Fred Borsch.

He is buried in Vinegar Hill cemetery not far from his friend Seth Galvin, a prominent silver miner who died in 1939. Because Galvin had extracted a promise before he died, Fred Borsch dug his friend's grave at a 75-degree angle so Seth could see the sun come up.

Yes, Galena has its share of picturesque ghosts.

Cascade, Cascade Springs

Cascade resembled a smiling debutante waiting to greet her guests—but nobody came to the party. And without her wealthy patrons, the debutante was desolate and heartbroken.

It's an incredible tale. Cascade, founded in 1888, and located about ten miles south of Hot Springs, expected to become a health resort rivaling Hot Springs. Speculators from Chicago and the southern Hills selling options on the dream had spent thousands of dollars creating a setting to entertain hordes of wealthy tourists and health-seekers the new railroad would surely bring to Cascade.

For reasons that no one clearly understood, the Burlington and Missouri railroad decided not to build through Cascade even though it was the shortest and most logical route for the rails to be laid to Hot Springs; instead the Burlington decided to cut over to Edgemont, 25 miles longer, and then go north. Who would have believed it?

Obviously, the capitalists had taken no stock in the country proverb: "Don't count your chickens before they're hatched."

It all began with the Cascade Medicinal Spring Company. In 1891, the company sponsored free excursions for visitors who wanted to inspect Cascade Springs and see for themselves why they should buy lots and invest in the exciting enterprises in beautiful Alabaugh Canyon.

River Street, Cascade Springs, with sanitarium in background. About 1891. Promoters invested a fortune to build a health spa hoping to attract crowds of wealthy tourists and health-seekers. But the customers never arrived. The railroad did not build through Cascade and the dreams died. *Photo credit —South Dakota State Historical Society.*

The Company provided free accommodations at the elegant hotels for the potential investors and sponsored tours of the six springs and their cool waters said to contain great curative properties for countless diseases. The Bower Family Band accompanied one excursion and enlivened the tour day with music.

The Cascade Geyser, the newspaper named in honor of a geyser three feet high, listed all the new structures going up and predicted great prosperity in Cascade's future. "Parties wishing to settle here and go into business should come at once to get in on the ground floor and make money," urged the promoters.

In 1892, the expanding resort town had three hotels, the four-story Cascade House with a five-story tower being the fanciest with porches and verandas overlooking the spas and pavilions. The Cascade House had black marble bathtubs with gold fixtures, marble halls, and paneling of marble, bronze, and rare woods.

The two-story sanitarium-bath house combination had parlors for both men and women, a large number of Turkish baths with hot air, steam and cooling rooms "all of which the public will be allowed to enjoy." Plans for a hospital and another sanitarium were under way.

That the railroad went the other way was a numbing realization for everyone, and the national financial panic added to the woes. Despite all the marvelous enticements, the tourists never did arrive in Cascade. Why

The handsome sanitarium at Cascade which had parlors for both sexes, Turkish baths, steam and cooling rooms. But no tourists ever used the facilities because the railroad went the other way. *Photo credit—Helen Magee.*

should they ride on a bumpy stagecoach when they could travel on a comfortable train to Hot Springs where the accommodations were excellent and the healing waters were warmer and already famous?

Thus, the party for the debutante never came off, and all the Chicago speculators and local promoters lost their investments. Sadly, people moved away, beginning in 1893.

Construction stopped, and some buildings which had never been used

Cascade Falls a few miles down the road from the ghost town. According to the old newspaper, the **Cascade Geyser,** the stream used to drop eighty feet in a mile. Probably still does. *Photo credit—Rapid City Chamber of Commerce.*

by any customer—rich or poor—were torn down stone by stone and hauled into Hot Springs for use in building the library, the Catholic Church, and the Sisters Hospital.

By 1900, the Cascade post office served only 25 people. By 1915, the post office had been moved to Hot Springs.

Today, only a corner of the luxurious Cascade House remains. In Keith Memorial Park, a charming picnic area beside a little creek decorated with watercress, the great geyser bubbles softly instead of throwing water three feet into the air. A few miles down the road is the pretty cascade about twelve feet high and forty feet wide. According to the old newspaper, the **Cascade Geyser,** it used to drop eighty feet in a mile. Probably still does.

Summer tourists continue to stop along SD 71 to see the Ghost Town Deluxe, as the South Dakota Historical Society labeled Cascade Springs in 1950. However, now the entire area is owned by Mark Lamphere and Cindy Reed who raise registered Texas Longhorns on their "Cascade Ranch." Visitors should get permission before they tramp around searching for ruins of fairy tale castles, a waterfall and a geyser rivaling Yellowstone's, and warm rivers flowing with medicinal waters.

Mark and Cindy live in the imposing W. Allen bank building, the only remaining structure still intact, which they have remodeled into attractive living quarters with lace curtains on the big windows.

Cindy complained, "Tourists ignore our 'Private Property—Keep Out!' signs and charge right in without even knocking. They don't even notice us—you'd think we were ghosts or something."

The W. Allen bank building on the left is the only remaining structure still intact in Cascade Springs. Now a private residence. The owners of the ghost town raise cattle on their "Cascade Ranch." *Photo credit—South Dakota State Historical Society.*

IV.
NATURAL AND MAN-MADE WONDERS

THE BLACK HILLS: WHERE THE BUFFALO ROAM IN CUSTER PARK

Custer State Park in the Black Hills of South Dakota is an amazing example of the oft-repeated observation that the Black Hills offer more variety than any area of comparable size in the world. Sharp ecological contrasts appear throughout the 72,000-acre park, a blend of grass and pine and mountain, and one of the largest state parks in the contiguous United States. It is also a game preserve that is home on the range to the country's largest buffalo herd (1,300).

Here, the tawny plains roll up to the meadows which then sweep up to the precipitous pine-covered slopes of granite mountains over 6,000 feet high. The park ranges through 4,000 feet of altitude, and each zone has its characteristic flora and fauna, preserved in its primitive beauty as much as possible despite the hotels, lodges, campgrounds, picnic areas and recreational activities of many kinds.

Not barren hills at all, as the name implies, the Black Hills bloom in an area about 100 miles long and 50 miles wide in western South Dakota and eastern Wyoming. These "hills" are actually the highest mountains between the Rockies and the Atlantic.

By Helen Rezatto

Within Custer State Park and close to it is some of the most colorful scenery in the hills. Two of these attractions, Mount Rushmore and Harney Peak (7,242 feet), the highest mountain east of the Rockies, loom up just outside the park, and may be glimpsed from overlooks throughout the park. Two mountain roads, especially designed to show off the scenery both inside and outside the park, are marvels of engineering skill: the Needles Drive and Iron Mountain Road.

Through the Forest

The 14-mile Needles Drive, in the northwest corner of the park, begins at its lower end near Legion Lake, with comfortable curves through a forest of ponderosa pine, spruce, birch and aspen; then abruptly the elevation rises so swiftly that you seem to be riding at a level with the tops of the tallest evergreens. Before you know it, your car is making hairpin curves and passing in and out of narrow rocky tunnels within a granite city of sky-piercing monoliths; these are the Needles, a jagged mountain range of purplish granite. The Needles Drive, completed in 1922, is a thrilling but safe road for sensible drivers. Architect Frank Lloyd Wright, an admirer of the Black Hills, commented: "The Needles is an endless supernatural world more spiritual than Earth but created out of it."

Cathedral Spires on the Needles Drive in Custer State Park. Mountain climbers love to climb these jagged pinnacles of purplish granite. *Photo credit—South Dakota Tourism.*

The climax of the drive is where Sylvan Lake (6,250 feet) gleams among the giant rocks and cliffs at the base of Harney Peak. Sylvan Lake, variously called turquoise or emerald or zircon, is a lovely example of what man and nature can create when they cooperate intelligently. Although you would never suspect it of this mountain tarn, the lake is man-made; an unobtrusive dam keeps the water pooled within the deep natural basin formed by the elephant's foot rocks and broken granite lances. Three other lakes within the park are also man-made: Legion, Stockade, and Center.

Road to Mount Rushmore

The 17-mile Iron Mountain Road begins in the park and ends at Mount Rushmore. This is the dramatic approach newcomers should take for their first introduction to Mount Rushmore, the most popular tourist attraction in the Black Hills. Your car will pass through three tunnels; and in each one, as you gaze toward the light at the far end, there you will recognize the likenesses of Washington, Jefferson, T. Roosevelt, and Lincoln framed like a classic miniature. Each successive tunnel will present a closer and sharper telescopic view.

The road, which goes up one side and down the other of Iron Mountain, eventually curls around and down-down-down on three pigtail bridges constructed of native logs and natural stone; these bridges are designed for fast drops in road elevation. Finally, you are at the bottom of Grizzly Creek Canyon and soon arrive—perhaps a little breathless—near the foot of Mount Rushmore National Memorial for a close-up inspection of sculptor Gutzon Borglum's masterpiece.

Vantage Points

Be sure to stop at the various pull-outs throughout the park, especially on the summit of Iron Mountain (5,445 feet). Climb the stairway to the wooden platform, the Norbeck Memorial Overlook, from where the green curves and valleys and peaks of the Black Hills are visible for miles. To the east are panoramic vistas over the plains where the eroded and jagged battlements of the Badlands National Monument are silhouetted 60 miles away.

Peter Norbeck, the man for whom the overlook is named, was both a governor and senator of South Dakota. Called the Father of Custer Park, Governor Norbeck, in 1919, persuaded the State Legislature to create it.

As soon as his life-long dream of Custer State Park became a reality, Governor Norbeck went to work. Over and over again, the Governor, who weighed 240 pounds, tramped through the mountain wilds to show engineers how he wanted to build the Needles Drive and later, the Iron Mountain Road, always insisting on preserving the scenery. When the engineers scoffed at his ideas and labeled them engineering nightmares, he responded by calling them "diploma boys"; if they said flatly that it couldn't be done, he fired them on the spot.

Peter Norbeck holding the burro's reins. With Clyde Jones in Custer State Park, 1927. Norbeck, both a governor and senator of South Dakota, became known as the Father of Custer State Park. He persuaded the State Legislature to create it and worked endlessly for its development. *Photo credit—South Dakota State Historical Soceity.*

"Get Out and Walk"

"This is a scenic road, not a commercial one," he roared in his Norwegian accent. "You're not supposed to drive 60 miles an hour. To do the scenery half justice, people should drive 20 or under; to do it full justice, they should get out and walk."

Through the years the Governor battled the Legislature to get state funds for the construction of scenic highways with hairpin curves, with hardrock tunnels framing Mount Rushmore, with pigtail bridges of native materials. The two roads are a tribute to his persistence and imagination.

Not far from the beginning of Iron Mountain Road are some surprising traffic-stoppers: about 25 wild burros who will eat anything the tourists feed them. These freeloaders hang around the highway during the day waiting for cars to stop with handouts. Maybe the aggressive burros try harder because they are the second most popular animals in the park.

Wild burros hoping for a hand-out are traffic-stoppers on the Iron Mountain Road which begins in Custer State Park. *Photo credit—Rapid City Chamber of Commerce.*

The most popular is the buffalo—or more correctly—the bison. A large bull may weigh a ton, stand about six feet tall at the hump and measure 10 feet from the massive, horned head to the ridiculously short tail, the entire animal a shaggy mass of muscle and power. The bison are dangerous and unpredictable; tourists are warned to observe them and to photograph them from inside their cars.

Where the Buffalo Roam

Stray buffalo from the main herd can always be seen on the Wild Life Loop road which leaves the higher elevations and the forests of the north for the more sparsely wooded foothills and rolling plains of the southern park. Here, where the mountains and prairies meet, is the range on which buffalo live much as the bison did centuries ago. The buffalo has been saved from extinction mostly through the efforts of the park, of adjoining Wind Cave National Park to the south, and of a few other state and national parks in the United States and Canada.

Buffalo are dangerous and unpredictable. Tourists should observe and photograph them from a distance. This bull charged the photographer right after this close-up shot was taken. *Photo credit—Earl Chace.*

Stray buffalo from the main herd can always be seen on the Wild Life Loop which leaves the higher elevations and forests of the north for the more sparsely wooded foothills and rolling plains of the southern park. *Photo credit—South Dakota Department of Game, Fish and Parks.*

To keep the buffalo from becoming too numerous for the amount of grazing land, rangers hold yearly buffalo auctions and hunts. Hunters, whose names are drawn by lot, are permitted, for a $1,000 fee, to shoot trophy buffaloes, under close supervision by the rangers. Buffaloes are the main source of revenue for the park, and their tasty meat is served at all of the park restaurants.

Movie Stars

Park bison have performed in many movies, almost learning to stampede on cue. The herd and the varied terrain of the park, most of it unmarked by civilization, have appeared in "How the West Was Won," "The Vanishing Prairie," "A Man Called Horse," and other Westerns. In 1978, the television show, "The Wild Kingdom" shot scenes for a "Prairie Spring" feature in the park.

Other animals frequently spotted on the Wild Life Loop and on gravel side roads are the pronghorn antelope, deer, elk, bighorn sheep, Rocky Mountain goats, prairie dogs, wild turkeys, coyotes, and an occasional rattlesnake.

Antelope on Wild Life Loop, Custer State Park. Flashing rump patches of the running antelope reflect the sun and make the animal visible for miles. *Photo credit—Earl Chace.*

Typical of the contrasts within the park is the fact that the modern airstrip used by both rangers and tourists is on the east Wild Life Loop, only a few miles from the entrance to the primitive area of the French Creek wilderness, a narrow and tortuous 12-mile canyon twisting approximately through the center of the park. The canyon challenges experienced hikers. About halfway through the gorge is the Narrows where the canyon walls are so close to the creek that there is no room to pass between them; the determined backpacker has to decide whether to take a swim in the cold deep water of French Creek or try the precipitous climb straight up the canyon walls.

Hiking in French Creek wilderness, a narrow, tortuous 12-mile canyon twisting approximately through the center of Custer State Park. About half-way through the gorge is the Narrows where the canyon walls are so close to the creek that there is no room to pass between them—except in the water. *Photo credit—South Dakota Tourism.*

Park Museum

The main thoroughfare through the park is Route 16A; on this road are the park office, the Park Museum and Welcome Center, Coolidge Inn and the State Game Lodge. On the eastern side of the park, Route 16A becomes the Iron Mountain Road; on the west side, Highway 87 going south toward Wind Cave National Park passes by the side road to Mount Coolidge (6,032 feet), with a lookout tower on top and marvelous views of the area.

The State Game Lodge is a picturesque old hotel, used as a summer White House by President Calvin Coolidge in 1927 and visited by President Dwight Eisenhower in 1953. *Photo credit—South Dakota State Historical Society.*

The State Game Lodge is a picturesque old hotel, used as a summer White House by President Calvin Coolidge in 1927 and visited by President Dwight Eisenhower in 1953. You can sit on the veranda where Grace Coolidge used to knit while watching the buffalo roam across the lawn—as they still do. You can catch fish in the nearby creeks which were kept stocked with starving trout for the two Presidents. In the dining room, where stuffed pheasants adorn the light fixtures, guests can dine on buffalo, elk, native Dakota pheasant and rainbow trout.

A Lofty Retreat

The highest resort in the Black Hills is Sylvan Lake Hotel where visitors sip cocktails on the flagstone terrace among the tall pines. Guests are confronted with the delightful dilemma of not knowing where to look first: below to Sylvan Lake, straight out at the Needles, or up at the lookout tower on nearby Harney Peak. Here, too, buffalo and other native delicacies are served.

In the park, there is summer theater at the Black Hills Playhouse; square dancing at the Barn; a free movie, "Paha Sapa," which dramatizes the history and geology of the park and of the Black Hills (called Paha Sapa by the Sioux Indians); jeep rides to the middle of the biggest buffalo congregation; fishing in lakes and streams; swimming and boating in the lakes, horseback riding on trails, and just plain sightseeing.

Sylvan Lake Hotel, the highest resort in the Black Hills, overlooking Sylvan Lake (6,250 feet), provides spectacular views of the lookout tower on Harney Peak and the Needles. *Photo credit—Black Hills and Badlands Association.*

One of the best ways to get to know the Black Hills is to pack a picnic lunch, take along a trail map, and go on a hike. You are sure to see a myriad of wild flowers: the star lily, the bluestem pricklypoppy, the butter and eggs snapdragon. You can't miss the kinnikinnick or bearberry, the forest's main ground cover which provided smoking material for the Indians. You will also see magpies and deer and mica rocks that glitter like gold.

There are easy trails for strollers and medium-rugged marked trails for hikers, and in addition one can follow one of the two long trails beginning at Sylvan Lake that lead to the summit of Harney Peak. The first white men to attempt to climb the peak (on horseback) were General Custer and his staff in 1874 and they were frustrated at not being able to scale the steep cliffs to the summit. Today, from atop the lookout tower on a clear day, you can see into Nebraska and Wyoming.

Fossils of marine creatures can still be found on top of Harney; the Black Hills, one of the oldest mountain ranges in the world, were once at the bottom of an inland sea.

Search for Gold

Custer State Park is named for General George Custer whose military report actually became the first publicity brochure advertising the attractions of the Black Hills. He and his ill-fated Seventh Cavalry had been commissioned by the United States Government, in the summer of 1874, to explore this relatively unknown region and to find out whether rumors of gold were true. The general was so captivated with the "enchanting scenery" and the "magnificence of the views," that not until the end of this official report did he get around to mentioning that "gold has been found in several places."

The Custer Expedition encamped for five days along French Creek, west of the park (on Route 16A), and this is where gold was discovered. Custer's widely publicized report of gold discoveries on French Creek was mainly responsible for the Black Hills Gold Rush of 1876. Now it's the tourist rush; over one million people visited the park in 1977.

The late Badger Clark, Poet Laureate of South Dakota, at his cabin "The Badger Hole" near Legion Lake. He lived an idyllic existence in Custer State Park for thirty years. *Photo credit —South Dakota State Historical Society.*

An absorbing place to visit is the Badger Hole, a cabin in the pines near Legion Lake. Here the late Badger Clark, poet laureate of South Dakota, lived an idyllic existence for 30 years. Some of his verse seems addressed to all visitors:

"But leave me the song in the pine tops
The breath of a wind from the snows
With mountains of green all around me
And mountains of white above."

and

"It's only lovely, free and big
And isn't worth a cent.
I pray that them who come to spoil
May wait till I am dead."

MOUNT RUSHMORE NATIONAL MEMORIAL

"There's the place to carve a great national memorial. American history shall march along that skyline," prophesied Gutzon Borglum, the noted sculptor, in 1924, when he first beheld the granite uplift known as the Harney Range, the highest mountains in the Black Hills of South Dakota. And he was right. But the memorial was not completed until seventeen years later, after many delays caused by a lack of financing, by complex engineer-

Mount Rushmore before sculptor Gutzon Borglum went to work on it. When he first saw this mountain, he prophesied, "American history shall march along that skyline." *Photo credit—Rapid City Chamber of Commerce.*

ing and artistic problems, by personality conflicts among the leaders of the project with Borglum, the personification of the temperamental artist, in the center of endless controversy.

During Borglum's preliminary exploration of the area, he hiked, climbed, and rode horseback through the magnificent scenery of the Harney Range, which he called "a garden of the gods," while searching for imperishable granite on which to carve a memorial to honor his beloved country. A fervent patriot, Borglum believed that his America deserved colossal art which would outrank the Sphinx of Egypt and classic monuments of Greece and Rome. Furthermore, he had the utmost confidence in himself as the artist-engineer who could create such a marvel.

Doane Robinson, long-time South Dakota state historian, was the man credited with conceiving the idea of carving huge monuments in the Black Hills. He invited Borglum to come to the Hills to discuss the nebulous plan. Borglum, always dominant and self-assured, turned down Robinson's concept of western heroes being memorialized, insisting that the figures should be of national importance. Eventually Robinson agreed.

Doane Robinson, South Dakota State Historian, conceived the idea of carving huge monuments of historical figures in the Black Hills. *Photo credit—South Dakota State Historical Society.*

Gutzon Borglum and his son Lincoln with friend Theodore Shoemaker. Lincoln later worked closely with his father on Mount Rushmore. After Gutzon Borglum's death, Lincoln Borglum completed the final detailing on the famous heads. *Photo credit—South Dakota State Historical Society.*

After considerable exploration with local guides and prominent leaders like Senator Peter Norbeck, Borglum, accompanied by his 12-year-old son, Lincoln, decided on a square, flat-topped mountain, 6,000 feet high, with few noticeable imperfections.

An obscure mountain, known only by local people, it had been haphazardly named "Rushmore" for a Charles Rushmore, a New York attorney who had mining interests at Keystone, the nearby mining town. Both Robinson and Norbeck pointed out that the mountain was inaccessible with not even a dirt road leading to it, only horse trails. The strong-willed Borglum overcame their objections and persuaded them that Rushmore was the right kind of granite on which to make his dream a reality, in a dramatic setting with a southeast exposure for the best lighting.

John Gutzon de la Mothe Borglum was born to Danish immigrants in 1867 in the mountainous frontier town of Bear Lake, Idaho. Early in life young Borglum showed a strong talent for art and an equally strong dislike of authority and supervision. Eventually, the independent youth attended art school in Paris where he became a good friend of Rodin, the renowned sculptor. It wasn't long before Borglum made his name known in the art world, in both Europe and the United States, by demonstrating his dramatic flair for sculpturing and painting western subjects—cowboys, horses, Indians.

At the time Borglum first came to the Black Hills in response to Robinson's invitation, he was involved in carving a large monument to the Confederacy at Stone Mountain, Georgia, featuring Generals Robert E. Lee and Stonewall Jackson with their troops. Borglum had many disagreements with the Stone Mountain Association mainly over the handling of finances and the basic question of who was in charge. When the Stone Mountain Association became so exasperated that they fired Borglum, he was furious at what he considered unjust treatment. In retaliation, he ordered workmen to destroy his unfinished carving on the mountain and smashed to bits his studio models, leaving the Stone Mountain fiasco amidst threatened law suits and bad publicity which would haunt him forever.

Senator Norbeck, who became the leading figure in promoting the Mount Rushmore Memorial, was already known as the "father of Custer State Park." He had taken the lead in the conservation of the Black Hills and in preserving areas for public enjoyment. Norbeck was a highly successful well-digger who had become a highly respected politician. He had been Governor of South Dakota before becoming an influential Senator in Congress.

Senator Peter Norbeck of South Dakota, leading figure in persuading Congress to appropriate funds for the Memorial, was the peace-maker in the endless controversies between temperamental Borglum and his colleagues. *Photo credit—South Dakota State Historical Society.*

From their first meeting, the well-digger and the artist liked and respected one another. Borglum was amazed that a man who had been a common laborer without much formal education was knowledgeable about art and appreciated creative ideas. Norbeck was indeed a remarkable man, and he provided invaluable leadership throughout the troubled years of getting federal appropriations for the memorial while doing his best to keep Borglum from alienating everyone connected with the project, from ordinary workmen to Presidents of the United States.

By the time Borglum was free to come to the Black Hills and get started on carving the mountain, there was still no money. Robinson and Norbeck, the principal promoters, were as yet unable to produce financial backing for the expensive and controversial undertaking.

Borglum suggested that they should focus attention on the project by presenting a dramatic ceremony to capture public imagination. He contributed $500 and the Rapid City Commercial Club donated $1,000 for expenses.

Thus, the first of many colorful dedication ceremonies took place on October 1, 1925, on what was later named Doane Mountain, across the canyon from Mount Rushmore. The estimated crowd of 3,000 had tramped through the mountain wilderness from Keystone, determined to find out just what this crazy artist was up to.

Borglum, a master showman, had arranged a first class pageant: band music, speeches, Sioux Indians, 21-gun salutes, flag-raising ceremonies symbolizing the mountain's various owners—France, Spain, England, climaxed with the Stars and Stripes waving possessively over the historic site. The audience loved it, and newspaper reporters wrote glowing features about both the ceremony and the proposed project.

Energetic and patriotic Gutzon Borglum placing the Stars and Stripes near Mount Rushmore for the first dedication in 1925. *Photo credit—South Dakota State Historical Society.*

Raising the flag of the Bourbons near Mount Rushmore at the first of many colorful dedication ceremonies directed by Gutzon Borglum, master showman. October, 1925. *Photo credit—Rapid City Chamber of Commerce.*

A colorful speaker, Borglum promised the crowd that if they would return in a year the first figure, that of George Washington, would be completed. (It was five years before Washington was unveiled.)

The delays were not Borglum's fault. He was eager to begin working. However, the sculptor was too optimistic in thinking that many wealthy philanthropists would immediately come through with large donations—and some of the possible benefactors were apprehensive because of the Stone Mountain debacle. Neither the state of South Dakota nor the Congress of the United States was willing to appropriate any immediate funds. And the people of the Black Hills weren't enthusiastic about contributing money.

Borglum shocked Rapid Citians by announcing that they should raise $50,000 just to get the carving started. Earlier, Borglum had promised these same people that they wouldn't be asked for even one dollar. Now the $50,000 he requested made them panic-stricken—even if the carving would improve the tourist trade. Maybe the whole thing was ridiculous—whoever heard of cutting up a beautiful mountain anyway?

Borglum often created confusion and hostility by contradicting not only himself, but also the official announcements and promises of both Robinson and Norbeck, the two most loyal and influential supporters

Borglum had. Many South Dakotans who had been against vandalizing a mountain in the first place, decided Borglum must be completely irresponsible to expect so much money from the Black Hills.

The year of 1926 passed with no progress being made on either the funding or the carving.

Then along came 1927 and President Calvin Coolidge decided to spend his summer vacation in the Black Hills and to make his headquarters at the State Game Lodge in Custer State Park. Wealthy donors perked up and came through with some donations for Rushmore, and Black Hillers decided they had better dig up some money.

Herbert Myrick of Boston, publisher of agricultural journals, including **The Dakota Farmer,** led the way with a $1,000 donation, followed by the Homestake Mining Company of Lead, SD, by three railways with lines into the Black Hills, and by Charles Rushmore for whom the mountain was named. By July, 1927, $50,000 had been donated to the Rushmore dream.

That was enough to get started. A fearless Borglum, by dangling from a cable while being suspended over the cliff, had already completed many tests and measurements of the granite on Mount Rushmore. Now with available money, supplies delivered by pack horses and wagons began arriving at the site. And the miners whom Borglum had to train to become mountain-carvers and blasters doubled as carpenters to construct scaffolding and sheds. The busy place looked like a mining camp that had just struck gold.

Borglum was so excited by Coolidge's arrival that he flew in an airplane over the Game Lodge to drop flowers on the lawn, thus welcoming the President and Mrs. Coolidge to their summer home.

The master showman arranged another dedication ceremony at Mount Rushmore with Coolidge, reputed to be reticent, as the star performer.

President Calvin Coolidge wearing cowboy boots while speaking at a dedication ceremony at Mount Rushmore in 1927. He rode horseback to the ceremonies on a road blasted out of the wilderness. Moustached Borglum seated on platform. *Photo credit—South Dakota State Historical Society.*

Although self-conscious, Coolidge was a good sport, wearing cowboy boots and a ten-gallon hat, and riding horseback to the ceremony in the wilderness. Since no cannon was available for a presidential salute, Borglum had ordered stumps to be blasted from the right of way to build a road to Rushmore, and thus to honor the President of the United States.

Speaking to the crowd sitting on rocks and pine logs, Coolidge, from a crude platform, said in his twangy monotone: "We have come here to dedicate a cornerstone that was laid by the hand of the Almighty." He praised Borglum and his dream, orating that "the people of the future will see history and art combined to portray the spirit of patriotism." He emphasized that the monument "deserved the sympathy and support of private benificence and the national government." Reporters said it was the best speech Coolidge ever made.

Borglum was ecstatic. Reticent—like Hell! Coolidge was outspoken and enthusiastic. A million dollars worth of publicity. Hurray for the President!

Coolidge then turned to Borglum and ceremoniously handed him a set of drills. Soon, across the canyon, the attentive crowd saw Borglum's tiny figure, supported only by a slender cable, descending over a steep cliff with a heavy drill in hand. People watched in thrilled apprehension while 60-year-old Borglum, maneuvering like a circus acrobat, drilled master points on the virgin granite for the visage of George Washington, the stacatto rat-a-tats signaling to the world that work on Mount Rushmore had at last begun.

Although Coolidge's enthusiastic support gave tremendous impetus to the project, Borglum and his inexperienced crew had to complete countless preparations before concentrated work could begin. They needed electric power, winches, cables, saddle-chairs, stairways, roadways, a cook shack, an art studio, a blacksmith shop where 400 drills could be sharpened every day, and all kinds of machinery and supplies.

Borglum set up small-scale models of the heads of four presidents in his log cabin studio with a large picture window overlooking the site. Extensive blasting and drilling did not actually begin until October 4, 1927. Work came to an end on December 7th of the same year because of exhausted funds and the severe winter weather. However, Borglum and his men had made considerable progress on Washington, except a casual visitor might see only an unsightly scar on the side of a granite cliff.

Unfortunately, Borglum got into an embarrassment with President Coolidge, publicized by newspapers throughout the country, over an inscription for the monument summarizing the nation's history, which the sculptor at the 1927 dedication ceremony had impulsively and publicly asked Coolidge to write.

Coolidge, although neither a writer nor a historian, accepted the challenge. Borglum, an eloquent writer, openly criticized Coolidge's prosaic writing and composed his own draft for posterity. Naturally, President Coolidge was offended. However, an inscription summarizing the nation's history in 500 words never was engraved on Mount Rushmore, mostly because of space requirements.

Finally, through the dedicated efforts of Senator Peter Norbeck and of South Dakota Congressman William Williamson, Congress, in 1929, after many delays, enacted a national law authorizing $250,000 on a matching basis for carving Mount Rushmore and organized the Mount Rushmore National Commission. The law was signed by President Coolidge.

John Boland, a Rapid City businessman, became the chief administrative officer. In this capacity, Boland contributed outstanding services in handling the finances and also raised large sums of money from private sources. Borglum, always unconcerned about how the bills would be paid for his tremendous expenses, detested being restrained from work because of financial deficits. When he needed a new machine, he demanded it immediately. Thus, the impractical artist and the conservative Boland were in constant conflict until Borglum forced Boland to resign from his administrative position.

From the very beginning of the floundering project, a pattern of ups and downs emerged, of starts and stops, caused mainly by the lack of a steady cash flow. Borglum was perpetually frustrated and wanted to get on with his holy work—money or no money.

Senator Norbeck frequently acted as mediator in the countless disputes between Borglum and his colleagues who were not perfect human beings either. This persuasive senator came to the rescue many times when it looked as though the project was dead. He was skillful at convincing Congress to appropriate money from various sources for his favorite enterprise.

Wealthy philanthropists did occasionally contribute large sums, often because of Borglum's efforts. Towns in the Black Hills and throughout South Dakota did their bit to fill the coffers. During the Great Depression of the 1930's, fund-raisers solicited school children of South Dakota to deposit dimes and quarters in the donation box sitting on every teacher's desk to help with the great endeavor.

Whenever money was available, Borglum kept forging ahead. He devised many innovative procedures for the workmen who wore leather harnesses attached to saddle chairs, the entire apparatus connected to cables which were controlled by hand-operated winches that raised and lowered the occupants of the saddles. Even if a worker became unconscious, it was impossible for him to fall out of this safety harness. Wooden cages attached to cables in the same way as the saddle chairs, enabled the sculptor and his helpers to range freely over the faces emerging from the cliff. Borglum was very proud that no serious injuries or fatalities ever occurred on the job.

Workmen dynamited tons of stone layers from the cliff to get down to granite suitable for the actual carving. Washington's head was recessed by twenty feet, Jefferson's head and part of Lincoln were recessed 120 feet behind the original outer rock.

Borglum had the exacting task, incomprehensible to most laymen, of transposing the complicated measurements of the plaster-cast studio models to the granite heads. Then the supreme challenge for the sculptor and the craftsmen he had trained was to refine the expressions into life-like and heroic representations of the four great Presidents.

Gutzon Borglum riding in a cage which allowed him to range freely over the faces emerging from the cliff. Borglum designed saddle chairs and wooden cages for workmen to use on the project. No employee was killed while working on Mount Rushmore. *Photo credit—South Dakota Historical Society.*

At last, five years from the first dedication, the head of Washington, although incomplete, was ready for inspection, and automobile roads to Mount Rushmore had been constructed for the crowds. On July 4, 1930, the huge American flag covering the face of Washington, was dynamited away thus unveiling the first carving for public scrutiny.

This colorful Borglum ceremony provided an airplane flying overhead, gun salutes, and impassioned speeches. The verisimilitude and grandeur of Washington's massive countenance gazing out from the mountains to the prairies thrilled and overwhelmed the audience. Chairman Joseph Cullihan presided and referred to the entire work as a "Shrine for Democracy," a name which stuck.

Despite staggering problems involving money, engineering, art, and personalities, work continued to progress in spurts. Then came a major setback. The head of Jefferson, on which $10,000 had already been spent, and originally located on Washington's right, had to be blasted off because there wasn't enough usable granite left to complete it. Borglum eventually reconstructed the head on Washington's left.

Jefferson was unveiled ceremoniously in August, 1936, with President Franklin D. Roosevelt giving a brilliant speech, emphasizing that Mount Rushmore could be an inspiration for democratic government in the United States and throughout the world. Although Borglum had been furious

A close-up of Washington's head, the first one completed. Washington's head, though unfinished, was dedicated in July, 1930, five years after the first dedication ceremony at Mount Rushmore. *Photo credit—Deadwood Chamber of Commerce.*

because the presidential party had arrived too late to view the two figures in the best morning light, he did not scold FDR—to everyone's relief. Roosevelt lent his powerful support to the completion of Mount Rushmore.

The American flag covers the head of Thomas Jefferson before the unveiling at the dedication in August, 1936. Jefferson's head was originally located on Washington's right. *Photo credit—South Dakota State Historical Society.*

On September 17, 1939, Lincoln was unveiled and dedicated with Senator Edward Burke of Nebraska as the principal speaker. From atop Washington's head, taps sounded in memory of three outstanding supporters of Mount Rushmore who had died: President Calvin Coolidge, Senator Peter Norbeck, and Joseph Cullihan, the first president of the Mount Rushmore Commission. Although the mercurial Borglum had at

President Franklin D. Roosevelt listening to sculptor Gutzon Borglum explain his work. FDR spoke at the unveiling ceremony for Thomas Jefferson, August, 1936. *Photo credit—Rapid City Chamber of Commerce.*

times quarreled with all three men, he was undoubtedly sincere in his wish to honor their contributions to his success. He exclaimed dramatically to the crowd: "They are with the Gods. We must keep their faith. We will carry on!"

And Borglum did. At last, on July 2, 1939, Theodore Roosevelt, the fourth and last figure to be completed, was unveiled and dedicated. The celebration was also to commemorate South Dakota's Golden Jubilee of statehood. South Dakota Governor Harlan Bushfield was the main speaker, but some of his comments didn't suit the occasion: he criticized the growing dependence upon government donations.

A very large crowd was present to celebrate the dedication of Teddy, the Rough Rider and cowboy president, the one most closely associated with the Dakotas. Rain spoiled the afternoon festivities, but by nightfall, a glorious moon shown down on the memorial. Sioux Indians in native dress and Hollywood celebrities added to the excitement. Then suddenly rockets and aerial bombs exploded while powerful searchlights highlighted the immortals on their pedestal. Clearly, Borglum was still running the show.

The Shrine of Democracy with its four heads of Washington, Jefferson, Lincoln, and T. Roosevelt was almost complete.

Then on March 6, 1941, Gutzon Borglum died unexpectedly of a heart attack. His doctor said the sculptor's heart had probably been damaged by his exhausting work in the high altitude. Although several national and state leaders suggested that Borglum be buried in an unobtrusive spot on his mountain, he was not. Gutzon Borglum is buried in Forest Lawn Cemetery in Glendale, California, under the epitaph, "He made a mountain chant." According to his wishes, his name is not engraved anywhere on the memorial.

The Mount Rushmore National Memorial Commission asked Borglum's son, Lincoln, to take over the final duties on the memorial. He had worked with his father from the first exploration and had long before mastered the techniques necessary for refining the face of Theodore Roosevelt and for finishing the lapel on Washington's coat. Young Borglum continued the final detailing on the figures and cleaned up the site until the treasury was empty—again.

In his final report, Lincoln Borglum wrote: "I do not think any more thould be done on the figures . . . with the possible exception of more work on the hand of Lincoln to make it stand out more." He thought the memorial was just as effective as if the figures had been completed to the waist, as his father had originally planned. A strong recommendation was that the 400,000 tons of rock debris below the grouping should be removed. He emphasized that the Hall of Records and the stairway should be completed. Lincoln Borglum finished the final drilling on October 31, 1941.

Gutzon Borglum had elaborate plans for a Hall of Records, an 80 by

100-foot room, with an 800-foot stairway leading to a small canyon behind the faces where the great hall would be located. He planned that accounts of the accomplishments and history of America would be stored in sealed, weather-proof cabinets, with gold-plated bas-reliefs dramatizing the adventures and explorations of the western world decorating the walls, and at least twenty-five busts of notable men and women adorning the hall. For posterity, there would also be a well-written explanation of why and how and by whom the memorial was conceived and built. He thought the Hall of Records should be the most elaborately finished archives in the world. Borglum never thought small.

In 1938, Borglum had the tunnel blasted 75 feet into the mountain for the Hall of Records, but before any more work was done, his colleagues were able to convince him to finish the Roosevelt figure first. Ever since 1941 when the activity stopped completely on Mount Rushmore, mountain goats have made their home in the $16,000 cave.

The entire cost of the undertaking which spanned fourteen years, with only six and a half actual working years, was not quite a million; the cost was $989,992.32, including Borglum's salary of $170,000. Eighty percent of the money came from federal grants and 20 percent through private donations. The South Dakota legislature never appropriated a cent, although they were willing to spend thousands of dollars on building roads to Rushmore.

A revealing story about Borglum goes like this: one day a friend said to him, "At the rate you're spending money on that rock pile, it's going to cost a million dollars." "Well," Borglum replied nonchalantly, "It will last a million years and that's only a dollar a year. How much do you want for your money anyway?"

Most Americans think they got their money's worth. There has been no charge to the fifty million Americans and foreign visitors who have viewed the largest monument in the world.

The heads are approximately sixty feet from chin to forehead; figures completed on the same scale would be 465 feet high. The noses each twenty feet long, are longer than the height of the Egyptian Sphinx. The life-like glint in the eyes is a jutting piece of original granite about three feet long.

Close-up view of Thomas Jefferson's eyes. The life-like glint is a jutting piece of granite about three feet long. *Photo credit—South Dakota Historical Society.*

Borglum, who said he always dreamed of remodeling a state or making over a mountain, never did want to create "just a damned big thing." Although some critics have insisted that he ruined a mountain, others praise the artistry of his creation. Architect Frank Lloyd Wright thought it "wonderful" and said: "The noble countenances emerge from Rushmore as though the spirit of the mountain heard a human plan and itself became a human countenance." Cecil B. DeMille, the Hollywood director, commented, "Not only do you look at those four faces—they look back at you as well."

Many visitors comment that it is not just the colossal size that makes Mount Rushmore unforgettable, it's the life-like representations of the four Presidents and the emotions they evoke.

One young woman summed it up: "I love to gaze and gaze at our great Presidents. It makes me feel so patriotic and proud of our country. I feel as if I am communing with the soul of America."

And that's what a genius named Gutzon Borglum had in mind all along.

Mount Rushmore National Memorial. Over fifty million visitors from many countries have viewed this largest monument in the world. *Photo credit—Deadwood Chamber of Commerce.*

HARNEY PEAK AND THE BLACK ELK WILDERNESS

Harney Peak, the highest peak in the Black Hills (7,242 feet), is also the highest peak east of the Rocky Mountains.

Dr. Cleophas O'Harra, the late renowned geologist and president of the South Dakota School of Mines, explained the geology of Harney Peak in his pleasing scientific style: "Its lofty storm-swept surface was in ages gone by thousands of feet beneath the sea, and from it in subsequent time, along with the process of uplift, the huge, thick blankets of sandstones, shales and limestones which covered it, and much also of the granite itself, have been removed with indescribable care by countless centuries of rain and frost and wind."

On Harney Peak Above the Clouds. Taken from South Dakota School of Mines Bulletin 14, **The Geology, Mineralogy, and Scenic Features of Custer State Park, South Dakota** by Cleophas O'Harra and Joseph Connelly. *Photo credit—d'Emery, Courtesy of Archives, Devereaux Library, South Dakota School of Mines and Technology.*

Sighting the peak from a distance in 1857, Lt. G. K. Warren, who made a topographical survey of the region surrounding the Black Hills, named the ancient granite crag "Harney Peak" in honor of General William S. Harney, who had conducted military operations throughout the region. The Sioux Indians called General Harney by two names, "White Beard" and "Squaw Killer."

The mountainous area over which Harney Peak presides, in 1980, was designated the Black Elk Wilderness whose 10,700 acres are also part of the larger Norbeck Wild Life Preserve, thus honoring great South Dakotans of two races.

Peter Norbeck, who was both governor and senator of South Dakota, was a leader in conservation and known as the Father of Custer State Park.

Black Elk was a warrior and medicine man of the Oglala Sioux who had prophetic visions while on the summit of Harney Peak. Before the Indian prophet died in 1950, he related the story of his life through a translator to John G. Neihardt, author and Poet Laureate of Nebraska. Neihardt wrote the mystical and philosophical account of Black Elk's life in the acclaimed book, **Black Elk Speaks.**

Governor Peter Norbeck loved wearing khaki coveralls, especially when he tramped through the Black Hills wilderness showing shocked engineers where he wanted them to build scenic roads. He personally supervised a 40-mile fencing project for the game preserve in 1914. *Photo credit—South Dakota State Historical Society.*

Black Elk in 1947 at Pine Ridge reservation. A warrior and medicine man of the Oglala Sioux, he had a vision from Harney Peak when he was a nine-year-old boy. He recalled: "Then I was standing on the highest mountain of them all, and round about beneath me was the whole hoop of the world." *Photo credit—South Dakota State Historical Society.*

Black Elk was the second cousin of Crazy Horse, the famed Oglala chief. When Black Elk was thirteen years old, he saw the Battle of the Little Big Horn in 1876 when Crazy Horse and his cohorts wiped out Custer. In 1877, he witnessed the tragic killing of Crazy Horse at Fort Robinson, Nebraska. In 1890, Black Elk participated in Wounded Knee, the final confrontation between Sioux Indians and whites, and he was wounded, both physically and spiritually. "A people's dream died there. It was a beautiful dream," said Black Elk.

After the power of the Sioux Indians had been destroyed, Black Elk, in an effort to understand the white man's ways, joined Buffalo Bill Cody's

Wild West Show. He visited England where he danced for Queen Victoria, whom he greatly admired.

When Black Elk was a boy of nine, he experienced a vision in which he stood on Harney Peak. Black Elk recalled: "Then I was standing on the highest mountain of them all, and round about beneath me was the whole hoop of the world. And while I stood there I saw more than I can tell and I understood more than I saw; for I was seeing in a sacred manner the shapes of all things in the spirit, and the shape of all shapes as they must live together like one being."

In 1931, Black Elk wanted to ascend Harney Peak again which he did, accompanied by his son Ben Black Elk and John Neihardt. On the summit, as Black Elk began to speak, the clear cloudless sky changed to rain and low thunder, as he had predicted it would.

In a thin, pathetic voice almost lost in the vast space, he spoke: "Great Spirit, a pitiful old man, you see me here, and I have fallen away and have done nothing. Here at the center of the world, where you took me when I was young and taught me; here, old, I stand, and the mightly flowering tree is withered . . . O Six Powers of the World, hear me in my sorrow, for I may never call again. O make my people live."

This was Black Elk's last pilgrimage to Harney Peak, the center of his universe.

The first white men to climb Harney Peak were General Custer and his staff (on horseback), in 1874, but the towering cliffs on top prevented their reaching the actual summit.

The steep cliffs on Harney Peak prevented Custer and his staff from reaching the top in 1874. Dr. V. T. McGillycuddy, topographer for the Jenney-Newton Expedition in 1875, was the first white man to reach the summit where the lookout tower was built in 1938. *Photo credit—Rapid City Chamber of Commerce.*

The next year, in 1875, Dr. Valentine McGillycuddy with the Jenney-Newton Expedition, made it to the top by cutting down a tall pine which fell against the cliffs, thus enabling him to reach the topmost pinnacle.

Today, many people hike up the trails to Harney Peak which begin at Sylvan Lake. Now a stone stairway leads to the summit, and a novel pigtail footbridge continues upward along the edge of the rocky precipice to the lookout tower.

Here, from the lookout tower, hikers are rewarded for their three-hour climb by the spectacular panorama of the Black Hills spread beneath them—forests, lakes, peaks, valleys, the Needles, and—here and there—great, gray granite outcroppings resembling the bodies of whales.

Hikers are rewarded for their three-hour climb to Harney Peak with a spectacular panorama of the Black Hills spread beneath them. The lookout tower from where rangers used to watch for forest fires is no longer manned; helicopters are used instead. *Photo credit —South Dakota State Historical Society.*

The Harney Peak Lookout Tower where rangers used to watch for forest fires is no longer manned; helicopters are used instead. The picturesque stone tower, built in 1938, whose stones were hauled up by horse-drawn bobsleds and wagons from French Creek far below, has recently been listed on the Register of Historic Places.

For years, the National Forest Service, while trying to keep the trash accumulations picked up, did its best with the use of volunteers stationed on top to preserve the log shelter house with its stone fireplace and the outdoor privy. Despite constant rebuilding, the structures continued to be vandalized until they became unsafe for people to use. During the winter of 1980-1981, the Forest Service had to destroy the deteriorating shelter house and privy for the safety of the public.

"Man marks the earth with ruin," wrote Lord Byron.

DINOSAURS IN THE BLACK HILLS

Travelers approaching Rapid City have been startled, especially on a moonlit night, to recognize the silhouette of a dinosaur standing on a high ridge overlooking the city, like an invader from a forgotten age. On a clear day he is visible for thirty-five miles. Eighty feet long and twenty-eight feet high, the monster is a life-size replica of a **Brontosaurus,** a prehistoric reptile who lived in the water, weighed about fifteen tons, had a small brain, and probably a smooth skin.

Dinosaur Park on Skyline Drive above Rapid City. The **Brontosaurus** in the rear is the only one of seven cement dinosaurs visible for miles. The Horned **Triceratops** and **Tyrannosaurus Rex** are facing each other, as though preparing for deadly combat. *Photo credit—South Dakota State Historical Society.*

Seven dinosaurs inhabit Dinosaur Park on Skyline Drive above Rapid City, SD. They were built by the Works Progress Administration during the depression years under the direction of Emmett Sullivan of Rapid City, designer for the project which was dedicated in 1936. With steel frames covered by cement these replicas were built to accurate measurements scaled from small models provided by the American Museum of Natural History.

The **Triceratops,** with some features resembling a present-day rhinoceros and elephant, was a land reptile with forty-inch horns.

Tyrannosaurus rex, the largest flesh-eating dinasour with many six-inch-long teeth, is standing upright on his hind legs and using his tail for balance with his short front legs held like a kangaroo's.

The **Triceratops** and **Tyrannosaurus rex** are facing each other, as though preparing for deadly combat.

The **Stegosaurus** is a smaller dinosaur, only eleven feet long, with huge alternating plates covering his body and four horns on his tail.

The **Anatosaurus** dinosaur, known as the duckbill, is about seventeen feet high and thirty-three feet long with web feet and a large bill.

Added later to the prehistoric collection are two small cement monsters across the road from the main park area. One is a **Protoceratops** with eggs, a horned dinosaur from Mongolia, and the other a flesh-eating reptile, the **Dimetrodon,** which lived millions of years before the true dinosaurs.

Geologists and observant ranchers have found dinosaur fossils both in the Black Hills and the northwestern plains area of South Dakota.

Dinosaurs roamed the vast swamps and jungles over 63 million years ago during the Mesozoic era.

Dinosaur Park is appropriately located: geologists have found dinosaur bones not fifty feet from the park. They have also found footprints of a small meat-eating dinosaur about two miles north of the park on the same range of foothills.

Dr. Cleophas C. O'Harra, president of the South Dakota School of Mines in Rapid City from 1911-1935, is credited with suggesting the idea for a dinosaur display in a public park.

Dr. Cleophas C. O'Harra, former president of the School of Mines in Rapid City was an educator, geologist, paleontologist, author, and editor. This versatile scientist is credited with suggesting a dinosaur display in a public park. *Photo credit—Alumni Office, South Dakota School of Mines and Technology.*

O'Harra was a nationally known authority on geology and paleontology (the study of fossils and ancient life forms). Before the turn of the century he led the way in scientific explorations of the Badlands, sixty miles east of the Black Hills, which are a vast burial ground of vertebrate animals that lived and died there in prodigious numbers. Under his leadership geologic expeditions, traveling in horse-drawn wagons, discovered skeletons of a saber-toothed cat, a three-toed horse—even a small camel. All of these fossils are displayed in the Museum of Geology.

The Badlands of South Dakota, sixty miles east of the Black Hills, are a vast burial ground for prehistoric vertebrate animals including a saber-toothed cat, a three-toed horse, and a small camel. No dinosaur fossils have been found in the Badlands. *Photo credit—Rapid City Chamber of Commerce.*

Today, the Museum of Geology, in the O'Harra Building at the School of Mines in Rapid City has one of the finest collections of Big Badlands fossils and Black Hills minerals found anywhere in the world. Displayed are a complete skeleton of an **Anatosaurus** dinosaur and the huge head of a **Tyrannosaurus rex,** both found in western South Dakota. To find the free museum, visitors follow the dinosaur tracks painted on the campus sidewalks.

The Museum of Geology at O'Harra Building on the campus of the School of Mines at Rapid City has a wonderful collection of fossils including this complete skeleton of an **Anatosaurus** dinosaur. In the foreground is the huge head of a **Tyrannosaurus rex,** both found in western South Dakota. *Photo credit—Rapid City Chamber of Commerce.*

Dr. O'Harra, who died in 1935, was an amazing man. A classical scholar and gentleman of the old school, he was a gifted speaker and writer. A geologist, teacher, administrator, and editor, he found time to write over eighty scientific and historical works including the **Badland Formations of the Black Hills Region,** the **White River Badlands,** the **Custer Expedition,** and **O'Harra's Handbook of the Black Hills.**

O'Harra wrote like a scientist who loved nature and was able to communicate his knowledge and feelings to the average reader. Here is a typical O'Harra paragraph: "The Badlands with their array of fossilized remains tell an entrancing nature story; a story of strange climates, strange geography, and strange animals of jungles, and marshes, and tranquil rivers; of fierce contests for food, and life and supremacy; of a varied series of events through ages and ages of time showing the working out of well-laid plans with no human being to help or hinder." He called dinosaur tracks "footprints on the sands of time."

This versatile educator was said to have tramped every foot of the central and southern hills while studying their geology and enjoying nature. Whenever he went to the cabin he built himself at Pactola Lake, he stopped the car on the top of Rockerville Hill (now Mount Rushmore Road) so he could revel in the beauty of the scene.

He wanted the public to appreciate and understand the educational values to be learned from geology and fossils. The contributions Dr. Cleophas C. O'Harra made to the development of Dinosaur Park are just a part of the legacy he bequeathed to the people of his beloved Black Hills. Truly, he left his own footprints on the sands of time.

CRAZY HORSE MOUNTAIN CARVING

Crazy Horse was the noted Indian chief for whom the stupendous carving-in-progress on Thunderhead Mountain in the Black Hills is named. Ironically, it is located just five miles north of the town of Custer, named to honor the controversial white general whom Crazy Horse and other Indian leaders annihilated at the Battle of the Little Big Horn in 1876.

Although Korczak Ziolkowski, the ambitious and talented sculptor of the Crazy Horse carving, died in October, 1982, his sons vow to complete their father's unfinished dream of the largest monument in the world and dedicated to the epic of Indian history. Twenty-two miles up the road is Mount Rushmore, the Shrine of Democracy with the likenesses of four American Presidents, and currently holding the title of the "largest sculpture in the world."

Modern Sioux Indian chiefs selected Crazy Horse as the native American hero they wanted to honor by a mountain memorial in the Black Hills. Crazy Horse was the Oglala Sioux leader and military tactition who devoted most of his short life to fighting the white invaders of Indian territory. "For me there is no country that can hold the tracks of the moccasin and the boots of the white man side by side," he said.

Crazy Horse, first known as Curly, the light-haired one, was born on Rapid Creek about 1843. Crazy Horse was the name of his father; and during the father's vision quest on Bear Butte, the Great Spirit in the form of a bear appeared to give him spiritual power to conquer the enemy. The aging father, a holy man, asked permission to bestow the gifts of spiritual power and leadership on his promising young son, thus preparing him to become a great leader of the Sioux Indians.

This momentous occasion happened at the Grand Council of the Teton Sioux in 1857 at Bear Butte on the eastern edge of the Black Hills. Legend has it that not long afterwards when the young brave had killed his first buffalo and had taken two scalps from an enemy tribe, the elder Crazy Horse decided his son had earned a new name. Crazy Horse's father, walking through the huge camp of tepees and council fires for a victory dance, chanted a song ending with these words: "I throw away his old name and give him a great name—I call him Crazy Horse!"

The young Crazy Horse vowed to the Great Spirit, to his father, and to himself that he would never cease fighting the white man to protect his people, the Oglala tribe of the Seven Teton Council Fires of the Lakota Sioux. "We will fight!" became Crazy Horse's motto almost to the end of his short life.

Although there is no documented photograph of Crazy Horse, he has been frequently decribed by both white and Indian contemporaries: about five feet, eight inches tall with a lithe, sinewy figure, a classic profile, and a melancholy yet aggressive expression on his handsome face. He wore the skin of a red-backed hawk in his long flowing hair and tied a small brown stone behind his ear for protection in battle.

During his adolescent training period, Crazy Horse, who had been blessed by the Great Spirit, began mastering strategies for tricking soldiers into ambushes and for launching surprise attacks on the enemy. He soon became renowned for his reckless horsemanship, daring hand-to-hand combats in battles, and for surviving unharmed in death-dealing situations. Young Crazy Horse also learned how to shoot a breech-loading rifle with deadly accuracy.

During the Moon of Popping Trees (December, 1866), near Fort Phil Kearney in Wyoming Territory, Crazy Horse led the decoy party that tantalized Lt. William Fetterman into disobeying orders and following the yelping Indians into a trap where all the blue coats were killed. This Indian victory became known as the Fetterman Massacre.

Thus through the 1860's and 1870's on the expanding and bloody western frontier of the white man, Crazy Horse again and again proved his courage and skill as a warrior chief. Crazy Horse, ever conscious of being the chosen leader, believed that men on earth lived in the shadow of the real world. Therefore, he sought visions to guide him into the psychic arena of conflict and struggle for victory. Often known as the Strange Man of the Oglalas, he was eventually recognized as a charismatic chief among all the seven tribes of the Sioux Nation.

Crazy Horse vowed revenge for the grievous wrongs perpetrated by the whites against the Indians: the broken treaties and false promises; the unprovoked attacks on villages which killed women and children; the invasion of their lands; the slaughter of the buffalo, the mainstay of the Plains Indians; the building of illegal forts on the hereditary hunting grounds; the selling of strong liquor to the Indians which brought much sorrow, including the debauchery of their daughters; and the spreading of small pox and cholera, the dread white man's diseases, among the vulnerable Indians.

The Fort Laramie Treaty of 1868, designed to open the way for more western expansion while granting to the Indians undisturbed occupancy of vast territories, became the most controversial Indian treaty of modern times. White leaders drafted the terms at a council at Fort Laramie, Wyoming, with a few Indians in attendance.

Among the treaty's provisions were that the Indians should cease attacking wagon trains, opposing railroad construction, and killing white

Peace Commission at Fort Laramie, WY, 1868. General William Harney with white beard. This group drafted the Fort Laramie Treaty of 1868, the most controversial Indian treaty of modern times, still the focus of court battles between the Sioux Indians and the whites in 1983. *Photo credit—South Dakota State Historical Society.*

people. In return, the whites agreed to abandon the forts on the Bozeman trail in Montana; and guaranteed the lands to the Indians between the Missouri River west to the summits of the Big Horn mountains and north to the Yellowstone River. This area included the Black Hills of western Dakota and eastern Wyoming. The treaty stipulated that "no white person or persons shall be permitted to settle upon or occupy any portion of the same; or without the consent of the Indians first had and obtained, to pass through the same."

The Indian chiefs who were there could not understand English, spoken or written; the contents of the treaty and the speeches were explained to them through the interpreters before the chiefs reluctantly scratched their X's on the document. The Indians believed that these marks on paper had meaning "for as long as water should run and grass should grow and trees bear leaves."

Treaty Council at Fort Laramie, WY, 1868, with a group of Commissioners and Indian chiefs who could not understand English. Crazy Horse did not attend. Legend says he never signed his X to a white man's treaty or had his picture taken. *Photo credit—South Dakota State Historical Society.*

Crazy Horse was not present at this treaty signing; and according to historic legend, he refused to sign a treaty or touch the pen.

In 1874, the Custer Expedition, without any permission being sought from Indians, was authorized by the United States government to explore the sacred Paha Sapa of the Sioux and to look for gold in the Black Hills. The nationwide gold publicity brought a horde of illegal and frenzied goldseekers which the United States army soon gave up trying to keep out of Indian territory.

With prospectors swarming into the Paha Sapa, the United States government tried to solve the dilemma by offering to buy the Black Hills from the Sioux. During a council of Indian chiefs when several leaders were considering this offer, Crazy Horse said scornfully, "One does not sell the earth on which the people walk."

Many Indians, dissatisfied with broken treaties and reservation imprisonment, began slipping away to rejoin the malcontents who were still trying to preserve their free life-style of roaming and hunting.

In January, 1876, the government sent messengers to the forts and agencies to announce far and wide that all Indians must return to the reservations; otherwise, they would be considered hostiles, and soldiers would be sent after them. Crazy Horse and his warriors were in winter camp at Bear Butte. He ignored the ultimatum which was completely unrealistic, especially because of the deep winter snows.

The spring campaign of the military was directed by General Phil Sheridan whose popular slogan was "the only good Indian is a dead Indian." The three-pronged movement of the armies to round up hostile Indians included the Second and Third Cavalry, led by General George Crook, and the Seventh Cavalry led by General George Custer.

On June 17, 1876, Crazy Horse clashed with General Crook in Montana. This Battle of the Rosebud was said to be the first organized Indian battle with mounted charges and the Indians following commands of the leader. Crazy Horse and his warriors drove General Crook and his troops into a retreat from the upper Rosebud.

General George Crook, the noted white general whom Crazy Horse and his warriors forced to retreat at the Battle of the Rosebud. The Rosebud was said to be the first organized Indian battle with mounted charges and Indians following the commands of the leader. *Photo credit—South Dakota State Historical Society.*

Sitting Bull and Buffalo Bill Cody when the Sioux medicine man was touring with Buffalo Bill's Wild West Show. The two showmen were billed as "Foes in '76—Friends in '85." *Photo credit—South Dakota State Historical Society.*

Five days later, on June 25, 1876, in the area where the Sioux and Cheyenne were encamped in the greatest concentration of Indians since the Teton Council at Bear Butte, occurred the Battle of the Little Big Horn. Sitting Bull, the powerful medicine man and military strategist, had had a prophetic vision of dead soldiers falling into camp—a good omen. Both Chief Gall and Crazy Horse were ready to fight. An over-confident Custer divided his troops and attacked the Indian village, expecting the Indians to run away and not put up much of a fight. Instead, the Sioux and Cheyenne, led by Crazy Horse, the supreme war chief, annihilated General George Custer and 294 of his Seventh Cavalry at the Battle of the Little Big Horn.

Legend has it that Crazy Horse rode unarmed into the thickest of the terrible battle and that his voice roared above the smoke and dust and din: "This is a good day to fight—a good day to die. Strong hearts, brave hearts to the front! and weak hearts and cowards to the rear! Hokay Hey! Hokay Hey!"

Crazy Horse believed that if he were wrong in his determination to wipe out the white soldiers, he would die; that if he were right, the Great Spirit would permit him to live. Crazy Horse lived. Custer died. Crazy Horse's victory at the immortal Battle of the Little Big Horn was the climax of his career.

In addition to being a great war chief, Crazy Horse demonstrated modesty, generosity, and thoughtfulness. Always, he showed great concern that the lives of the Indians were being changed by the increasing pressures of the white man. Except for weapons, he never kept possessions for himself and was beloved by hundreds for his charity toward the poor.

In August, 1876, Congress cut off all rations for the Sioux until they ceded the Black Hills to the government and relinquished their right to hunt outside the reservations. In February, 1877, Congress ratified the treaty of cession and opened the Black Hills to legal white settlement.

At last, in the fall of 1877, even Crazy Horse saw that it was hopeless to continue fighting the white man. Crazy Horse, leading a band of Oglalas, surrendered to General Bradley at Fort Robinson, Nebraska. Talking through Frank Grouard, an experienced interpreter, Crazy Horse said: "We are tired of war; we came in for peace." The interpreter told General Bradley that Crazy Horse had said: "We will go north and fight until not a white man is left."

Dr. V. T. McGillycuddy, the frontier surgeon whom the Indians trusted, and the famous agent at Pine Ridge reservation, wrote a detailed account of Crazy Horse's last hours. McGillycuddy believed that Grouard deliberately misinterpreted Crazy Horse's words. Crazy Horse had come into the fort under a flag of truce; and when he saw that he was going to be jailed behind bars, a degrading insult for a chief, took out a knife and fought his way through the crowd. An army captain grabbed one arm and his one-time Oglala friend Little Big Man the other. Both Red Cloud and American Horse, Sioux chiefs who had always been jealous of Crazy Horse's power shouted, "Kill him! Kill him!"

While Crazy Horse struggled to free himself, a white guard lunged at him with the fixed bayonet of his gun. Crazy Horse fell to the ground writhing in agony.

Despite the ministrations of Dr. McGillycuddy, Crazy Horse died later that night, age about 34, a victim of the white man's deception and of his own people's treachery.

No one knows where Crazy Horse is buried. After his death, his parents claimed his body and placed it on a death scaffold, as was the Sioux custom, for embalming by the natural process of drying the body. His parents later buried his heart and bones in secret, probably within sight of the Black Hills near a creek called Wounded Knee.

Ben Black Elk and Henry Black Elk point out travois trail over which Crazy Horse's parents transported his body to secret burial place (trail visible on right of road) probably within sight of the Black Hills. *Photo credit—South Dakota State Historical Society.*

History suggests an epitaph; Crazy Horse in all likelihood chanted this Sioux song in his youth:

The Paha Sapa is my land
And I love it.
And whoever interferes
Will hear this gun.

****

"My fellow chiefs and I would like the White Man to know the Red Man had great heroes, also." So wrote Sioux Chief Henry Standing Bear inviting the New England sculptor, Korczak Ziolkowski, to the Black Hills to carve a mountain memorial honoring the American Indian. The Indians chose Crazy Horse to be the subject.

Korczak came to the Black Hills in 1947. Although he had no professional training in art, his marble bust of Paderewski, the Polish pianist, won top honors for sculpture at the 1939 New York World's Fair. He had also worked briefly at Mount Rushmore as an assistant to sculptor Gutzon Borglum whom he greatly admired.

Korczak arrived in the Black Hills with only $174 to start the monumental project. He established a non-profit Crazy Horse Memorial

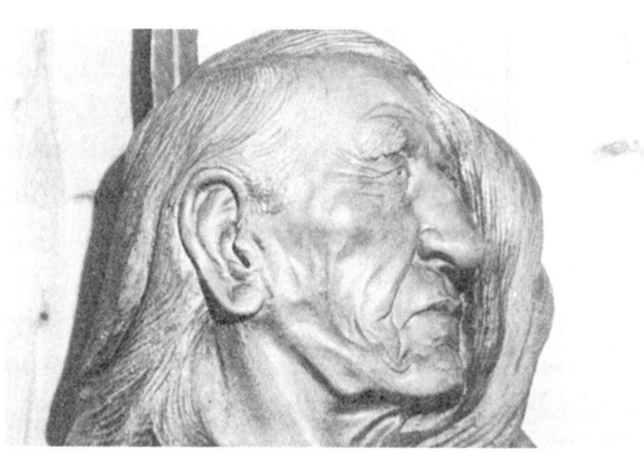

Korczak Ziolkowski sculpted this mahogany portrait of Chief Standing Bear who invited Korczak to the Black Hills to carve a mountain memorial honoring the American Indian. The Sioux Indians chose Crazy Horse to be the subject. *Photo credit—South Dakota State Historical Society.*

Foundation, obtained the land on Thunderhead Mountain and 328 acres around it through a land exchange with the federal government. Twice, Korczak turned down ten million dollars in federal grants, fearful that he would lose control of the monument and of his great dream. The humanitarian project is supported by private donations and by tourist fees of five dollars a carload.

The unfinished Crazy Horse memorial is the focus of a proposed North American Indian center embracing a university and a medical complex. Although these goals are far from realized, the Indian museum in the spacious visitors' complex has an impressive collection of 1,000 artifacts, representing more than thirty Indian tribes. In 1979, the Foundation awarded thirty-one scholarships for books and tuition for Indian students from nine South Dakota reservations.

Korczak worked strenuously for twenty-seven years on the memorial to Crazy Horse which will be a sculpture in the round with incredible dimensions: 563 feet high and 641 feet long. The horse's head is 219 feet high and Crazy Horse's arm extends to 263 feet, longer than a football field. Korczak removed seven million tons of excess granite by blasting and drilling, constructed more than four and a half miles of road up and down the mountain, and built a stairway of 741 steps.

Most viewers gazing at the mammoth rock with barely discernible outlines of a man on a horse have difficulty visualizing just how the largest monument in the world will look when completed. For reference, there is a twenty-foot high model on the visitor's terrace one mile from the carving.

The head of Crazy Horse is not meant to be a lineal likeness; instead it is a symbolic depiction of the noted Oglala chief. His left arm is outstretched to the east, the direction from which the white invaders came. "Where are your lands now?" taunted a white soldier. Crazy Horse replied, "My lands are where my dead lie buried."

Sculptor Korczak Ziolkowski died in October, 1982, several months after a heart by-pass operation.

Korczak was a rugged, bearded mountain man who mesmerized audiences and the press with his enthusiasm, confidence, and colorful language. Despite two heart attacks, four back operations, and other injuries, the indomitable sculptor kept doing hard physical labor. During the last three weeks of his life, Korczak painted an outline of the horse's head on the dangerous mountain as a guide for continuing work.

Crazy Horse Memorial Now in Progress—Comparing the mountain in 1947 with the mountain today shows the great progress blocking-out Crazy Horse. Sculptor Korczak Ziolkowski's Crazy Horse 1/34th scale model is inserted for reference. More than 8.2 million tons of granite have been blasted off the 600-foot-high mountain which will be carved in the round. When completed, Crazy Horse will be 563 feet high and 641 feet long. The horse's head will be 22 stories high. For size perspective, all four heads on nearby Mr. Rushmore would fit inside just Crazy Horse's head. *(Photos: Crazy Horse Memorial Archives)*

Ziolkowski family members are dedicated to carrying-on the Crazy Horse dream—as Korczak planned. From left, standing, are Monique, Mrs. Korczak (Ruth) Ziolkowski, Jadwiga, Anne, Casimir and, seated, Dawn and Adam. In the background is Korczak's 1/34th scale model for the mountain carving now in progress. Crazy Horse is pointing over his horse's head, proclaiming, "My lands are where my dead lie buried." *(Crazy Horse Memorial Archives photo by Robb DeWall)*

The last words of the sculptor-engineer to his family were these: "You must keep building. The only good is in building. Crazy Horse must be finished. You must work on the mountain—but slowly—so you do it right."

Korczak's wife Ruth did more than respect his dream; she was a working partner in supporting and promoting his life-time work. Six of his ten children plan to carry on by working at the Crazy Horse Memorial, following the detailed blueprints and plans for the completion of the gigantic project. Korczak said: "The story of the American Indian is an epic that requires an epic scale; it is an ancient tradition to pass along an epic work for another to finish."

Sculptor Korczak Ziolkowski died in October, 1982. His five sons plan to carry on his dream. The dynamic man's last words to his family were "Crazy Horse must be finished." *Photo credit—South Dakota State Historical Society.*

Korczak is buried in a tomb on the mountain which he and his five sons blasted out of the granite. On the outside of the door is a plaque with these words: "Storyteller in Stone—May His Remains Be Left Unknown." **Inside** of that door is the brass door knocker which Korczak placed himself.

The public funeral for Korczak Ziolkowski, held on the viewing terrace with the Crazy Horse Memorial in the background, was attended by many whites and Indians, including a large delegation from Pine Ridge Indian reservation. The Sioux participated in the ceremony, singing death honor songs and chanting traditional Lakota prayers. Korczak's widow Ruth carried an American flag in one hand and an eagle feather in the other.

The white clergyman emphasized that people were there to "celebrate a life, celebrate a work, celebrate a man."

Tribal executives of the Oglala Sioux Indian tribe said: "Two races of people have lost a great man. Crazy Horse Monument is our shrine of freedom and nationhood. At a time when our people are down-trodden, we can look to this man and be a proud people."

Korczak and his wife Ruth talking with their Indian friends. Ruth Ziolkowski did more than respect her husband's dream; she was a working partner in supporting and promoting his life-time work on the Crazy Horse Memorial. *Photo credit—South Dakota State Historical Society.*

A LABYRINTH OF CAVES

Underneath the edge of the pine-forested Black Hills is a dark underground world of caves created in what is called the Paha Sapa limestone formation, which geologists believe was deposited in the vast inland sea that covered the region about 300 million years ago.

During the passage of incomprehensible centuries of time, volcanic action forced the Black Hills uplift from the bottom of the sea. The accepted scientific theory is that the land rose and fell several times. The last upheaval occurred about sixty million years ago and that's when the caves were created—give or take a century or two.

In an age that was ancient even before mammals roamed the earth, acidic water seeped endlessly through the cracked and hollowed out sedimentary layer and partially dissolved the soluble limestone to form the caverns and their fantastic decorations.

Today, nine caves honeycombed with passages in the Paha Sapa limestone are accessible to the public, each sharing basic similarities but having distinctive features. The explored part of these known caves is only a small portion of the vast subterranean world whose extent cannot be accurately determined.

Of the explored caves, Wind Cave, ten miles north of Hot Springs, SD, has been known the longest to both red men and white men. For centuries, the Indians claim to have known about **Washun Niya,** "the breathing hole."

Underneath the edge of the pine-forested Black Hills is a dark underground world of caves created in what is called the Paha Sapa limestone formation. The caverns and their fantastic decorations were formed about sixty million years ago—give or take a century or two. *Photo credit—South Dakota Tourism.*

According to James LaPointe in his book, **Legends of the Lakota,** the Lakota Sioux have many legends about Wind Cave, believing that the whispering, sighing and hissing noises coming from the hole were made by mysterious people who lived far below. The Indians made flutes to imitate the musical tones which blew through the noisy hole like a cool breeze.

The legend of Taopi Gli, son of a chief, tells of the day when he and a friend (kola) were hunting deer. Taopi Gli left kola to investigate a faraway moving object. When Taopi Gli did not return to camp, the kola went searching for him. He saw Taopi Gli talking to a bewitching maiden who was enticing him to follow her into a dark canyon.

The kola tried to shout warnings to Taopi Gli but found that he was unable to make a sound or to move. The kola then fell into a trance. When he came to his senses, he ran down into the canyon but Taopi Gli and the maiden had disappeared. He found the spot where he had last seen the young couple and there was a small hole hissing a steady flow of cold air. Near the hole were the tracks of the girl's moccasins beside those of Taopi Gli. The kola was sure they had both disappeared into the breathing hole.

When the kola told his friends what had happened, the Indians decided that Taopi Gli had been abducted by an evil "double woman" and was probably dead. The chief who was the father of Taopi Gli grieved so long for his son that the medicine man recommended he seek comfort in a special prayer called the **Hanblecheya** which might reveal his son's fate after the chief underwent a dangerous and grueling fast.

The chief prayed for his vision quest on top of a high mountain called **Hechinskayapi Paha** or goat mountain, which was later named Mount Coolidge by the whites.

After four days of fasting and praying, the chief had become very weak. Suddenly, he felt stronger when he recognized Fallen Star standing before him, the god-son of a Lakota mother. Then before his eyes, the chief saw a vision of his son who was alive and happy, now married to the maiden, who was not an evil "double woman," but a good woman. Taopi Gli had become a powerful high priest and he could never return to the upper world; he was destined to remain always underground.

Relieved and comforted, the chief thought the strange marriage a good omen because those who lived underground were the keepers and breeders of all game animals. Never again would the Lakota fear famine because **Washun Niya,** the breathing hole, was the connecting link between the upper world and the underground world.

The fortuitous marriage of Taopi Gli and the honorable maiden of the underground assured the absence of famines for ages because hordes of buffalo and deer continued to come through the opening of Wind Cave. The animals became small as ants when they passed through the entrance, then expanded to their natural size when they breathed the invigorating air of the upper world.

Today legendary Wind Cave with 34 miles of explored passages is the sixth longest cave in the United States and the eleventh longest in the world. In 1903, President Theodore Roosevelt and Congress created the Wind Cave National Park.

The buffalo herd of Wind Cave's upper world and the buffalo of adjoining Custer State Park comprise the largest buffalo herd in the country. The rolling prairies of Wind Cave, where the mountains meet the plains, are dotted with the holes and mounds of huge prairie dog towns. The barking

Black-tailed prairie dogs inhabit many prairie dog towns in the upper world of Wind Cave National Park where the rolling plains are dotted with the holes and mounds of these barking rodents. *Photo credit —Earl Chace.*

prairie dogs are small enough to pass through the original ten-inch opening of Wind Cave without first changing into ants. Other animals who live in the wild-life sanctuary are the deer, pronghorn antelope, elk, coyote, badger and raccoon.

The first white man to discover Wind Cave was Thomas Bingham in 1881. One day while hunting deer on a calm day, he was terrified when a gust of wind blew off his hat. Because of this hair-raising situation, he discovered the currents of air blowing out of a hole among some rocks.

Jesse McDonald and his two sons, Elmer and Alvin, were the first white men to explore Wind Cave; by using candles that the wind often blew out and balls of twine, they explored hundreds of passages. Alvin McDonald kept a careful record of his explorations, and the McDonalds named many passages, caverns, and formations. Alvin McDonald, who died at age twenty, is buried near the entrance to Wind Cave.

Wind Cave is often compared to a human lung breathing in and out. The phenomenon of strong currents of air rushing in and out of the cave entrances is caused by changes in atmospheric pressure. There are about 34 mapped miles in Wind Cave which is noted for its delicate box-work honeycombs of calcite resembling paper-thin shapes; and unusual "frostwork" and "popcorn" formations and huge helicite "bushes."

Two elevators and hard-surfaced trails lead to the lighted rooms in the cave with names suggestive of their appearance: Pearly Gates, Fairgrounds, Blue Grotto, Monte Cristo Palace, Temple Room, Garden of Eden, Post Office and Devil's Lookout.

Jewel Cave National Monument, the other Hills cave in a federal preserve, was at first thought to be a small cave; however, because of recent explorations, Jewel Cave is now rated the second longest cave in the United States and the fourth longest in the world; it has 69 miles of explored passageways on four levels. There are reports of this cave as early as 1886, but no one knows for sure when white men first discovered it because they noticed air rushing out of a hole.

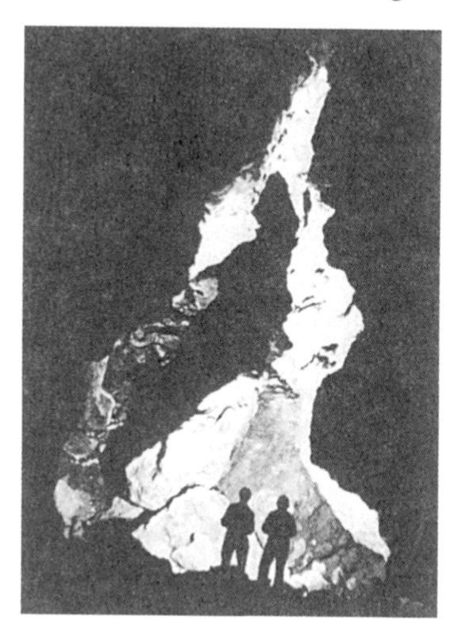

Two cavers or spelunkers are silhouetted in Penn Station, one of the large rooms discovered in Jewel Cave, near Custer, SD. The multi-colored cave acquired its name from the scintillating calcite crystals, called dogtooth spar, which line most of the passages and rooms. *Photo credit—South Dakota Tourism.*

The multi-colored cave got its name from the scintillating calcite crystals, called dogtooth spar, which line most of the passages and rooms. Stalactites hang from the ceiling and some are joined with stalagmites growing upward. Most unusual are the flowstones that resemble mashed potatoes and gravy, the hollow balloon formations and gypsum "flowers." Elevators, lighted metal stairways and trails enable visitors to view the wonders of Jewel Cave, located on US 16 west of Custer.

Since 1959, a husband and wife team of spelunkers, Herb and Jan Conn—just for fun—have explored, surveyed, and mapped sixty-four miles of passageways in Jewel Cave and written a fascinating book, **The Jewel Cave Adventure.** Many spelunkers and speliologists believe there are at least 100 miles of unexplored passages in this cave.

Herb Conn follows his wife Jan up through a chimney formation. Although Jewel Cave became a National Monument in 1908, it remained little known until these two expert spelunkers began their explorations in 1959. Eventually the Conns discovered and mapped 64 miles of new passages and rooms. Jewel Cave is now ranked the fourth longest cave in the world. *Photo credit—Dave Schnute, South Dakota Tourism.*

The Conns, who are expert spelunkers, wear old army fatigues, a hard hat to support a carbide lamp (they also carry candles and waterproof matches), thus leaving their hands free. They wear pads on their hands, knees, elbows, shins and hips to protect their bodies when they squeeze through narrow openings in the rocks. The cave is deadly quiet except for the roaring wind and dripping water. They hear nothing from the upper world.

The Conns describe their activities as an "ever-changing succession of maneuvers varying from mountain-climbing techniques to the undulating oozing of an earthworm. There are chimneys to climb up or down and great blocks to scramble over or squeeze under. Everywhere broken slabs of crystal roll underfoot or hang menacingly from the ceiling."

The Conns have discovered and named innumerable new passages, rooms and formations: Gyp Joint, Blessed Relief, King Kong's Cage, Wall Street, Hurricane Corner, Brink of Eternity, Paul Bunyan's Feet, and the Miseries.

Jan Conn emerging from a tight squeeze in Jewel Cave. Her hard hat supports a carbide lamp, thus freeing her padded hands. The Conns also wear pads on their knees, elbows, shins and hips to protect their bodies when they work their way through narrow openings. *Photo credit—Larry Dilts, from* **The Jewel Cave Adventure.**

Jan Conn has written cave music to be sung to guitar accompaniment. Both Conns write cave poetry. Herb Conn wrote this verse:

A chorus of crystals
A travertine cast.
The footlights are mounted
And lighted at last.
The curtain will rise
On a scenic tableau.
Come to the cave
For a Jewel of a show.

Seven other Black Hills caves which are open to the public are privately operated.

Wonderland Cave, near Nemo, SD, was not discovered until 1931. It has an Icicle Fence of stalactites forty feet long and a huge underground lake.

Rushmore Cave, near Keystone, SD, has "the Big Room," the largest cavern in the northwestern United States.

Stagebarn Crystal Cave, northwest of Rapid City, SD, displays brilliant colors and unusual growing formations in "Nature's Painted Room."

Sitting Bull Crystal Caverns, southwest of Rapid City, feature dogtooth spar and unusual fossilized sea creatures embedded in its walls.

Black Hills Caverns, west of Rapid City, are noted for rare and beautiful frost crystals. Hole in Ceiling Room and Moonshine Cavern are colorful chambers.

Wonderland Cave, not discovered until 1931, has an icicle fence of stalactites and an underground lake. The fantastic formations in all the limestone caves in the Black Hills are millions of years old. *Photo credit—Rapid City Chamber of Commerce.*

Bethlehem Cave (formerly Crystal Cave), northwest of Rapid City, was discovered in 1890 and used to be reached by visitors riding the narrow-gauge railway up spectacular Elk Creek Canyon. An entire room was stripped of its glittering crystals and brilliant stone flowers for a display at the Chicago World's Fair in 1893. There are plenty left.

Diamond Crystal Cave, west of Rapid City, has a profusion of crystals of many varieties. When the cave opened in 1929, the owners discovered a skeleton, believed to be that of a small Indian boy who fell to his death through the cave opening 400 years ago. His skull is displayed.

Many speleologists and spelunkers have suggested that all the caves, known and unknown, located in the Paha Sapa limestone of the Black Hills are probably connected by passageways. Some openings are undoubtedly so small that spelunkers would have to be only six inches tall, like the Lilliputians in **Gulliver's Travels.**

Imagine if a person, first utilizing the Indian magic of **Washun Niya,** the breathing hole for a reduction in size, could enter Wind Cave in the south, then take many side trips in the underground labyrinth, and eventually walk out at Wonderland Cave in the north.

What a thrilling adventure that would be!

V.

PIONEERS AND PERSONALITIES

JEDEDIAH SMITH—FIRST WHITE MAN IN THE BLACK HILLS

An impressive mural in the South Dakota state capitol building at Pierre depicts a large keelboat, the "Yellowstone," floating on the Missouri River. In the center of the painting are figures of fur traders and trappers in the prow with the focus on a man kneeling in prayer. It was "a powerful prayer that moved us all greatly," reported Hugh Glass, one of the listeners.

The man delivering the prayer is Jedehiah Smith, Bible-toting fur-trader and trail-blazer, who asked the Lord's blessing for the dead and wounded after the Ashley party had a fight with the Arikara Indians. Smith's celebrated prayer became known as the first recorded act of Christian worship in the land that is now South Dakota.

Jedediah Smith was born in New York state in 1799 where he received an education suitable for a teacher or a minister. As a boy, he read the journals of Lewis and Clark which stimulated him to seek adventure and fortune in the unknown and beckoning west.

When a young man, he traveled to St. Louis, the bustling frontier town where the boats of the fur traders and adventurers crowded the Missouri River. A strapping six-footer, Smith, at age 23, joined General William Ashley's second fur-trading expedition. He was a devout Methodist, prayed every day, and carried his Bible with him wherever he went in the uncharted wilderness.

After the Arikara fight, Jed Smith volunteered to carry the news of the battle to Ashley's partner on the Yellowstone River. General Ashley was so impressed with the young volunteer's bravery and the speed with which he accomplished the arduous mission that he made Smith a captain.

In the early fall of 1823, Captain Jed Smith led a party of fifteen men from Fort Kiowa on the Missouri River (near present-day Chamberlain, SD) across the plains to the southern Black Hills, their destination being the Wind River country of Wyoming.

While traveling through or near the southern Black Hills searching for water and respite from the heat, they were trudging single file through plum and chokecherry thickets. Then without warning, a grizzly bear sprang out of the brush, knocking Jed to the ground, and the animal's claws almost tore off the man's entire scalp and left his ear dangling. The other men managed to shoot the bear.

Although prostrate and wounded, Jed was able to coolly give instructions to his stunned comrades, especially to James Clyman, whom he asked to get out his emergency kit and begin sewing the scalp back into place. Clyman cut away the blood-matted hair and clumsily did as he was told. Although Clyman said he could do nothing for the mangled ear, Jed Smith ordered, "Try!" Clyman did. The crude surgery worked, and in ten days Jed had recovered enough to mount his horse and keep riding west.

Jed Smith usually kept a diary full of observations about the natural history seen on his travels, but on this trip he did not, perhaps because of his injuries.

Fortunately, there is a written record. James Clyman, who had saved

The Buffalo Gap break on the southeastern edge of the Black Hills. In 1823, Jedediah Smith and his men rode their horses through this historic gap. They were the first white men to penetrate the Hills. *Photo credit—Earl Chace.*

Smith's life, many years later wrote an account of this trek from the Missouri River through the southern Black Hills and into Wyoming. Historians have analyzed Clyman's vague descriptions of the terrain, rivers and landmarks and have come up with at least three different conclusions of the routes the Jed Smith party took. Did they follow the White River and then cut over to French Creek? Or did they cross the south fork of the Cheyenne River in the southern Hills, probably near the present location of Hot Springs and Edgemont with perhaps an entanglement in Hells Canyon? However, most readers of the Clyman report believe that from whichever direction they came, Jed Smith and his men passed through the Buffalo Gap break into the Black Hills.

Clyman recalled in his report that when they arrived in the Black Hills, "We entered a pleasant undulating pine Region cool and refreshing so different from the hot dusty planes." This was to be an oft-repeated reaction of many explorers to follow.

From this Clyman report also comes the story told by a Moses Harris which has been the source for some colorful folklore about the wonders of the Black Hills. Harris claimed that he had seen a petrified forest with trees, branches and leaves all turned to stone, "wild cherries peetrified into rubies of reddest hue and peetrified birds a-sittin' on the branches of a tree a-singin' peetrified songs." Perhaps Harris, who publicized this tall tale around many campfires, had been drinking wine in the petrified forest north of what is now Edgemont, SD.

Jedediah Smith, throughout his short, active life, proved himself to be a leader with great endurance and determination, and ranged over the entire western United States. He and two others, William Sublette and George Jackson, eventually purchased the productive Ashley fur business and did well with their venture, trapping beaver, muskrat and all kinds of fur-bearing animals in the wild country.

Smith frequently sent money home to his parents and to his younger brothers for their education. In this letter to his brother, he reveals his religious beliefs: "As it respects my welfare, I hardly durst speak. I find myself one of the most ungrateful, unthankful creatures imaginable. O, when shall I be under the care of a Christian Church! I have need of your prayers. I wish our Society to bear up to a Throne of Grace." No wonder Smith was regarded as a true Christian.

In 1831, while scouting alone for water for his wagon train on the Santa Fe trail, a hunting party of Comanches killed the 32-year-old Smith on the Cimarron River in southern Kansas. His body was never recovered and details of his death were later learned from the Indians. Reportedly, his distinctive silver pistols turned up in Mexican pawn shops.

During his brief lifetime, Smith had made a remarkable record as an explorer and trail-blazer. He made the first complete exploration of the

South Pass in Wyoming, later the gateway to the far west used by thousands of emigrants in their covered wagons. He was the first American to cross the Sierra Nevada mountains into California. He was the first white man to explore the entire Pacific coast from Canada to Mexico.

Throughout his years on the frontier, this Christian man had consistently opposed giving or selling liquor to the Indians. An official national law, enacted in his memory in June, 1832, prohibited traffic in intoxicants in Indian territory.

Today, South Dakotans honor Jedediah Smith because he was the first white man to enter the Black Hills. Although there were no navigable rivers to attract the fur trade, the Black Hills, from time immemorial, were destined to bewitch several races of people with their charms, both real and fabled.

SARAH CAMPBELL—FIRST NON-INDIAN WOMAN IN THE BLACK HILLS

Sarah Campbell, a Negro, was the only woman with the Custer Expedition of 1874, which had been commissioned by the United States government to explore the Black Hills and to check up on the rumors of gold in this mysterious and unknown region. "Aunt Sally"—as the men called her—was cook for John Smith, the sutler for the expedition. She was thus the first non-Indian woman, white or black, to see the Black Hills.

Aunt Sally was probably just as delighted as were the men—many of whom recorded their reactions in diaries, letters, military reports, and newspaper accounts—to discover that the Black Hills were really not black and gloomy as they appeared from a distance; instead the mountains were covered with thick, green pine forests which made them look dark; and they were full of marvelous surprises—sparkling streams, flower-filled meadows, painted canyons—a cool, welcome paradise after the hot alkaline northern Dakota plains and their ever-present hordes of mosquitoes and swarms of grasshoppers.

Probably, Aunt Sally rode in the sutler's wagon which, like all the wagons, was pulled by a team of six mules and driven by a whip-cracking, profane driver. As likely as not, Aunt Sally, being the only woman in this summer wilderness trek, must have had numerous problems involving her own privacy and meager comforts.

Aunt Sally's job was to cook for civilian John Smith, the post trader commonly called "sutler," who accompanied the expedition and sold whiskey, food, and other special provisions to the soldiers.

Presumably, Aunt Sally was expected to exercise her ingenuity to create culinary treats he could sell. The government rations included hard tack, bacon, rio coffee, rice, sugar, vinegar, salt and pepper, supplemented by occasional fresh beef from the herd with the expedition and occasional venison from the antelope and deer the men shot along the way.

There is no record of how ingenious Aunt Sally was in concocting appetizing meals from the frugal supplies or whether she could make soup out of stones. The routine procedure called for the cooks to respond to the first reveille at 2:35 a.m. and to begin unloading the mess gear kept in the big chests in the wagons, to build fires, and to begin preparing breakfast.

One wishes Aunt Sally had been able to record her feelings, but no doubt she enjoyed the myriad charms of the Black Hills as much as did the eloquent observers whose reactions are preserved in writing about the spectacular scenery, the cool weather, and the delightful band music echoing from peak to peak.

At French Creek, near the present town of Custer, SD, Horatio Ross, an experienced miner with the Custer Expedition, made the historic gold discovery. Then everyone went wild digging and scratching and panning gold with shovels, knives, picks—any available implement—whether a mule-whacker or a scientist or a sutler's black cook.

The Horatio Ross monument honoring his discovery of gold in the Black Hills. Main street, Custer, SD. Aunt Sally Campbell, black cook for the Custer Expedition of 1874, was an excited prospector in French Creek and located claim No. 7 Below Discovery. *Photo credit—Fielder Collection, Devereaux Library, South Dakota School of Mines and Technology.*

The bearded Horatio Ross on the right standing in front of W. J. Thornby's cabin in Custer. Thornby, discoverer of Minnekahta in middle. Gold-discoverer Ross died in poverty. *Photo credit—Centennial Archives, Deadwood.*

William Curtis, the 23-year-old star reporter for the **Chicago Inter-Ocean** and the **New York World** reported the gold discovery at French Creek. In the same issue in which the momentous gold discovery in the Black Hills was announced to the country is published his exclusive interview with Aunt Sally, in the August 27, 1874, issue of the **Chicago Inter-Ocean:**

"The most excited contestant in this chase after fortune was 'Aunt Sally,' the sutler's colored cook, a huge mountain of dusky flesh, and 'the only white woman that ever saw the Black Hills,' as she frequently says. She is an old frontiersman, as it were, having been up and down the Missouri ever since its muddy water was broken by a paddle wheel, and having accumulated quite a little property, had settled down in Bismarck to ease and luxury.

'Money didn't done brung dis chile out hyar, now, I tells ye dat; dis hain't no common nigger, now I tells ye: not it ain't, now hyar me; and ye wouldn't cotch dis gal totin' chuck out hyar now, I tells ye, if it haadn't bin for seein' dese hyar Black Hills dat Custer fetched us to. I'se heered 'bout dese here hills long 'fore Custer did. Now I'm talkin'. When I was on de Missouri—cooked on first boat dat ever run up dat stream, an' I hain't had no hard luck, neither, now I tells ye folks. But I wanted to see dese Black Hills—an' dey ain't no blacker dan I am and I'm no African, now you just bet I ain't; I'm none of yer common herd, I've got the money to back it, now I have, I tell you.'

Aunt Sally's Dream of Gold

Aunt Sally expected to find the Black Hills in some indefinite way or other adapted to the colored race, and was terribly disappointed; but the gold discoveries compensated for the lack of any distinctive mark of her race, and she joined in the development with religious fervor. She talked incessantly about them from morning to night, and when she packed her mammoth body into a little wagon that provided for her and her 'traps,' her dreams were of gold mines, and ' 'ery thing dats on his dis hyar earth, now I 'low.' She went to the stream when the strike was made, 'scratched grabble,' and staked out her claim, and she says she's coming here as soon as anybody, 'now you hyar me.' "

Aunt Sally, along with the rest of the miners, experienced and inexperienced, staked out her illegal claim, recorded as "No. 7 Below Discovery." Later, these claims in Indian Territory were probably taken over by more prospectors who unlawfully invaded the region within the next year.

Whether or not Aunt Sally had a hand in trying to tenderize and cook the tough bear meat provided by General Custer for the officers' mess, it is probably safe to assume that she became an expert at cooking the plentiful venison. One can easily visualize huge Aunt Sally in a covered wagon, loaded with rattling pots and pans, jouncing over the pine-clad mountains and rocky outcroppings and emerald meadows, and driven by a teamster swearing at the balky mules.

According to the Curtis interview, from the time Aunt Sally was the first excited female tourist in the Black Hills and then participated in the French Creek discovery, she was determined to return. Gold! That was the magnet that attracted her—as well as thousands of other gold-seekers.

Aunt Sally kept her vow and return she did, but there is no conclusive record of just when. Several reports state that she walked beside an ox-drawn wagon train from Bismarck to the Black Hills, establishing herself first at Crook City, then at Galena, cooking and midwifing for various families. There is no record of whether she ever returned to the French Creek area to check on "No. 7 Below Discovery." Eventually, she filed a claim at Elk Creek near Roubaix in Lawrence County and lived on a little ranch there.

Rumors and contradictions abound concerning Aunt Sally. Some old-timers reported that she claimed her father had been a Cherokee Indian and her mother a Negro, that she and her mother had spent the Civil War years in Canada until Custer sent her money to return to the United States.

Aunt Sally also claimed that she was a personal cook both for General Custer and for Captain Miles Keogh, the owner of Comanche, the famous horse who survived the Battle of the Little Big Horn. Although it is possible that, at various times, she may have cooked for these officers, there is no record of it.

Several sons and daughters of Galena pioneers, the old silver-mining town, remember stories their parents told and retold about popular Aunt Sally whom they loved and respected. How she enjoyed relating colorful anecdotes about her adventures with the Custer Expedition, while puffing on her pipe, her ample sides shaking with merriment. The main character in all her tales was her hero, George Armstrong Custer. She had the reputation of being a good midwife, a superb cook, and a lover of children.

An unusual aspect of Aunt Sally's life was that she found a hungry, ragged 10-year-old white orphan boy crying on the streets of Deadwood. She took him home and adopted him as her son. His name was Anthony Herr or Wier. He never smiled so she called him "Sad."

Aunt Sally, who was her own best press agent, lived happily among other pioneers in the Black Hills, mostly white people who settled Crook City, Galena, Elk Creek, and Roubaix areas—all in Lawrence County, South Dakota.

She died on April 13, 1888, at age 73 or 75, and two Deadwood newspapers published complimentary obituaries. **The Deadwood Daily Pioneer** concluded: "Everybody knew her, everybody liked her, and not a few will learn with deep regret that death has claimed her."

She was buried on Vinegar Hill, a beautiful little mountain cemetery in the tall pines west of Galena. Seth Galvin, a Galena native who knew her as a boy and wrote about her in his unpublished memoirs, kept her grave in good condition. He placed the first simple wooden marker on which was carved: "Aunt Sally—First Woman in the Black Hills," which is now displayed in the Adams Museum in Deadwood.

Mr. Galvin's interpretation of why Aunt Sally always said she was the first **white** woman in the Black Hills was this: "She was not very literate, and the term 'white' was the only she knew. She meant 'civilized.' "

In 1934, Seth Galvin enlisted the aid of Fred Borsch, another Galena native, and the two men built a simple wooden fence around Aunt Sally's grave to keep out wandering cattle and erected a larger and improved marker.

Fred Borsch with niece Jeri Fahrni and Ramona Hultman, Vinegar Hill cemetery, Galena. Borsch and Seth Galvin, Galena pioneers, placed the sign on Aunt Sally Campbell's grave and took care of the gravesite for many years. She was a popular cook and midwife for many pioneer families in Galena, a silver camp in Lawrence County, SD. *Photo credit—Ed Baier.*

The name of Sarah Campbell will live forever in Black Hills history; for as her grave marker says, "She Ventured with the Vanguard of Civilization."

Likewise, the name of "Aunt Sally," a wonderful friend and neighbor to many, lives on in the long memories of the sons and daughters, even the grandchildren, of the pioneers of Lawrence County in the Black Hills of South Dakota.

ANNIE TALLENT—FIRST WHITE WOMAN IN THE BLACK HILLS

Annie Tallent was the first white woman to enter the Black Hills, and ever since she had been honored and revered for this "first" in addition to other accomplishments of a more uncontroversial nature. At age 47, she was the only woman with the 28-member Russell-Collins or Gordon Party, as it is variously called. These gold-seekers made secret preparations in Sioux City, Iowa, for their trek to the Black Hills in 1874, violating both the Laramie Treaty of 1868 and the express orders of the United States government not to invade them, for the Black Hills were supposed to be strictly off limits to whites.

Annie Tallent was born in New York state, was educated in a female seminary, and eventually moved westward. She married David Tallent, a lawyer, and it was with him and their nine-year-old son Robert that she embarked on her perilous and celebrated march to the forbidden El Dorado.

Annie Tallent in center. She was the only woman with the Russell-Collins or Gordon Party, which illegally invaded the Black Hills in 1874. Thomas H. Russell, the leader of the group, was elected first president of the Society of Black Hills Pioneers. *Photo credit—Centennial Archives, Deadwood.*

Twenty-five years later Mrs. Tallent wrote the Bible of regional histories, **The Black Hills** or **Last Hunting Grounds of the Dacotahs,** in which she described the adventures and hardships of the perilous 78-day journey to the Black Hills when she walked mile after mile beside the heavily loaded wagon train into Indian Territory.

Constantly tormented by visions of the scalping knife, she described a hazardous journey across the barren plains in late fall, the arguments among the disgruntled men, the desolation of the Badlands, and the practical reason for tying gunny sacks around her worn shoes which was to protect her feet from the cold.

Annie Tallent wrote the Bible of regional histories, **The Black Hills** or **Last Hunting Grounds of the Dakotahs,** in which she describes the adventures and hardships of her perilous walk to the Black Hills. *Photo credit—South Dakota State Historical Society.*

In vivid detail, she recalled how the first glimpse of the shadowy Black Hills and of the Bear Butte landmark "guarding the entrance to the unknown land" made every heart sing "paeans of joy and thankfulness." Despite the wintry weather, the heartened group finally located the Custer wagon trail out of the Black Hills and noted traces of civilization such as a few kernels of corn and discarded army gear. At this point, Annie Tallent confessed that she sat down on a log and cried from sheer homesickness.

By backtracking Custer's route, made five months earlier, the party arrived on French Creek near the present site of Custer city on December 23rd in heavy snow. They spent a miserable Christmas, dreaming of home, and eating "coarse everyday fare" not turkey and plum puddings. A forest of Christmas trees surrounded them, but there were no decorations—"nothing but picks, shovels, gold pans, and an ox chain for ornamentation," wrote Mrs. Tallent.

Except for listing the individual members of the group at the beginning of her book, the author never mentions the presence of her husband and little boy throughout the entire ordeal. However, the men soon began constructing seven cabins inside the famous Gordon Stockade while hoping for reinforcements and praying not to be discovered by the military contingents they knew were searching for violators of the law.

General Crook's soldiers in 1875 at Gordon Stockade on French Creek. Crook's men arrested the trespassers and escorted them back to Fort Laramie, WY. Annie Tallent rode out of the Black Hills on a government mule. *Photo credit—South Dakota State Historical Society.*

About a month later, United States Army officers arrested the trespassers and escorted the unhappy group to Fort Laramie, WY, where they were all released without punishment. Annie Tallent rode a government mule out of the Black Hills; thus she was the first woman to enter and to exit.

But it wasn't long before the United States government and the relieved army patrols gave up trying to stop the Black Hills Gold Rush as thousands of fortune-hunters began pouring into the Indian reservation from all directions.

Not until 1876 did the Tallents return to the Black Hills where they settled first in Custer, then in Deadwood, and finally in Rapid City. David Tallent eventually deserted his family and disappeared from the region. Mrs. Tallent, ever resourceful and self-sufficient, taught school in log schoolhouses at Tigerville and Hill City, then became postmistress and teacher at Rochford. Always interested in education, she served as superintendent of public instruction in Pennington County, proving herself to be an active community leader and church worker wherever she lived.

Annie Tallent spent her final years living with her son Robert in Sturgis where she researched and wrote her book. Her chronicle includes detailed histories of all the Black Hills settlements, accounts of mines and other industries, sketches of prominent people, including Wild Bill Hickok, who she thought looked like a Quaker minister instead of a gunman. She wrote colorful descriptions of memorable events like the devastating Deadwood fire of 1879. Included are lengthy, dramatized narratives of the Battle of the Little Big Horn and the Wounded Knee uprising; however, she provides few sources for most of the voluminous information presented on a variety of subjects.

In her history book, Mrs. Tallent writes at length about the Custer Expedition of 1874, but she does not state that Sarah Campbell, or "Aunt Sally"—as she was called—a cook with the expedition, was the first non-Indian woman to visit the Hills. Her only mention of the Negress is in this context: "Aunt Sally, who claimed the distinction of being 'de fustest culled lady in the Brack Hills,' was one of the early settlers of Crook City." Whether or not Mrs. Tallent felt any rivalry with Aunt Sally about who had the prior claim, white or "culled," she does not elaborate.

Mrs. Tallent's attitude toward Indians reflected the white attitude of that era: the Indians were savages and "the only good Indian was a dead one." Definitely, she suggests that their legal rights to a rich land coveted by the greedy whites should not have been taken seriously and that "a long list of fancied wrongs, treasured up for years" contributed to the bitter hostilities, resulting in the crowning tragedy of the Little Big Horn.

In 1974, Brevet Press published the second edition of the Tallent history with a special introduction by Virginia Driving Hawk Sneve, a Brule Sioux Indian, who is a teacher, writer, and editor. Mrs. Sneve strongly objects to many of the book's discussions of Indian life and beliefs, including the author's biased reporting of the conflicts between Indians and whites. Mrs. Sneve believes that "Annie Tallent's malicious, bigoted treatment of the Dakota or Sioux Indians, would best serve mankind if it were burned rather than reprinted in this edition to continue to perpetuate a distorted, untrue portrait of the American Indian."

However, in the white world Annie Tallent is a favorite heroine, hailed as the personification of the ideal pioneer woman. Many schools and prestigious awards have been named in her honor. The Society of Black Hills Pioneers erected, near the town of Custer, a statue dedicated to her memory with the inscription: "The world is better because she lived and worked in it."

When Annie Tallent died in 1901, aged 74, in Sturgis, SD, she was reported to have been given the most impressive funeral ever held in the history of the Society of Black Hills Pioneers. She was buried in a family plot at Elgin, Illinois.

In arriving at a fair assessment of Annie Tallent's contributions to the development of the Black Hills and the significance and influence of her book, historians would do well to recall the words of a writer named Froude: "To be entirely just in our estimate of other ages is not only difficult, but is impossible."

WILD BILL HICKOK AND HIS MAGIC TOUCH

Wild Bill Hickok, as everyone knows, was the fastest gun in the Wild West. He was also an accomplished magician. He lived in a tent in Deadwood, Dakota Territory, for only about six weeks while prospecting for gold during the Black Hills Gold Rush in 1876. An inveterate gambler, this famous Kansas marshal, carelessly sitting with his back to the door, was shot in the back while playing poker in the Saloon No. 10 in Deadwood.

And that's it—that's the extent of his accomplishments in the entire Black Hills. He didn't even shoot anyone. Yet, Wild Bill is hailed as the most illustrious person ever to be a Black Hills resident, however briefly. There must be magic somewhere to explain how his personality has dominated Black Hills history and legend, which are hopelessly entangled and can never be clearly separated, especially about Wild Bill Hickok.

An old woodcut depicting the most famous event in Deadwood history, on August 2, 1876. Jack McCall shot Wild Bill Hickok in the back of the head while he was playing poker in the No. 10 Saloon. Hickok, who died instantly, was holding black aces and eights, known forever after as the "Dead Man's Hand." *Photo credit—Fielder Collection, Devereaux Library, South Dakota School of Mines and Technology.*

Maybe he had a magic wand, a secret weapon that still transmits powerful signals. Or sleight-of-hand tricks that have mesmerized the populace for over a century. Something like that.

Wild Bill Hickok was saluted as the Prince of Pistoleers. His friend and one-time employer, Buffalo Bill Cody, said: "He was the most deadly shot with rifle and pistols that ever lived." A great many other eye-witnesses to his shooting prowess said the same thing. Wild Bill was the gunman par excellence with an estimated 100 shootings to his credit or discredit, not counting Civil War rebels and Indians.

Wild Bill was born James Bulter Hickok in Troy Grove, Illinois, in 1837, and early in life demonstrated great talent in using guns. When he became a youthful stagecoach driver in Nebraska, he got into a fight with the McCanles horse-stealing gang and single-handedly, with lightning-like rapidity, shot and killed nine of them. Some say three victims were innocent bystanders. The lenient frontier jury acquitted him on self-defense. From that time on, everyone on the frontier began calling him "Wild Bill" very admiringly.

During the Civil War, Wild Bill acquitted himself well as scout and sharpshooter for the Union Army. After the war, to earn a living, he tried homesteading, bullwhacking, stagecoach driving, scouting, and gambling, his obsessive occupation.

In 1867, Hickok scouted for General George Custer in Kansas, and the two controversial long-hairs became good friends. In Custer's only book, **My Life on the Plains,** he wrote: "Wild Bill was a strange character, just the one which a novelist might gloat over. . . . He was one of the most perfect types of physical manhood I ever saw, the most famous scout on the Plains." Custer was convinced that Wild Bill never killed a man except in self defense and concluded "that his skill in the use of rifle and pistol was unerring."

Wild Bill Hickok as he dressed while scouting for Custer in Kansas. Wild Bill always carried two pearl-handled revolvers and a knife. A handsome man with charming manners and a clean appearance, he captivated the ladies. *Photo credit—South Dakota State Historical Society.*

Various biographers relate many thrilling episodes in which Hickok killed countless Indians and outlaws and had many narrow escapes, including a fight with a grizzly bear. But he led a charmed life—for awhile.

Everyone who ever knew him or wrote about him agrees that his shooting prowess was spectacular. He could hit a dime tossed into the air nine out of ten times; he could drill bullets into the cork of a bottle without hitting the glass, and all at twenty-five paces or more. Although he had to cock the hammer each time he shot and never appeared to aim, he could handle two guns, firing simultaneously from the hips and never miss, whether in target practice or in life-or-death situations.

Wild Bill and his fast guns were just what some of the lawless frontier towns wanted—a peace officer. He was appointed deputy United States marshal to clean up the rip-roaring towns of Hays City and Abilene, both in Kansas. And he did, acting as judge, jury, and executioner for suspicious characters and thus fulfilling his murderous duties as peace officer. He left innumerable corpses strewn throughout Kansas, all presumably killed in self-defense.

Women were always attracted to charismatic Wild Bill and his handsome, clean appearance and charming manners. He had a number of romances but Calamity Jane wasn't one of them. Then he became enamored of a daring circus acrobat and equestrienne, Agnes Lake Thatcher. Widow Thatcher was eleven years older than he; and, according to her photograph, was not pretty. Nevertheless, Wild Bill married her in March, 1876, in Cincinnati, Ohio. He gallantly gave his age as 45 instead of 39 so he would be older than the false age his bride assigned to herself.

After a two-week honeymoon, Agnes went to stay with her daughter in

MARRIAGE CERTIFICATE

This is to Certify

That ... of ... in the State of ... and ... of ... in the State of ... were by me joined together in

HOLY MATRIMONY

on the ... day of ... 1876 in ...

Wild Bill Hickok married Agnes Lake Thatcher, a daring circus acrobat and equestrienne, in March, 1876. Although Widow Thatcher was eleven years older than he and not pretty, she must have had charisma to capture this ladies' man. *Photo credit—From Adams Museum, Deadwood, by Al Gunther.*

Cincinnati. Wild Bill left on the train for Cheyenne, WY, to make plans for joining the Black Hills Gold Rush.

On a memorable day in June, 1876, Wild Bill Hickok and Calamity Jane, all duded up in fringed buckskins and white stetsons, galloped into Deadwood Gulch as outriders for the long, Colorado Charlie Utter wagon train from Cheyenne which delivered the first whores to Deadwood. The cumbersome ox-train blocked the traffic in the gold camp, jammed with an estimated 10,000 to 25,000 prospectors, reputed to be the entire floating population of the west.

Wild Bill and the Utter brothers set up headquarters in a tent in the crowded, twisting gulch packed with gold-crazed prospectors and a jumble of wagons with oxen, horses, and mules trampling manure into the muddy, stinking main street. The sounds of pounding hammers and screechy music mingled with the cries of hawkers selling soap and peanuts and knives. Gamblers and hustlers exhorted the men to try their luck at faro, poker, and other games of chance. Adding to the bedlam were the oaths of bull-whackers, the cracks of their long black whips, the bawling of cattle, and the braying of mules. These were the sounds of Deadwood when Wild Bill Hickok arrived in the rambunctious gold camp.

In lawless Deadwood, Wild Bill kept a low profile, not capitalizing on his already widespread reputation as a gunfighter, scout, and lawman. He prospected a little, wrote loving letters to his wife Agnes, did some target practice. But he spent most of his time gambling, his greatest obsession.

On August 2nd, a significant date in Black Hills history, Wild Bill was playing poker with his friends in the Saloon No. 10. Inexplicably, the Kansas marshal with many enemies, sat with his back to the door. In burst Crooked Nose Jack McCall, a common gunslinger, and shot Wild Bill in the back of the head. Wild Bill Hickok died instantly. He was holding black aces and eights, known forever after as the "Deadman's Hand."

Several Hickok promoters claimed for years that Wild Bill had both guns out and cocked before he fell over the poker table. Others say he never had time to reach. So go the contradictions of the legend.

Jack McCall ran out of the saloon with his gun smoking, and outraged citizens chased the assassin yelling "Wild Bill's been shot! Wild Bill is dead!"

The assassin was eventually captured in a much-disputed location on Deadwood's main street—without Calamity Jane's help, as she later insisted.

Jack McCall was tried the next day in the Bella Union theater before a packed house, eager for entertainment. Because Deadwood was legally Indian territory, the judge and jury had no jurisdiction; they just went through the motions of the fake trial. Jack McCall testified that he had shot Wild Bill to avenge the death of his brother by Wild Bill's gun in Kansas.

Judge W. Y. Kuykendall accepted the revenge motive and acquitted McCall in a farcical trial typcial of frontier justice. McCall did not leave town until he was good and ready. Eventually, he was arrested in Wyoming, United States territory, where he bragged about killing Wild Bill Hickok. He was arrested and brought to Yankton, the capital of Dakota Territory. In this second trial, Jack McCall was convicted in a federal court, and on March 1, 1877, was hanged for the murder of Wild Bill Hickok and buried with the rope around his neck.

After Hickok's murder, Colorado Charlie Utter and his brother Steve carried Wild Bill's body to their tent where Doc Peirce, a loquacious barber acted as undertaker "on the prettiest corpse I've ever seen." Everyone in the gulch, including a wailing Calamity Jane, traipsed through the tent to see if the fastest gun in the west was really dead.

The Utter brothers buried Wild Bill in the Ingleside area of Deadwood, the first boot hill, and placed a wooden marker above the grave with this inscription:

Wild Bill
J. B. Hickok
Killed by the assassin Jack McCall
Deadwood, Black Hills
August 2, 1876

Pard we will meet again in the
Happy Hunting Grounds to part no more
Good bye
Colorado Charlie, C. H. Utter

Three years later, in 1879, the Utter brothers returned to Deadwood and with John McClintock and another Deadwood man, dug up Wild Bill's coffin and struggled up the steep hill carrying the wooden coffin to Mount Moriah, the new cemetery.

After Hickok's murder, Colorado Charlie and Steve Utter buried their friend in Ingleside, the first boot hill in Deadwood. The brothers erected a wooden headboard which didn't last long. The inscription is famous in western history. *Photo credit—Centennial Archives, Deadwood.*

McClintock, who many years later wrote **Pioneer Days in the Black Hills,** described opening the casket and finding that both Wild Bill's carbine and his corpse were in a perfect state of preservation. His clothes were decomposed and the body was exposed to the hips and coated with lime. McClintock poked the corpse with a stick in many places but did not discover any soft spots.

This well-publicized story gave rise to the rumor that Wild Bill's body was petrified and impervious to ordinary decomposition presumably because of the god-like status of the deceased. Or Doc Peirce must have been a better undertaker than anyone thought.

Through the years several gravemarkers and statues were destroyed by vandals in Mount Moriah cemetery, including two large monuments, one a bust and the other a life-size statue of Wild Bill.

Mount Moriah cemetery, Deadwood. The sculptor Riordan beside his huge bust of Wild Bill whose epitaph is "Custer was lonely without him." Vandals eventually destroyed this bust in addition to a full-size statue of Wild Bill and two other large Hickok monuments. *Photo credit—Centennial Archives, Deadwood.*

Wild Bill's friends and enemies, including the first Black Hills tourists, began to make pilgrimages to the grave. Hickok's widow Agnes came, as did Buffalo Bill Cody and Captain Jack Crawford, the poet-scout, who wrote several poems about Wild Bill while sitting on his grave. And of course Calamity Jane came often, even having her picture taken at the grave site.

Like his friend Custer, Wild Bill's death, a violent death, complete with dramatic irony, conferred on Wild Bill Hickok an immortality he could never have earned even if he had lived to be one hundred years old with his shooting skill intact.

Another reason for Wild Bill's increasing notoriety is that in 1885, nine years after his death, author Edward Wheeler (pseudonym Ned Buntline) used his name for a hero of numerous dime novels with a western setting which featured well-known western characters as fictionized heroes and heroines.

Wild Bill was also the subject of countless articles in western pulp magazines whose editors were not concerned about facts and historical accuracy. Eventually serious historians and biographers wrote about Wild Bill Hickok, each presenting his or her version of a much-disputed life. Was he a fair, dedicated peace officer who killed only in self-defense, as Custer insisted? Or was he an instinctive killer who gloried in using his magic gun at the slightest provocation? Who knows?

Almost every author who wrote a newspaper or magazine feature about Deadwood or a history of the Black Hills openly admitted to having known Wild Bill personally—or else the writer's grandfather had. The number of people who claimed to have been kibitzing at that celebrated poker game in Saloon No. 10 when the Kansas marshal was murdered would suggest that the log cabin saloon, which later burned, must have been larger than a Roman amphitheater.

In the twentieth century, the motion picture industry discovered both Wild Bill Hickok and Calamity Jane. Many movies dramatized the make-believe romance between them. The movie screen also added new dimensions to Wild Bill's exploits while cleaning up and prettifying Calamity Jane.

Ever since Wild Bill was murdered in 1876, Deadwood residents have been proud that he died there and delighted to claim this six-weeks-resident as a native son.

A few spoil-sports have pointed out that Wild Bill did nothing for Deadwood except to die there. But that was plenty. He has become the patron saint of commerce throughout the Hills, and especially in Deadwood, where all types of stores and miscellaneous merchandise have been named for Wild Bill Hickok. The commercial exploitation combined with ersatz history provides signs, often contradictory, about the exact location

of the original Saloon No. 10 and the exact spot where assassin Jack McCall was captured. The graves of Wild Bill and Calamity Jane high above Deadwood in Mount Moriah cemetery are popular tourist attractions.

Calamity Jane finally caught up with Wild Bill Hickok in Mount Moriah cemetery, Deadwood. Their graves are Deadwood's most popular tourist attraction. *Photo credit —Al Gunther.*

Yes, there are many understandable reasons why this sleight-of-hand artist has become one of the most enduring legends in American folklore. Wild Bill personified the ideal hero of the west: he was both a gunfighter and a lawman on horseback, the supreme role of command and influence, endowed with the phallic symbolism of the towering horseman with a pointed gun. He lived by the gun and he died by the gun—and that's frontier justice. Today, he is a dominant figure in western mythology, one to be cherished and remembered, like the Wild West itself.

There is also another reason why Wild Bill Hickok will live forever—he had the magic touch.

Gravesites of Wild Bill Hickok and Calamity Jane before vandals destroyed the statue of Wild Bill and the large urn on Calamity's side. The urn was donated by brothel madam Dora DuFran. *Photo credit—South Dakota State Historical Society.*

"THAT'S NO MAN—THAT'S CALAMITY JANE!"

"I was considered the most reckless and daring rider and one of the best shots in the western country. And I was at all times with the men where there was excitement and adventures to be had." So says Calamity Jane in her autobiography written by a ghost writer.

Truer words than these were never spoken by that frontier roustabout and inventive liar known as Calamity Jane. Perhaps this quoted example of her truthfulness is the exception to prove the rule because much of what she publicized about herself was simply gross exaggeration or an outrageous lie—like the sensational fib about her and Wild Bill Hickok being lovers.

Separating fact from fiction about the woman (even some doubt about that) who is undoubtedly "Queen of the Wild West" is mostly impossible. Calamity Jane has become a legend. And legends are notoriously difficult to pin down to origins, verifiable facts, and clear-cut roles.

Take the contradictions about her appearance; she has been described as both beautiful and ugly, with both red hair and black raven tresses. Authors have described her as "roughest-looking human I ever saw" and "extremely pretty." Undoubtedly, she aged quickly from the degenerate life she led.

Reputed to be a rare photograph of Calamity Jane when she was young and pretty. "The men all liked her, being the only woman in camp," wrote brothel madam Dora DuFran of the gold rush days in Deadwood Gulch. *Photo credit—W. H. Over Museum, Vermillion, SD.*

At last, historians have decided that Calamity Jane was born Martha Canary around 1850—give or take a year or two—in Princeton, Missouri. When she was a young girl she began frolicking around the frontier in Montana, Utah, Colorado, Kansas, Wyoming, and Dakota Territory (particularly in the Black Hills).

During her lifetime she was at various times a bullwhacker, a scout, a teamster, a prostitute, a howling drunk, a laundress, a cook, a sharp-shooter, a prospector, and a home nurse. "Reckless" and "daring" she certainly was, especially where there were men, excitement and adventure—as she says in her spurious autobiography.

A youthful Calamity Jane. During her lifetime she was at various times a bullwhacker, scout, teamster, prostitute, howling drunk, laundress, cook, sharp-shooter, prospector, and home nurse. *Photo credit—Centennial Archives, Deadwood.*

However, this rare little pamphlet which she sold on the streets and in saloons when she was down and out can be mostly discounted as history. It is a tall, tall tale typical of the frontier and an example of Calamity's often boozy imagination.

In her autobiography, which should be labeled "fiction," Calamity explains how she acquired her name. During an Indian ambush, her comrade, a Captain Eagan, was injured in the fight, but dare-devil Calamity galloped up beside him and lifted him onto her own horse. Then she raced for the fort holding the wounded man in front of the saddle. Later, she claimed the grateful captain bestowed her nickname as though he were crowning a queen: "I name you Calamity Jane, the Heroine of the Plains."

Dora DuFran, a notorious brothel madam in the Black Hills, and a close friend of Calamity's later wrote a book about her, **Low Down on Calamity Jane.** Madam DuFran had another explanation of how Calamity acquired her name: "If anyone was sick in camp, it was 'send for Jane!' Where calamity was, there was Jane; and so she was christened Calamity Jane."

Watson Parker, dean of Black Hills historians, suggests that the most likely story about how she got her name was that Calamity Jane's paramours were generally visited by some venereal "calamity."

Even though at various times she worked as a prostitute, especially when she needed money for drinks, Calamity often dressed like a man in buckskins, a big campaign hat hiding her hair, and packing six-shooters which she was an expert at using. How she relished the huge joke of passing herself off as a man, especially when she wanted a job as a bullwhacker or teamster. Like the typical macho image of the western hero, she could drink, cuss, ride horseback, shoot, and chew tobacco. Sometimes she even danced with the "soiled doves" in the hurdy-gurdy houses.

No wonder a common refrain on the frontier when an exhibitionist in pants shot up a saloon, put on a show cracking a bull whip, or won all the turkeys in a shooting match was, "That's no man—that's Calamity Jane!"

Perhaps it is true, as some biographers have suggested, that Calamity's fondness for playing both feminine and masculine roles indicated bi-sexuality.

Dressed like a man, Calamity Jane first entered the Black Hills in 1875 with the Jenney-Newton scientific expedition, whom the government had commissioned to verify the glowing reports of the Custer Expedition of 1874 about gold discoveries in the Black Hills.

Calamity Jane all dressed up like the lady she was not. Some biographers have suggested that Calamity's fondness for playing both feminine and masculine roles indicated bi-sexuality. *Photo credit—South Dakota State Historical Society.*

She probably got herself hired as a teamster driving a supply wagon and impressed the boss with her working vocabulary of obscenities. Then someone said, "That's no man—that's Calamity Jane!" and sent her back to Fort Laramie. But she sneaked back, and therefore first came into the Black Hills with the Jenney-Newton Expedition.

Thus, Calamity Jane was the third non-Indian woman to penetrate the

Black Hills: the first was Sarah Campbell (Aunt Sally), a Negro cook for the Custer Expedition in the summer of 1874; and the second was the revered Annie Tallent, a white woman with the illegal Russell-Collins Party in late 1874. Therefore, Calamity was certainly a Black Hills pioneer of 1875; and depending on whether from a white or from an Indian point of view, she deserves some credit for that distinction.

Calamity was a versatile liar. She lied when she said she scouted for General Custer; she probably never met the ill-fated general. She lied about being a scout for General George Crook in 1875 when he ordered the illegal prospectors out of the Black Hills which belonged exclusively to the Sioux Indians.

At least once, she told the truth about her scouting; she really was a scout for General Crook at Fort Fetterman in May, 1876. The proof is that her name was listed on the records of Frank Grouard, chief of scouts, and she is also mentioned as being there in the diaries of several of the soldiers with Crook.

Calamity Jane. Although she lied about many aspects of her life, Calamity really was a scout for General Crook at Fort Fetterman, WY. Frank Grouard, chief of scouts, listed her name on the records and several soldiers mentioned her as being there in their diaries. *Photo credit—Centennial Archives, Deadwood.*

Undoubtedly, she was an excellent scout. She knew the terrain and the wagon ruts and the saloons at the end of the trails. An expert shot with both rifle and pistol, she was a roughneck with characteristics of both sexes, a dramatic concoction of good and bad; certainly she could cope with the hardships of the wilderness as well as any man.

Calamity Jane made a spectacular entrance into Deadwood Gulch at the height of the gold rush in June, 1876, when she and Wild Bill Hickok were both outriders with the Colorado Charlie Utter wagon train from Cheyenne, Wyoming. Reporters wrote that Calamity was youthful and pretty, and that she and Wild Bill were both dressed in buckskins with long fringe, white stetsons, and clean boots. Calamity, described as an "Amazonian woman of the frontier" waved and yelled at all the excited prospectors crowding Deadwood's narrow, winding main street. No wonder the 190-person wagon train powered by ox-teams stopped the traffic in the gold camp.

Calamity and Wild Bill weren't the only attractions. It was an historic occasion: the first whores had arrived in Deadwood, riding on their wagons like queens greeting the cheering male populace. Two experienced madams and faro dealers, Madam Mustachio and Madam Dirty Em, soon set up brothels in what quickly became a thriving red-light district that lasted for over 100 years in Deadwood.

During that wild summer of 1876, Calamity made Deadwood, Dakota Territory, her headquarters because "Sin City" had the most action—brawls and shootings, saloons and hurdy-gurdy houses, roistering gold-seekers and professional gamblers. She swaggered into the bars ordering "Give me a shot of booze and slop her over the brim."

Sometimes, she provided free entertainment to anyone who would listen by telling fantastic tales of her exploits, like robbing stagecoaches and fighting Indians, with herself in the chief male role. And when Calamity got drunk, watch out!

Madam DuFran, her friend and frequent employer, wrote: "She even had a band of coyotes beat for howling when she was drunk and that was most of the time. The Hills reverberated to the wild howling of Calamity Jane, the untamed woman of the wild, wild west."

This untamed woman certainly got around the frontier. In Cheyenne, WY she shot out the lights in a saloon; in Miles City, MT, she was arrested for brawling, and it took three strong men to drag her to jail, no doubt howling all the way.

Every town in the Black Hills knew her well. In Rapid City, whooping and hollering, she rode a red bull up main street to the delight of the onlookers. In Hot Springs, she was blasted in the newspaper for putting on a "drunken exhibition of horsemanship and shooting." In a Deadwood theater, she strode up to the footlights and spit tobacco juice all over the leading lady's gown.

The following news items appeared February 8, 1879, in the **Black Hills Daily Times:** "It is reported from Sturgis City that Calamity Jane walloped two women at that place yesterday. Calamity can get away with half a dozen ordinary pugilistic women when she turns loose, but she never fights unless she is in the right, and then she is not backward to tackle even a masculine shoulder hitter."

Understandably, once a person had an encounter with Calamity Jane, that person never forgot her. Her bizarre behavior and escapades in the border country always made for fascinating conversation and lively reading. Calamity Jane was news.

During the summer of 1876, Calamity Jane followed Wild Bill Hickok around like a puppy, but the elegant Kansas marshal had no time for this vulgar woman, being a newly married man who spent his time writing loving letters to his bride, prospecting for gold, and gambling. Calamity did her best to spread the gossip that there was a romance between them, but few believed her.

After Wild Bill was shot in the back during a poker game in the Saloon No. 10, Calamity later bragged that she was the one who had captured the assassin, Jack McCall, in Shoudy's meat market with a meat cleaver. But this was another lie, according to many witnesses of the murder.

Calamity did set herself up as the chief mourner of Wild Bill, wailing and crying while the motely gang of the gold camp filed through the tent where the handsome corpse was laid out. Even though she behaved like a bereaved sweetheart of the dead man, she didn't fool anybody.

Calamity Jane wearing a red dress and a red hat at Wild Bill Hickok's grave in Mount Moriah. She loved to brag that they had been lovers—especially after he was dead and couldn't defend himself. *Photo credit—Centennial Archives, Deadwood.*

However, there definitely was another side to the roughneck Calamity—a kind, tender, caring side. Her contemporaries agree that she was an angel of mercy to the sick. She frequently helped nurse the sick with Dr. L. F. Babcock, an early Deadwood doctor, who praised her as "beautiful and brave" for her nursing work.

During the terrible small pox epidemic of 1878, it was Calamity who nursed a great many contagious patients. According to Madam DuFran, Calamity had small pox when she was a youngster and was thus immune.

Nevertheless, it was a remarkable act of mercy, day after day, week after week, to care for the small pox victims in filthy tents and shacks with no running water or sanitary conveniences of any kind. The only medicines were epsom salts and cream of tartar.

Madam DuFran related how Calamity volunteered to nurse eight sick men who were quarantined with small pox in a shack on White Rocks mountain above Deadwood. Probably because of her ministrations, five of her patients survived.

When a patient died, Calamity wrapped him in a blanket and yelled down the mountain for someone to dig another grave. Then she conducted the burial rites and recited the only prayer she knew, "Now I Lay Me Down to Sleep."

During the small pox epidemic, Calamity Jane was much more than a nurse: she was a doctor, cook, chambermaid, water boy, undertaker, sexton, and preacher. Brown and Willard, two authors who knew Calamity, summarized her nursing activities in their book, **Black Hills Trails**: "It made no difference to her that she knew them not, or that no gold would be there to repay her for the labor, the sacrifice, the danger. They were fellow beings in distress and needed help."

No wonder contemporary writers labeled Calamity Jane as "The West's Joan of Arc," "The Black Hills' Florence Nightengale," and "Lady Robin Hood."

The basic plot of the Lady Robin Hood story is that a penniless Calamity pulled a gun on a storekeeper to get groceries for a sick family who couldn't afford to buy food. Probably the storekeeper would have let her charge if she had asked politely. But Calamity always thought it was fun to wave a gun around. She consistently performed with showmanship with an eye to the audience. Maybe even with an eye on posterity—who knows?

Calamity left Deadwood in 1880 and for about fifteen years roamed the frontier playing her many roles. In 1898, an aging and weather-beaten Calamity Jane returned to Deadwood with a little girl in tow, announcing that she was married to Clinton Burke, a hack driver, and claiming the little girl was hers. The child was actually Burke's stepdaughter. Although Calamity claimed to have been married many times—and there were many men who claimed to have been her husband—there is no record or proof of her ever being legally married to anybody.

At last she got a job where she could show off, with Kohl and Middleton, an amusement company which traveled in eastern cities. She was billed as "The Famous Woman Scout of the Wild West and Heroine of a Thousand Thrilling Adventures." Although the aging tomboy could still shoot amazingly well, she was fired for excessive drinking and for her shocking language.

Back in Deadwood, Calamity lashed out at people who tried to reform her: "Why don't the sons of bitches leave me alone and let me go to hell my own route?"

Calamity Jane died of alcoholism in the little mining town of Terry, a few miles from Deadwood, on August 11, 1903, age about fifty-three years.

Newspapers reported another of the "largest funerals Deadwood has ever seen." A showperson to the last, she had made a dying request: "Bury me beside Wild Bill, the only man I ever loved." So she was.

And now the two graves, side by side in Mount Moriah cemetery, are

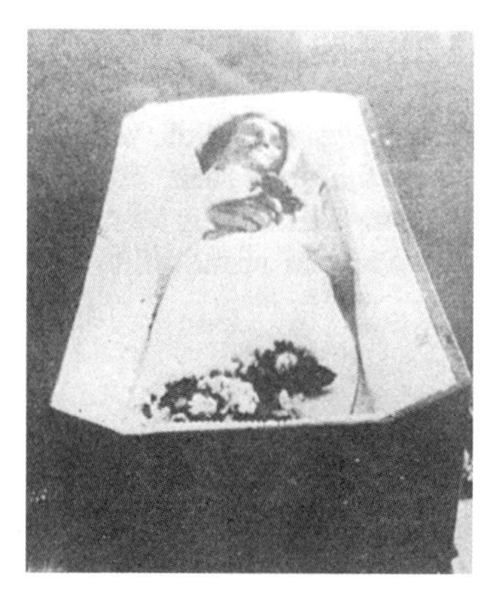

Deadwood's most popular tourist attraction. In death, she is closer to Wild Bill than she ever was in life. Many observers report that Wild Bill has been spinning in his grave ever since she caught up with him.

Calamity Jane in her coffin, 1903. Someone put a six-shooter in each hand so she'd look natural but the undertaker removed the guns. Several mourners (some still living in 1983) cut off locks of her hair until a bullwhacker friend built a wire cage over her head to protect the corpse. *Photo credit—Centennial Archives, Deadwood.*

How did Calamity Jane become so famous?

One reason is that everyone who knew this colorful woman inevitably had at least two stories to tell about her: one about the picturesque bad side and the other about her humanitarian side, her generosity and her nursing of suffering pioneers. These stories, often embellished with each telling, were handed down from generation to generation, especially in the Black Hills, which has always lovingly claimed her as its own.

Another reason for her notoriety is that in 1885, seventeen years before her death, author Edward Wheeler whose pseudonym was Ned Buntline, used her name for a fictional heroine of numerous dime novels with a western setting and featuring well-known western characters. **Calamity Jane, The Heroine of Whoop-Up**, was the title of one best seller.

Over and over again, Calamity Jane was mentioned in many diaries, sketches, and newspapers of the gold rush days and later. When the first authors began writing Black Hills history books, they always included a chapter on Calamity Jane. She was good copy.

In the twentieth century, the motion picture industry discovered Calamity Jane and glamorized her life while dramatizing that make-believe romance between Calamity and Wild Bill Hickok. Bearing no resemblance whatever to the original, actresses like Doris Day and Jane Russell portrayed plain Jane in fictional situations. But no matter—her fame grew.

Calamity Jane had always been a red-hot publicity hound. How she would have loved all the attention she has received from the media in the twentieth century. She would have enjoyed the publicity about being "Queen of the Wild West" and a "prostitute with a heart of gold."

How does one assess the contributions of this complex, masculine woman? Has she received more attention than she deserves? Why is she so unforgettable?

Her friend, Madam Dora DuFran, suggests the answer: "Calamity Jane was truly a Diamond in the Rough."

PREACHER SMITH—RELIGIOUS MARTYR

Preacher Smith, whose real name was Henry Weston Smith, was the first minister to come to the Black Hills during the gold rush. He was murdered during the violent summer of 1876 a few weeks after Wild Bill Hickok was shot in a saloon. Both men have achieved immortality but Preacher Smith is by far the more admirable of the two; he came to save men's souls with only his Bible for guidance and protection.

Preacher Smith, whose real name was Henry Weston Smith, was the first minister to come to the Black Hills during the gold rush. He was murdered during the violent summer of 1876 a few weeks after Wild Bill Hickok was shot in a saloon. *Photo credit—South Dakota State Historical Society.*

Preacher Smith heard about the gold rush in the Black Hills and decided that environment would provide many challenges for a servant of the Lord hoping to bring Christianity to the ungodly. He left his wife and three children in Kentucky, planning to send for them later to join him.

Smith walked beside a wagon train from Cheyenne, WY, to Custer City where he preached the first sermon in the Black Hills, a wild region which was said to have no Sunday, like the rest of the country west of the Missouri River, and no God west of the Cheyenne River.

Preacher Smith walked to Deadwood and began preaching on the streets and occasionally in the saloons to anyone who would listen—cutthroats, gamblers, prostitutes, speculators, and undoubtedly a few respect-

Preacher Smith, carrying his Bible, walked beside a wagon train from Cheyenne, WY, to Custer City where he preached the first sermon in the Black Hills. *Photo credit—South Dakota State Historical Society.*

able people. Rough, grizzled miners packing six-shooters paused on the muddy, crowded streets to listen to his sermon amid the shouts of the gamblers and prostitutes calling for business. Smith reminded his listeners that their ever-loving Father was present here in a strange, gold-mad country, and not to forget "the greater riches of God and of home ties."

On Sunday, August 21, 1876, Preacher Smith said he was going to walk ten miles to Crook City to preach a sermon in the streets there. Friends warned him not to go because of the danger of marauding Indians and urged him to carry a gun. Preacher Smith refused, insisting, "The Bible is my protection. It has never failed me yet."

Crook City, 1876 (town has disappeared). Preacher Smith with only his Bible for protection set out from Deadwood to preach a sermon in the streets of Crook City. His body was found on the trail, his hands clutching his Bible. His unsolved murder was blamed on Indians. *Photo credit—Centennial Archives, Deadwood.*

He left a note on his cabin door: "Gone to Crook City to preach, and if God is willing, will be back at three o'clock."

He never returned. His body was found on the trail, his hands clutching his Bible and the blood-stained notes for his sermon in his pocket. He had been shot through the heart but was not scalped or mutilated. His murder was blamed on the Indians, although many historians believe he was killed by lawless whites.

On the same day that Preacher Smith was killed, three other white men were found murdered, and a posse with needle guns went out after the Indians. A jubilant Texas Bill cut off the head of an Indian and paraded through the Deadwood saloons with his gruesome trophy.

According to folklore, Calamity Jane, who had frequently passed the hat to collect gold dust for Preacher Smith, helped to prepare his body for burial and made a memorable statement: "Ain't it a shame that the only man who came here to tell us how to live had to be killed by Indians." Then with tears streaming, she added, "And we sure needed the telling."

The gold camp shut down business for the burial in Deadwood's boot hill in Whitewood Gulch. Young Seth Bullock, who became Deadwood's first sheriff, drew the lot to say the prayer which he called "The toughest emergency of my life." Bullock later wrote a masterful letter to Smith's wife conveying "the sad intelligence" of his death.

Preacher Smith and Charles Mason, another murder victim of that terrible day, were buried in separate wooden coffins in one grave. Years later Bullock wrote that everybody sang "Nearer My God to Thee" whether they knew the words or not, "for it was the most serious business that ever happened in the Hills, a lot of wicked, illiterate miners burying a minister, a man of God. It was a scene worthy of the brush of a great artist."

Seven years later, a Methodist minister decided that Preacher Smith's body should be moved to Mount Moriah, the new cemetery, but he and the undertaker had to open eleven graves before they found the right one. Both Smith and his grave-mate, Mason, were re-interred with elaborate outdoor ceremonies. Four Methodist ministers took turns praying and reading from the Bible, and a choir sang "The Crown of Life Beyond This Vale of Tears."

In 1891, the body of Preacher Smith, which had been reburied eight years earlier near the boundary of the cemetery, was moved for the second time and reburied in the middle section of Mount Moriah.

Preacher Smith Statue, like all the statues in Mount Moriah cemetery, Deadwood, was destroyed by vandals. Preacher Smith's body was moved three times to its final resting place in the central part of Mount Moriah. *Photo credit—South Dakota State Historical Society.*

Then in November, 1891, the life-size statue of Preacher Smith, sculpted by Riordan and paid for by a subscription campaign, was dedicated in Mount Moriah. Said to be a perfect likeness, the statue was eventually destroyed by vandals. Included in the ceremonies was a reading of Preacher Smith's poem, "The Gold Hunter's Reverie" whose first two lines are:

> "I am sitting by the campfire now
> On wild Dakota's hills,
> And memories of long ago
> Steal o'er me like the rills."

Another monument to Preacher Smith, presented by the Society of Black Hills Pioneers, was dedicated in August, 1914, at the highest point on Highway 85, the Deadwood-Spearfish road not far from where Preacher Smith's body was found.

Preacher Smith is probably the most famous good guy buried in Mount Moriah cemetery in Deadwood where many prominent people rest. He did not live long enough to actually contribute much to the development of the area. Yet, he has been honored through the years for being the first minister in the Black Hills, and he has been memorialized as a religious martyr because of his tragic death. Mrs. Henry Weston Smith—Annie—many years after her husband was murdered, presumably by Indians, wrote a historical novel which condemned the whites and sympathized with the Indians for the racial strife depicted in her book.

SETH BULLOCK—FIRST SHERIFF

Seth Bullock was an accomplished jack of all trades; and contrary to the old saying, he was master of many. Known best as the first sheriff of Deadwood then of Lawrence County, he was also a United States marshal, first Black Hills Forest supervisor, president of Iron Hill Mining Company, Captain of Grigsby's Cowboys (known as the Black Hills Rough Riders), merchant, politician, rancher, and historian. He was instrumental in founding many villages including the cattle town of Belle Fourche, just north of the Black Hills. A pioneer of 1876, the magic year to be a pioneer at the height of the gold rush, he became one of the most influential leaders ever to seek his fortune in the new El Dorado.

Seth Bullock was a veteran of the Montana gold rush where he was elected to the Montana Territorial Senate when he was only 21 years old and elected sheriff of Lewis and Clark County when he was 24. In the legislature he was credited with introducing the resolution which resulted in the establishment of Yellowstone Park, the first national park.

Seth Bullock, first sheriff of Deadwood, was also U.S. marshal, first Black Hills Forest Supervisor, president of Iron Hill Mining Company, Captain of Grigsby's Cowboys, merchant, politician, rancher and historian. A Black Hills Pioneer of 1876, Bullock became an influential leader in the Hills. *Photo credit—South Dakota State Historical Society.*

Bullock and Sol Star, the man who was to be his life-long partner, arrived in Deadwood with the second Montana party which came by boat down the Missouri River to Bismarck, in northern Dakota; then they loaded their supplies and merchandise on an ox-drawn wagon and set off across the prairie wilderness. Bullock had first sent his wife Martha and baby on a Missouri riverboat, then by train, back to Michigan for safe keeping while he hit the gold trail to the Black Hills.

The two adventurous young men arrived in Deadwood on the first day of that memorable August of 1876; Wild Bill Hickok was shot the next day, and Preacher Smith was murdered a few weeks later. Bullock and Star set up shop on Deadwood's crowded main street and began auctioning off picks and shovels, other mining equipment, and Bullock gave an eloquent speech lauding the advantages of chamber pots. Instead of embarking on the search for placer gold along with the frenzied gold-seekers, they set to work constructing a fireproof log building for their hardware store and warehouse. The firm of Star and Bullock, with its 350-foot-high sign, became one of the most prosperous in the Black Hills, and the proprietors became two of the most successful and respected pioneers. Sol Star was appointed postmaster in 1879 and was elected mayor of Deadwood for twelve terms.

The two experienced graduates of the Montana gold rush soon recognized that Deadwood sorely needed law and order if any permanent settlement was to be established in the illegal gold camp where tents and shacks were mushrooming up and down the twisting gulch, overrun by a lawless mob. When several people came down with the dreaded small pox, Bullock and Star joined with other responsible citizens to organize a Board of Health which established a pest house for the quarantine of victims, and the Board sent for small pox vaccine via the pony express—and thus averted an epidemic.

The Board of Health took on many responsibilities in trying to keep the boisterous Sin City under control; they adopted ordinances to bring order out of chaos; they established a police force, a fire department, and the first cemetery; they drew up some ground rules about the layout of streets, settled gunfights and the endless disputes over claim jumping.

Seth Bullock with his background as sheriff in Montana was a natural choice for unofficial lawman. But it was not until the spring of 1877 when Congress opened the Black Hills to white settlement that he was officially appointed sheriff of Lawrence County by Gov. John Pennington.

When the first election for county positions was held in November, 1877, Bullock, a Republican, was defeated for sheriff in a wild election in which accusations flew—of stuffing ballot boxes and of people voting more than once. Some say there were too many Democrats for a Republican to win; others say that the majority of gold-seekers did not want such an efficient sheriff as Bullock. Bullock was not a gracious loser and at first refused to vacate his office to the winner, John Manning, a Democrat.

A prospector guarding his placer claim in Deadwood Gulch, 1876, where gold-seekers lived in tents and brush shelters. When Seth Bullock took over as unofficial sheriff, many arguments and gunfights were over claim-jumping. *Photo credit—W. H. Over Museum, Vermillion, SD.*

But Bullock was still a deputy United States marshal and continued riding horseback all over the rugged Black Hills tracking down stagecoach robbers and criminals with great success. Abandoned mining tunnels and dirt basements were used for a jail, but he had the reputation of treating the miserable prisoners with kindess and fairness.

Although Bullock was an expert marksman, the story goes that he never killed a man. He had a commanding personality which demanded respect, and his piercing gray eyes, according to observers, "could have outstared a mad cobra or a rogue elephant" and of course an accused criminal. Historians generally credit him with bringing the first semblance of law and order to Deadwood, the Sin City of the gold diggings in the northern Hills.

An oft-repeated story demonstrating Bullock's ingenuity is how he broke up a sit-down strike when about thirty miners holed up at the Keets mine in Hidden Treasure Gulch. Seth went shopping in Deadwood's Chinatown and then craftily dropped burning sulphur down the air shaft. Soon the striking miners came out in a state of sputtering surrender.

Estelline Bennett, author of **Old Deadwood Days** and daughter of Judge Granville Bennett, wrote in her book: "Father chuckled delightedly over that bloodless victory all the rest of his life. It verified and strengthened his high regard for Seth Bullock, who set a standard then to which all other sheriffs, as far as Father was concerned, had to measure."

When Bullock was a deputy United States marshal, he was riding the range on his Belle Fourche ranch when he ran into some suspicious-looking characters. The leader of the disheveled group turned out to be Theodore Roosevelt, a deputy marshal from the Badlands of northern Dakota. He had captured a horse thief named Crazy Steve whom Bullock was also trailing.

Years later in his **Autobiography,** Roosevelt summed up the confrontation by writing that "Bullock then inquired after the capture of Crazy Steve with a little of the air of one sportsman when another has shot a quail that either might have claimed." The two deputy marshals liked one another immediately and became life-long friends. Author Estelline Bennett commented: "Bullock's friendships could run the gamut from Roosevelt to Calamity Jane and back again without stumbling. That was the West and Seth Bullock."

Roosevelt, in his first year of office, appointed Seth Bullock a United States Marshal, a post Bullock held under three Presidents. One time when Roosevelt was campaigning in Montana, a well-armed Bullock acted as his bodyguard; TR described him as "a splendid-looking fellow with his size and supple strength, his strongly marked aquiline face with its big mustache, and the broad brim of his soft hat drawn down over his hawk eyes."

Through the years and during Roosevelt's presidency, TR often came to the Black Hills on hunting trips with Seth Bullock in Spearfish Canyon and the surrounding plains. The boisterous Roosevelt boys loved visiting the Bullock ranch, where they learned how to hunt and ride broncos and become rugged outdoorsmen under expert tutelage.

Through TR's influence, President McKinley appointed Seth Bullock the first forest supervisor of the Black Hills where he emphasized conservation of natural resources. Bullock built towns and hotels and mining shafts. He was Captain of Grigsby's Cowboys during the Spanish-American War which never saw action.

In 1905 when Roosevelt was inaugurated President of the United States, Bullock brought to Washington a group of about fifty cowboys who galloped their broncos up Pennsylvania Avenue during the inaugural parade, lassooing spectators, much to the delight of TR, the cowboy president.

When Theodore Roosevelt died in 1919, Bullock, who was suffering from cancer, was the moving force in the Society of Black Hills Pioneers which built a tower monument to Roosevelt on a mountain about five miles from Deadwood, now called Mount Roosevelt. It was the first monument in the United States to honor him. A few months later, in September, 1919, Seth Bullock died of cancer, joining TR in the "Great Adventure."

Bullock is buried on the high trail to White Rocks, above Mount

Moriah cemetery in Deadwood, across the broad, forested gulch from the Roosevelt Memorial. Theodore Roosevelt had hailed the first sheriff of Deadwood as "my typical ideal American." And Seth Bullock requested a one-word epitaph engraved on his own tombstone: "Pioneer." Both men had it right.

Tower on Mount Roosevelt near Deadwood, the first monument in the U.S. dedicated to Theodore Roosevelt, 1919. Largely through Bullock's efforts, the Society of Black Hills Pioneers erected the memorial. TR and Seth Bullock were close personal friends. *Photo credit—Centennial Archives, Deadwood.*

KITTY LeROY—BEAUTEOUS MURDER VICTIM

Kitty LeRoy, a jig dancer from Texas, reigned as queen of the Badlands of Deadwood, the red light district of the wild gold camp. A notorious "lady of the night" or "soiled dove," she wore diamond earrings which sparkled like her glorious eyes and always kept a dagger tucked into her long curly hair. She dressed in a gypsy costume with plenty of room to

No dresses visible in this picture of rip-roaring Deadwood, 1876, although a wagon-load of madams and "soiled doves" arrived in June, 1876. Until she was murdered, beauteous dancer Kitty LeRoy reigned as queen of the Badlands, as the red light district was called. *Photo credit —W. H. Over Museum, Vermillion, SD.*

conceal bowie knives and pistols to protect her from the love-starved miners. Men were said to have killed each other over her magnetic beauty. Reputed to be a murderess herself, she was also a professional gambler who conned many drunken miners out of their gold dust.

Some say she had five husbands, several at the same time. Legend has it that she married her first husband because he was her only lover reckless enough to let her shoot an apple off his head while she galloped by at full speed, a lady William Tell, Wild West style.

The setting for her fifth wedding was the Gem Theater, the most infamous of all Deadwood's combination brothels, gambling dens, saloons, and dance halls. The lucky man was Sam Curley, a faro dealer, who foolishly believed that Kitty would be a faithful wife while he was out of town.

Sam came home unexpectedly and found Kitty in their room at the Lone Star Saloon where she was conducting business as usual. The frightened customer escaped Sam's wrath, but Sam shot Kitty in her pretty breast, then turned the gun on himself. "A thrill of horror ran through the community," reported a Deadwood newspaper in December, 1877, who described in gory detail the murder-suicide in the blood-spattered room. There was a rumor that Kitty also had a husband and child in California.

The two ill-starred lovers were buried in separate pine boxes in a single grave in Deadwood's first boot hill, then later their bodies were moved up to Mount Moriah, Deadwood's permanent mountain-top cemetery where their final resting place is unknown.

A month later, the newspaper reporters claimed to have seen two spirits which markedly resembled Kitty LeRoy and Sam Curley hovering about the upper recesses of the Lone Star Saloon. But no one knew why their spirits had returned. Perhaps they were searching for a lost love.

Kitty LeRoy married Sam Curley, her fifth husband, in the Gem Theater, the most infamous of all Deadwood's combination brothels, gambling dens, saloons, and dance halls. The "ladies of the night" entertained men privately in small curtained rooms on the left. *Photo credit—Centennial Archives, Deadwood.*

DOC PEIRCE—POPULAR HUMORIST

Ellis T. Peirce, a versatile raconteur of the Black Hills, was called "Doc" by his many friends and admirers. Doc Peirce is probably best known for having laid out the body of Wild Bill Hickok after the poker-playing Kansas marshal was murdered in Deadwood in August, 1876. Doc Peirce wasn't a doctor or a mortician; he was an entertaining barber with some medical background and was thus the logical choice for the serious job of undertaking.

After Wild Bill's funeral, Doc Peirce settled down in front of his cabin to hold court, got out his guitar and began strumming and talking to the gathering crowd: "Yes, Siree," began Doc, reflecting on the recently departed celebrity. "When Bill was shot through the head, he bled out quickly, and when he was laid out he looked like a wax figure. I have seen many dead men on the field of battle and in civil life, but Wild Bill was the prettiest corpse I have ever seen. His long mustache was attractive, even in death, and—."

E. T. "Doc" Peirce, known as a "prince of good fellows," was the most entertaining and talkative barber in the Black Hills. As undertaker for Wild Bill Hickok, Doc was disappointed that he couldn't make Wild Bill laugh while preparing the holy body for burial. *Photo credit—From New York Public Library, Fielder Collection, Deveraux Library, South Dakota School of Mines and Technology.*

When Doc Peirce told a story, people listened.

Born a Pennsylvania Quaker, he served meritoriously for the Union in the Civil War. He joined the Black Hills Gold Rush and arrived in Custer City in February, 1876, as captain of a wagon train. During his fifty years in the Black Hills he led an exciting life while playing many roles. He was not only a barber and an undertaker; at various times, he was also a scout, a miner, a sheriff, a hotel proprietor, a state legislator, and a frontier doctor without a license. And no matter which role he was playing or which Black Hills town he called home, he was always a humorous storyteller, both orally and in writing.

Annie Tallent, the author of an early Black Hills history, said she was willing to wager a quarter "that Doc Peirce has spun more yarns than any other man who ever emigrated to the Black Hills."

Although one contemporary put him down as simply the "town clown, a bombast, and windjammer deluxe," Mrs. Tallent disagreed. She characterized the stocky man with the walrus moustache and steely eyes as a "prince of good fellows" and a staunch friend of the pioneers with an ability to see the silver lining in every situation, no matter how dismal.

In Custer City, Peirce's first home in the Hills, he built a log cabin along French Creek and began prospecting. He also scouted for wagon trains and helped chase the Canyon Springs robbers to the Missouri River where they disappeared. He turned all of his adventures into amusing conversation.

A humanitarian as well as a jokesmith, Doc Peirce established a free hospital in his cabin where he doctored and nursed the ailing miners, doubtless improving their spirits with his inexhaustible humor and optimism. At one time the Doc cared for fourteen sick miners in his cabin free of charge.

In June, 1876, when the big strikes up in Deadwood Gulch brought on a fresh epidemic of gold fever, Doc, along with most of Custer City, lit out for the new diggings. In the roistering gold camp, Doc built himself a small shack, spread a wagon canvas over the top, and opened a barber shop on Deadwood's crowded main street. His barber chair was a beer keg with a lean-back railing attached.

Even though Doc Peirce mixed a little axle grease with perfume for moustache wax and dispensed after-shave tonic that was a mixture of bad whiskey and bay rum, everyone liked his barbering and relished his colorful conversation.

He would begin, "You want to know how I escaped getting scalped in Red Canyon south of Custer where the Indians attacked every wagon and stagecoach?" Then the entertainer would build up suspense by stropping his razor and cutting off a hunk of grizzled hair before he delivered the punch line: "First I said every prayer I could remember and hoped Somebody Up There was listening. Then just to be sure, I nailed my scalp down to my block head before our outfit pushed into bloody Red Canyon. And that's why I'm here today." Bending over, he would show the top of his head to the customer, "You can still see the nails."

Doc was such a confirmed ham who loved to perform straight-faced for appreciative audiences, that the story goes how disappointed he was when he couldn't make Wild Bill Hickok laugh while he was preparing the holy body for burial.

After spending the tumultous summer of 1876 barbering in rip-roaring Deadwood, Doc Peirce went back to Custer to settle down. He opened up another barbershop and continued placer mining. That same year his reputation for being a fearless leader in the constant battle for law and order in the Black Hills earned him the appointment of deputy sheriff for Custer County. Another honor that he always cherished was that his good friend, an Oglala chief, christened him with the Indian name Mata Oye meaning "Bear Tracks"—for an unknown reason.

In 1878, Peirce moved to Rapid City where he managed the International Hotel for eight years. He was also elected sheriff of Pennington County for two years.

His best Rapid City story is his explanation of how a gold stampede got started in 1889 because the lawyers were bored and craved excitement. Peirce described the nefarious work of the scheming lawyers salting a gypsum bed with gold dust to hoodwink the gullible. Later, one of the barristers secretly dropped a large gold nugget into the creek which tricked his fellow conspirators into thinking they really had struck it rich. The promoters of the stampede went wild with excitement over the appearance of the big nugget. "Thus the salter was salted," concluded Doc.

Doc moved to Hot Springs for his health because the warm mineral springs improved his rheumatism. He set up a barbershop across from the fancy Evans Hotel. In 1902, he was elected a state representative from Fall River County and he did all he could to liven up the stodgy legislature with his wisdom and humor.

Doc Peirce is credited with being the original narrator of the well-known story about a free-lance freighter named Phatty Thompson who brought a wagonload of cats to Deadwood Gulch in 1876. Although the

The International Hotel in Rapid City, corner of Main and 6th, about 1900, with the popular horse-drawn trolley. Doc Peirce managed this hotel from 1878-1886 where he entertained customers with tales of how he escaped being scalped in Red Canyon. *Photo credit—Minnelusa Historical Museum, Rapid City.*

wagon overturned and Phatty had trouble rounding up all the howling felines by "using strange and fearful language," he finally reached the red light district of lower Deadwood. Here he quickly sold the two-bit cats for prices ranging from $10 to $25 to the delighted prostitutes whose bulging bags of gold dust were larger than their bosoms.

Doc didn't say so but is this why the brothels in Deadwood were also called "cat houses"?

Doc was as good a writer as he was a speaker; and in his later years, he wrote a column for the **Hot Springs Star** and also some sketches about the "Odd Characters and Incidents of the Black Hills." Doc wrote that some vigilantes hanged a known horse thief because they found a tree they couldn't resist.

For his birthdays, Doc always held huge celebrations in his home with the host performing on center stage for a captive audience and the guests were instructed to "wear anything but pajamas." Delicious victuals were always served by Doc's wife and daughter, who were undoubtedly quiet females, probably never having had a chance to talk.

Doc Peirce celebrated many birthdays and died in 1926 at age eighty, a beloved and respected Black Hills Pioneer of 1876—the magic year at the height of the gold rush.

A tribute to Doc Peirce should include a story with a moral:

A loud-mouthed stranger was sitting in a Hot Springs hotel lobby bragging about his early experiences in the Black Hills and the heroic part he had played in dangerous situations. Doc Peirce interrupted the long-winded tale to ask the offender what year he had come to the Black Hills.

"In '81," confessed the bore.

"You poor tenderfoot," said Doc Peirce.

Then everybody relaxed, knowing it was time to settle back, light up cigars, and enjoy another happy evening listening to Doc tell funny hair-raisers about how he was tricked into being locked up in the Rapid City jail until big Fred Evans bailed him out, or the shenanigans at the Hinch Murder Trial in Gayville in 1876, or the lugubrious demise of Fly-Speck Billy or—."

There was no way you could upstage Doc Peirce.

LAME JOHNNY—TALENTED HORSE THIEF

Lame Johnny, the most accomplished horse thief of the Black Hills, started out as a good guy, turned into a bad guy, and died ignominiously under mysterious circumstances. On the frontier, stealing horses from whites was considered a crime almost as serious as murder. A man's horse was often his only means of transportation, and woe to the thief who would deprive an early settler of his mount. Of course, pioneers didn't like stagecoach robbers either, and some historians insist that Johnny was also a daring "knight of the road."

Mock hold-up of Deadwood Stage in 1925. Lame Johnny was suspected of having held up the Sidney, NE -Deadwood Stage in 1879 or 1882. Various accounts about the hold-up and the hanging are contradictory and confusing. *Photo credit —South Dakota State Historical Society.*

Confusion and contradictions dominate the historical accounts of Lame Johnny's life and death. That old standby, **The Black Hills Trails,** by Brown and Willard, written when they were both old men, is the chief primary source for information about Lame Johnny, puzzling as it is. Jesse Brown, co-author of this popular history, was a young deputy guarding Johnny on his last stagecoach ride, and he admitted he really didn't know what happened when Lame Johnny was whisked off to eternity.

Another primary source is a collection of colorful sketches, "Odd Characters and Incidents of the Black Hills," written by Ellis T. (Doc) Peirce, the champion spell-binder of the Black Hills and a deputy sheriff of Custer County who interviewed Lame Johnny.

Much later, in 1949, Robert Casey, a well-known Rapid City writer, published **The Black Hills and Their Incredible Characters,** in which this perceptive author tried to make sense out of the so-called "facts" of Lame Johnny's career.

However, these three sources do agree that Lame Johnny was born Cornelius Donahue in Philadelphia; that when he was a boy, he was thrown from a horse and sustained a bad leg injury. Thus he acquired a limp and the name "Lame Johnny." After graduating from Girard College in Philadelphia, he went ranching in Texas.

There the agreement ends, and the historic trails, dimming and twisting through the years, obscure the true story of Lame Johnny and his exploits with horses and stagecoaches. The only thing that can be said for sure is that it all happened over a century ago.

Doc Peirce, always the humorist, wrote that Johnny was a splendid judge of a horse—no matter who owned it and that he was not addicted to the smaller vices. "There was something mysterious in that young man's make-up that excited my curiosity," wrote Doc.

In an interview, Lame Johnny told Doc Peirce that when he was ranching in Texas, the Comanches ran off with 700 head of his cattle. To retaliate, Johnny persuaded a group of Tongaway Indians to help him steal sixty head of horses from the Comanches. Revenge was sweet.

Lame Johnny confided to Peirce, "That trip gave me a taste for adventure, and I have been working ever since to get even for the loss of my cattle." Perhaps this experience was his motivation for becoming a professional horse thief.

Few whites saw anything wrong in stealing horses from the Indians, but stealing horses from whites was a serious crime, often punished by an impromptu lynching mob or "necktie party" throughout the border country from Dakota Territory to Texas.

Johnny, now using the alias of John Hurley, left Texas and headed north, presumably on horseback. Attracted by the glitter of the Black Hills Gold Rush, Johnny settled on Castle Creek in the Black Hills in 1876 and began prospecting for gold.

Johnny told Doc Peirce that Indians stole his horse when he was prospecting on Castle Creek. Angry at the Indians again, he had to borrow a horse and then rode alone down to the Red Cloud Agency where he sneaked up on a herd of about 300 horses, shot the Indian guard, and stampeded the herd. Single-handedly, he ran off the herd toward the Black Hills. When his mount became tired, he would rope another horse from the stampeding herd, jump on, and continue racing toward the Hills with 300 horses. He cached these horses in a "Robber's Roost" on upper French Creek. Johnny concluded his tale by saying "all summer long it was nip and tuck between myself and the Indians."

The story goes, according to Brown and Willard, that Johnny, now known as John Hurley, became a deputy sheriff of Custer County in 1878, and "proved to be a very efficient officer of the law." One wonders if he was especially adept at catching horse thieves. Doc Peirce, himself a deputy sheriff of Custer County, does not mention Johnny's brief tenure as a respectable law officer nor is there any official record of it.

According to Doc Peirce's account, Johnny enjoyed telling his interviewer all about his prowess in stealing horses from the Indian reservations, but there is no admission of his stealing horses from whites. Johnny said that he used an alias to protect his respectable relatives back east in Philadelphia.

When Johnny tired of "the stock business"—as horse stealing was called—he got an office job working as a bookkeeper for the Homestake Mining Company in Lead.

One day a Texan came into the office, recognized John Hurley as

"Lame Johnny" and announced to everyone that the quiet bookkeeper was a horse thief. Johnny quit his job at Homestake and disappeared for a time.

Not long after, rumors circulated that Lame Johnny had branched out: he was stealing horses from whites, an unforgivable crime. Then Ed Cook, the superintendent of the Gilmer and Salisbury stagecoach line, identified Johnny as being one of the road agents who held up the stage a few miles north of Buffalo Gap. Although Johnny was becoming known as a notorious outlaw, he never did confess to Doc Peirce that he was a road agent.

But he did entertain Doc Peirce with an account of one of his best-known escapades with cohorts Jim Brocky and Tony Pastor. They made a surreptitious visit to the Cheyenne agency, stampeded about 68 head of horses, with the enraged Indians in pursuit. The Indians wounded Brocky. A blizzard came up. The horse thieves were soon lost, freezing, and hungry trying to keep track of their horses in the swirling snow. Brocky, who was seriously wounded, begged to be shot but Johnny refused. Instead, he tied Brocky on a horse and gave him a threshing with his quirt hoping that he would make Brocky angry enough to survive. The wounded man still begged to die. So Johnny stopped, tied the best saddle horse to the sage brush, and laid Brocky down in the snow, hoping Brocky would gather enough strength to follow.

By the time Johnny and Tony Pastor made it through the snowy ravines to the mouth of Battle Creek on the Cheyenne River, they were about ready to expire. Brocky never did catch up with them. And only thirteen head of Indian horses were left to sell.

Not long after this episode, Tony Pastor was hanged on the Denver Road—but not for stealing horses from Indians. In 1881, a cowboy brought in a skull he had found on the exact spot where Johnny had said he had left Brocky with a good horse. Doc Peirce concluded: "There was nothing left to do but write 'Brocky' across that empty forehead and place it upon the mantel piece for ornamental purposes."

Another well-known personage involved in the Lame Johnny saga was Dr. Valentine T. McGillycuddy, the agent at Pine Ridge, formerly called the Red Cloud Agency. McGillycuddy claimed to be the person who ordered the arrest of Lame Johnny for stealing the horses of his Indian wards.

According to the McGillycuddy version of what happened, a Captain Crawford, on the agent's order, arrested Lame Johnny at Pine Ridge Indian reservation. The Captain and others handcuffed and shackled the prisoner, then pushed him into a stagecoach going up to Deadwood where he would be tried first for the federal offense of robbing the mails. Whispering Smith was the name of the deputy marshal accompanying Lame Johnny on his last ride.

Jesse Brown, who many years later became the co-author of **The Black**

Hills Trails, wrote a first-person account of Johnny's last stagecoach ride. Brown, a respected deputy, was an experienced guard of treasure coaches and of prisoners, but maybe he was an inexperienced writer. He related a strange story with little explanation of key points: "So Lame Johnny was placed inside the coach in my care," wrote Jesse Brown, "and the marshal (Whispering Smith) rode beside the driver." Apparently, Brown was riding on horseback on the side of the coach nearest the prisoner.

Brown explained, "Everything went along all right up to Buffalo Gap, when looking out toward the foothills toward the west, we could see a horseman riding parallel with us at a swift gallop. Johnny became restless and nervous, saying that he did not like the appearance of the stranger."

According to Brown, Johnny thought he recognized Boone May, and it did turn out to be Boone May, one of the guards. Why didn't Brown know that it was Boone May from the start? And why does he devote so much space to writing about Johnny's concern over the identity of the rider? Was Brown trying to hint that Boone May was responsible for what happened later?

No wonder Johnny was apprehensive. Boone May was a notorious trigger-happy law officer who sometimes rode shotgun or messenger, or was an outrider for stagecoaches carrying gold bullion or prisoners. He had the reputation of shooting prisoners for the fun of it, and had in fact been tried in court for this compulsion. May was acquitted because his stock defense was that the prisoner had tried to escape; therefore he was forced to shoot.

Boone May had once dug up the body of a bandit, wanted dead or alive. May cut off his head and put the trophy in a gunny sack, transporting it to the authorities in Cheyenne, WY, to claim the reward. But May was unable to collect because there wasn't enough evidence proving he had been the executioner for this outlaw.

So this was the Boone May who was galloping some distance apart from the stage and ahead of it, presumably to guard Lame Johnny, the prisoner, who had some rights even in the Black Hills.

For over fifty years, Brown insisted that he was unaware of impending trouble until he was near the little creek about four miles north of Buffalo Gap and heard the ominous command, "Halt!" given to the stage. Brown, who was then some distance from the scene of action, dismounted quickly and hid in the sage brush and tall grass until he could figure out what was going on.

Then Brown says he heard a voice telling him to go back. Just at that moment Brown "heard my wife and girls running back on the road, thinking that I was still behind." After quieting his hysterical family, Brown heard some shooting "on the creek where the coach stood."

Brown doesn't explain what the women were hysterical about, nor had he previously mentioned that his family was riding with the prisoner. Along came Whispering Smith, the marshal who had been sitting beside the driver on the stage. He asked to borrow Brown's horse "because he wanted to reconnoiter a little."

Then Brown with his frightened family got back on the stage. "But there was no prisoner there and I do not know up to this time just what happened," wrote Brown, the man whose duty it was to guard the prisoner, and who wrote what was supposed to be an accurate eye-witness account of Lame Johnny's death.

To add to the confusion, Brown tells the reader: "For it was very evident to me that whoever it was that had ordered me not to come any farther, knew that I was riding behind the coach and was watching for me. Or it might have been that they (the mob) expected me to protect Johnny, which would have been my duty."

Brown wrote that he never saw the marshal again who left Brown's borrowed horse at the stage station. Brown wondered how anyone knew Lame Johnny was on the stage unless Marshal Smith had told somebody before leaving Pine Ridge. He does not explain what Boone May, the other guard, was doing when the coach was stopped by a phantom mob. Or was Boone May the leader of the mob?

Brown concludes his puzzling and incoherent account with this offhand rambling statement: "Johnny was hanged to a limb of an elm tree, just where he had robbed the coach, and one of his gang, Lame Bradley, shot at Ed Cook, the bullet penetrating his left ear." Finis. The End.

Brown does not say that he actually saw a mob of vigilantes hang Johnny, or that he and his family saw Lame Johnny swinging from the elm tree when they boarded the stage; nor does he explain why he did not find out what the commotion was when he heard "shooting on the creek where the coach stood." And it was broad daylight and he was a guard.

Brown, renowned as a fearless deputy, relates a jumbled account, damaging to himself, of the Lame Johnny episode. Was Brown or May or Whispering Smith—or were all three—involved in a conspiracy to guarantee that Lame Johnny was hanged?

Author Robert Casey was the first imaginative historian to suggest that the only person to stop the stage carrying Lame Johnny was one Boone May—not a gang of vigilantes.

Brown's account of Lame Johnny's last ride added to the many other conflicting accounts of Lame Johnny's hanging illustrate the old maxim: "History is only a confused heap of facts." The major problem is to determine what the "facts" were.

Johnny was reputed to be personable, refined, and talented in music—not a common outlaw type. Doc Peirce liked him. Many of his contemporaries, including George Boland who ran a stage station at Buffalo Gap, were very fond of Johnny and insisted that he was a respectable horse thief, stealing only from Indians; that he did not rob stagecoaches; and that he should not have been hanged.

The First National Bank and citizens of Buffalo Gap, a stage stop on the Sidney-Deadwood stage route, 1892. George Boland, manager of the stage stop, did not believe Lame Johnny was a road agent, only an accomplished horse thief who stole only from Indians. *Photo credit—South Dakota State Historical Society.*

In any case, Lame Johnny, age 24, was hanged until dead. The story goes that a bullwhacker with poetic talent came along, cut down the body, buried it, and composed an epitaph he then posted on a wooden headboard over the grave. Loquacious Johnny was known for having a big mouth.

This is the first version of the epitaph:

"To Lame Johnny
Stranger, pass gently o'er this sod,
If he opens his mouth, you're gone, by God."

Second version of the epitaph:

"Pilgrim Pause!
You're standing on
The moldering clay of Limping John.
Tread lightly, stranger, on this sod.
For if he moves, you're robbed, by God."

Ten years after the hanging two local men dug up the grave. Doc Peirce reported that they found the high-heeled boot that Johnny wore on his short leg and the shackles with which his legs were bound. His remains were intact except for his head. That was missing.

Doc Peirce theorized that the head may have been taken by cowboys and shipped east as a curiosity. The shackles are now displayed in museums in Custer and Fort Pierre.

The head might have made a fine souvenir for Boone May, too, even if there was no bounty on it.

Horse Thief Lake, near Mount Rushmore, is named for Lame Johnny. He was rumored to have buried gold and gold watches he acquired from stagecoach holdups in the natural bowl or valley where he kept his stolen horses. Since then, a dam has created Horse Thief Lake. Now the legendary treasure is unrecovered "fairy gold" underneath the water.

Ever since that June day in 1879—or was it 1882—when Johnny was hanged near a little creek not long after he was supposed to have robbed the Sidney-Deadwood stage on that very spot, the creek has been known as Lame Johnny Creek. Today, it meanders out of Custer State Park, and as it always has, flows eastward to join the Cheyenne River.

Doc Peirce was right when he wrote that there was something mysterious about Lame Johnny, christened Cornelius Donahue, and alias John Hurley.

Dry Lame Johnny Creek, four miles north of Buffalo Gap, where Lame Johnny, a talented horse thief, was hanged by vigilantes for allegedly robbing the stagecoach. His body was buried here. Ten years later two curious locals dug up the body and discovered the head was missing. *Photo credit—Fielder Collection, Devereaux Library, South Dakota School of Mines and Technology.*

LANGRISHE THEATER COMPANY IN DEADWOOD

In the early days of Deadwood Gulch, the lust for entertainment rivaled the lust for gold. The motley crowd of fortune-hunters yearned for all kinds of amusement after a hard day in the diggings of the rough gold camp. In July, 1876, the populace was delighted when a theater troupe rolled in from Cheyenne, WY, with a wagonload of stage properties and actors.

The director-manager-leading actor was Jack Langrishe, the idol of western mining camps in Denver, San Francisco, Cheyenne, and Helena. His wife Jeanette, an accomplished actress herself, accompanied him as she had all his barnstorming tours throughout the frontier.

In the classic tradition of the theater, Langrishe arrived broke, but he went right to work setting up a make-shift theater on Deadwood's lively main street. He soon had a crude stage constructed which was lighted with kerosene lamps, surrounded by a high fence, and topped with a canvas roof. Eager volunteers nailed together odds and ends of pine logs for hard benches for the audience.

The first performance opened to a packed house in the improvised theater with a canvas roof that didn't stretch quite far enough. Despite rain pouring down during the performance, the cast and audience didn't let that dampen their enthusiasm for "Lillian's Lost Love" or "The Banker's Daughter."

During the time Langrishe was having a sturdier theater being built with a shingled roof, he leased the notorious Bella Union theater for his nightly performances. In August, the trial for Jack McCall who had murdered Wild Bill Hickok was held here, the trial almost as farcical as a Langrishe comedy. The Episcopalians also used the Bella Union for church services; in Deadwood, as in most mining camps, theaters were multi-purpose community centers used for sin, prayers, and theatrical productions.

Jack Langrishe, the idol of western mining camps, was the director-manager-leading actor of the Langrishe Theater Company. This legitimate theater group presented an extensive repertoire including: "Dutch Lovers," "The Banker's Daughter," "Ten Nights in a Bar Room," "The Mikado," "Uncle Tom's Cabin." *Photo credit—Denver Public Library, Western History Department.*

The Langrishe Company made a big hit in Deadwood, the entertainment capital of the Black Hills. The titles of the plays presented indicate the extensive repertory: "The Divorce," "Flies in the Web," "Dutch Lovers," "Jane Eyre," "Lucretia Borgia," "Ten Nights in a Bar Room," "Uncle Tom's Cabin," "Rip Van Winkle," and even "Othello."

These were plays of the legitimate theater—comedy, melodrama, tragedy. A man could take the whole family; there was no saloon, gambling den, dance hall, or brothel attached to the Langrishe theater offerings, unlike the Gem with its vulgar burlesques and vaudeville. No wonder the Langrishe theater style was called "legitimate."

Langrishe made colorful posters which he plastered over the boulders and cliffs in the gulch to advertise the performances. Charges were $1.50 for tickets in the first ten rows, and one dollar for a seat on the rest of the benches.

An Irishman by birth, he was said to have built more theaters on the frontier than any other man who ever lived. Although Jack and his wife Jeanette were middle-aged and not handsome, they were talented professional actors. **The Black Hills Pioneer,** the first newspaper in the Black Hills wrote: "Mr. and Mrs. Langrishe have been greeted with immense applause, and prove conclusively their title to the great praise awarded them in every city where they have performed."

Historian Annie Tallent wrote with perceptive enthusiasm: "As an all-round actor Langrishe was considered exceedingly clever, but in the area of old-style comedy, he was par excellence, and also a perfect master of the art of facial expression." Nor did she neglect Mrs. Langrishe: "an actress of no mean ability, and whether she impersonated an Irish servant girl fresh from the Emerald Isle, a dude, or a red-headed cowboy, she looked and acted her part to perfection."

When the troupe presented comedies, especially when Jack pantomimed, the audience laughed so hard at his antics that some fell off the benches into the sawdust.

However, the serious drama of "East Lynne" stimulated a different reaction: Calamity Jane was so displeased about the heroine's deserting her husband and child for her lover that the lady bullwhacker stomped up to the footlights and spat tobacco juice all over the leading lady's pink satin gown.

During his three years in Deadwood, Langrishe built a second theater which had boxes where fashionably-dressed society ladies showed off by using opera glasses, an affectation totally unnecessary for the small theater. One night an old bearded prospector came in lugging a two-foot-long board with two holes in the end where he stuck beer bottles. When Langrishe came on stage, the prospector made a commotion peering through his large homemade opera glasses. That was said to be the only time Langrishe forgot his lines. The actors broke up laughing and the side-show brought down the house. Even the society ladies in boxes laughed until they cried.

The Langrishes were extremely popular personages, well-liked by both the ordinary miners and the growing class of educated people who were settling in Deadwood. Many hailed the Langrishe theater as the first cultural influence in the Black Hills.

Langrishe, who had been a newspaper reporter on the **New York Herald Tribune** before he took up acting, occasionally wrote entertaining features for the **Black Hills Pioneer.**

Office of the **Black Hills Pioneer,** Deadwood, the first newspaper established in the Black Hills. Jack Langrishe frequently wrote entertaining features for its pages, including odes to the "beautiful stove. . . . She'll soon knock h--- out of the beautiful snow." *Photo credit—Centennial Archives, Deadwood.*

One cold wintry day when Langrishe came shivering into the Pioneer office, which was housed in a drafty log cabin, he composed an ode on the spot:

> Oh, the stove, the beautiful stove
> Heating the room below and above,
> Broiling, roasting and keeping warm—
> Beautiful stove you can do no harm.
> Fill her up to thaw your toes
> Fill her to thaw the end of your nose.
> Open the damper and let her go—
> She'll soon knock h--- out of the beautiful snow.

Jack Langrishe, who was well-known for his thoughtfulness and generosity, gave a special Christmas gift to Deadwood. On Christmas Day, 1877, he and a xylophone musician hauled the drill steel chimes he had bought from Star and Bullock on a bobsled up to Brown Rocks overlooking Deadwood. When the Bell Ringer sounded a bell-like tone and "Adeste Fideles" rang out on the cold mountain air, the people rushed unbelieving to the doors and windows of their log cabins, which were stacked in layers on the mountainsides.

Many homesick pioneers said they never forgot the intense joy of hearing the beloved carol ring out again and again over the snow-buried gulch. They thought it must be a miracle—but it was just another memorable Langrishe production.

In the devastating Deadwood fire of September 26, 1879, Langrishe's second theater burned to the ground along with most of Deadwood's main street district. While gazing sadly at the smoking ruins the next day, Jack was said to have remarked to stunned bystanders, "Well, I guess we'll have to put out the 'Standing Room Only' sign. There's not even a slab left to sit on."

According to Dr. Lawrence Stine who researched Deadwood's early theater days, from 1876-1890, there were 535 different performances of plays presented; 217 of these were Langrishe's.

After his theater burned and rival companies began moving in, the acting team went back to Colorado where they performed for the grand opening of the elegant Tabor opera house in Leadville, and later established a popular theater in Denver. Langrishe's many friends in Deadwood were glad to hear that at last he was making "barrels of money."

Jack Langrishe's last years were spent in northern Idaho where he edited a newspaper in the boom town of Wardner and was elected to the senate in Idaho's first legislature. The old pro had taken his last curtain calls during the 1880's, and his newspaper pals had to write "30" at the end of the Langrishe story in 1895 when he died at age seventy-one.

FRED EVANS—A REAL PAUL BUNYAN

Frederick Taft Evans was a big, broad-shouldered man, 6'4'' in height, a giant in both stature and accomplishments. The people of the Black Hills, especially in Hot Springs, have always idolized this promoter and benefactor.

Born in Ohio in 1835, Evans in his youth began moving westward, working in the timber of Wisconsin, cutting wood and logging for a living, like a genuine Paul Bunyan whose fantastic deeds became legendary.

Evans freighted to Pikes Peak, Colorado; rounded up wild horses in Washington; ranched in Nebraska before he moved to Sioux City, Iowa. Here he built a street railway and stockyards while helping to organize a bank.

When he heard about gold discoveries in the Black Hills, Evans was eager to strike it rich by becoming a supplier to the gold-seekers he knew would invade them. In April, 1875, he started freighting supplies to the Black Hills, even though the entire area was still an Indian reservation, off limits to the whites.

The great caravan of wagons and supplies, powered by mules, started out from Sioux City, Iowa, but the United States army intercepted them and forbade them to proceed. The soldiers destroyed their supplies and turned the mules loose on the prairie. A big disappointment for Evans.

But nothing could long deter this resolute man. Later in 1875 he organized another freighting expedition which made it through to Deadwood where the wagons had to be lowered into the gulch with ropes and chains.

In February, 1877, Congress, despite the Laramie Treaty of 1868, declared the Black Hills open to white settlement. Then there was no stopping Evans.

Frederick Taft Evans, a Paul Bunyan in size and accomplishments. He organized the first passenger and freight transportation train, powered by oxen and mules, from Sioux City, Iowa, to the Black Hills in April, 1875. Big Fred could swear an ox's horn off in two minutes. *Photo credit—From* **The Black Hills** *or* **Last Hunting Ground of the Dakotahs** *by Annie D. Tallent, Fielder Collection, Devereaux Library, South Dakota School of Mines and Technology.*

Even before Evans decided to make his headquarters in Pierre on the Missouri waterway, he had become president of the First National Bank in Pierre. He organized a steamboat line to run freight up the Missouri from Iowa to Fort Pierre, across the river from Pierre, and later to Chamberlain, down river in Dakota.

The Evans Transportation Company became the biggest freighting outfit in the west; it loaded countless wagon trains from the docks at Fort Pierre that were heading for the Black Hills, about a fifteen-day trip.

During the twelve years of its existence, from 1876 to 1888, the Evans Transportation Company hauled twelve million pounds of freight. The company could handle 400 tons at once. They employed from 1,000 to 1,500 men and wagons, and worked from 2,000 to 3,000 oxen and from 1,000 to 1,500 mules.

The varied freight included coal, machinery, dynamite, mining supplies, flour, sugar, bacon, beans, hardware, pianos, calico—even a thirty-ton narrow gauge train engine, the first one used by the Homestake Mining Company at Lead. On the return trip from the Hills, the wagon trains hauled gold bars from the Homestake and flour from the new mills.

The typical prairie bull team unit consisted of twenty head of oxen yoked into ten teams before three wagons, which were fastened one behind the other. Each unit had its own driver, the bullwhacker, who generally walked most of the way beside his slow-moving teams. The white-covered Evans wagon trains were the trail-breakers across western Dakota, carving out the first ruts on the famous Fort Pierre to Deadwood trail.

Trying to prove who was boss, the bullwhacker carried a wooden-handled leather whip about twenty feet long to guide and control the oxen, by flicking them expertly without injury while motivating them to respond to the commands of "Gee" and "Haw." Inevitably, the bullwhacker had a magnificient working vocabulary; and to accent his swearing and yelling, he would snake out the whip to make a popping sound, like a rifle shot, that was supposed to encourage the oxen to "git along." Although these patient beasts of burden were also stubborn, they surely deserve great credit for opening the west.

Fred Evans had the reputation for being able "to swear an ox's horn off in two minutes." When he put on a bullwhacking exhibition, "Big Fred" with curly dark hair, long beard, and side-burns was a colorful show with sound effects. Like a giant Paul Bunyan with more than one pet ox, Evans drove his white oxen team up and down the length of the supply train, often strung out for miles. He and his well-trained animals helped pull out wagons that had become mired in the terrible gumbo which clung to the huge wagon wheels and stuck like glue on the oxen's feet.

One time when Evans was using some rough bullwhacker language to get a mired team moving, a preacher friend of his chastised him for using such profanities.

Evans, a formidable man said to weigh as much as one of his steers, drew himself up to his full height and explained. He defended himself by pointing out that swear words were the only kind the oxen understood. He declared that trying to move oxen was a lot harder than the minister's work of freighting souls to heaven. Evans climaxed his defense by offering the preacher $1,000 if he could drive one yoke of maddening oxen for one day without cussing. The critic, who then had to put up or shut up, did not accept the challenge.

When the railroads reached the Black Hills in the 1880's, their arrival brought the colorful era of wagon-supply trains to an end. After Evans sold his freighting business, he moved to Hot Springs where he and four other men had already had the foresight to establish the Dakota Hot Springs Company.

Fred Evans' last bull train to Rapid City, 1886. The outfit is camped at St. Joseph and 11th streets, Rapid City. When the railroads reached the Black Hills in 1886, the colorful era of wagon-supply trains ended. *Photo credit—From C. Irwin Leedy Historical Collection, Minnelusa Historical Museum, Rapid City.*

Hot Springs was indeed fortunate that Evans thought the village the prettiest spot in the Hills, located in the most promising section, and endowed with the most potential for becoming the largest community in the Black Hills. Along with his boundless energy and abilities, Evans brought to Hot Springs one half million dollars to invest, plus connections with eastern financiers.

When Evans saw the Indians drinking the warm medicinal water of the thermal springs and bathing themselves in it to cure their ills, he immediately saw the possibilities of developing a health resort town which would attract many visitors.

His first project was in 1886 when he built the Minnekahta Hotel, a three-story frame structure which burned in 1891. During the height of the blaze, legend has it that Evans yelled to the firemen, "Let her go, boys! We'll build a better one for Hot Springs." And he did, on the same location.

While the new hotel was being built, Evans and his wife Theresa went to Europe to study hotel architecture. Eventually, they incorporated many European ideas in the design of the hotel as well as in their lavish home.

In 1892, the magnificent Evans Hotel opened its doors. Built with stone from the Evans quarries, the hotel was furnished in Victorian elegance with red lamps and velvet drapes, the guest rooms and lobby the utmost in comfort and luxury. The cuisine was excellent with a chef from Chicago, and black waiters stood at attention with starched napkins over their arms. An orchestra and roulette wheels provided entertainment for the guests.

The Evans Hotel looming up in the background, Hot Springs, SD. Fred Evans built the hotel with stones from the Evans quarries and furnished it with Victorian elegance. An orchestra and roulette wheels provided entertainment for the guests. *Photo credit—South Dakota State Historical Society.*

The Evans Hotel entertained many famous people and wealthy visitors who came by train to take the healing waters of Hot Springs and to marvel at Evans' steamer moored on Fall River. The Evans was said to be the most elegant hotel between the West Coast and Chicago until Denver built the Brown Palace.

The Evans Plunge was "Big Fred's" brain child which he built in 1890 over numerous small springs and the "Old Original Indian Spring." Since Evans' time, several improved structures have enclosed the plunge, but the new ones have incorporated his original approach with constant changes of warm water rising and flowing out of the plunge, with excellent accommodations for swimmers, and with a free gallery for spectators. The Evans Plunge is still advertised as "the largest indoor natural warm swimming pool in the world."

The warm water pool at Evans Plunge, Hot Springs. Fred Evans built the plunge in 1890 over numerous small springs and the "Old Original Indian Spring." *Photo credit—South Dakota State Historical Society.*

Among the other achievements of this tireless promoter of Hot Springs was that Evans was instrumental in getting the Elkhorn, Fremont, and Missouri railroad to come through his town.

An oft-repeated saying was whenever an improvement was needed for Hot Springs, Fred Evans would provide half the cost and the town would try to provide the other half. He donated land on which to build every church in town and also provided land for the State Soldier's Home. He organized the first bank and installed the first electric light plant. After a typhoid epidemic from impure water, he installed a modern water system. He provided complete financial support for the city band and baseball team.

Despite all the wealth he had accumulated and spent, often for the benefit of others, Evans died in 1902, a relatively poor man at age sixty-seven. His wife Theresa, a greatly beloved woman in Hot Springs, outlived him for fifteen years. She was the organizer of the society which erected the public library in the city developed by her husband.

Throughout Hot Springs, Fred Evans left stone monuments and far-sighted philanthropic projects. Like a skillfull bullwhacker cracking his whip over the slow advance of civilization, he also left a Paul Bunyan legacy of giant strides in the development of the entire Black Hills.

CAPTAIN JACK CRAWFORD—THE POET-SCOUT

Captain Jack Crawford christened himself the Poet-Scout of the Black Hills. Drawing on his own experience in the Civil War and throughout the frontier, he wrote numerous sentimental verses about the beauties of nature; the basic corruption of all Indians; pathetic tales of poor souls; the sad deaths of his mother, of Wild Bill Hickok, and of General George Custer. He also wrote a paean to the attractions of Rapid City when it was still a hay camp.

John Wallace Crawford was born in Ireland and immigrated with his parents to the United States. Although small for his sixteen years, he managed to enlist as a volunteer in the Union Army and was twice wounded in Civil War battles. He never attended school but was taught to read and write by a Sister of Charity in a Philadelphia hospital.

In 1876, he joined the Black Hills Gold Rush and came first to Custer where he became captain of the Custer Minute Men whose purpose was to protect the settlers from the Indians. According to humorist Doc Peirce, the reason for the name was that the Minute Men never went so far from town that they couldn't get back in one minute. The signal for an emergency was three pistol shots fired in rapid succession.

Captain Jack Crawford, captain of the Minute Men in Custer organized to protect the settlers from the Indians. He also wrote sentimental verse and gave dramatic readings. Captain Jack wrote several poems while sitting on Wild Bill Hickok's grave. *Photo credit—South Dakota State Historical Society.*

In the fabulous boom town of Rockerville, a diggings was named "Captain Jack's Gulch" in his honor, but he never had much luck as a miner. The Captain also claimed to have been a founder of Deadwood, Crook City, Gayville and Spearfish.

Always interested in writing and educating himself, Jack worked on his poetry and began giving dramatic presentations at gatherings in mining camps. Dressed in buckskins with a sombrero atop his long flowing hair, he became a picturesque and popular performer. Soft-spoken and emotional, he was an effective reader of his own poetry and plays. Sometimes he sang and did lariat tricks.

Because of Captain Jack's literary inclinations, he was frequently called upon to eulogize over a dead miner and to write a poem at the drop of a tear, which he could do in record time, to the amazement of the non-poets.

A correspondent for several newspapers, including the **Omaha Bee** and the **Cheyenne Leader,** he wrote copy designed to attract more fortune hunters to the Black Hills. His exaggerated claims proclaimed how civilized Custer City was with 100 homes already built and surveying underway for a school, courthouse, and park. At the time he wrote these fairy tales the town of Custer had not yet been officially established.

In July, 1876, when he was second in command of General Crook's scouts in the Indian campaigns, he carried dispatches on horseback through the Big Horn Mountains to the nearest telegraph at Fort Laramie, WY. He traveled almost 400 miles in four days through Indian country, riding hell-bent at night and hiding during the day, knowing he would be killed if the Indians caught him.

One time during a campaign with General Crook, he was given a bottle of whiskey to deliver to Buffalo Bill Cody, the famous scout who loved to drink. The grateful Cody stated that Captain Jack was the only man on the frontier who could be trusted with a bottle of whiskey.

Captain Jack and Buffalo Bill Cody were long-time friends and rivals for scouting honors, and in the fall of 1876 Jack joined Cody's Wild West show in a co-starring role as the Poet-Scout of the Black Hills. During a dramatic performance in 1877 in Virginia City, NV, they re-enacted the famous fight with Yellow Hand when Buffalo Bill Cody took "the first scalp for Custer." During the stage duel while Crawford was playing the part of Yellow Hand, he was wounded in the leg. Crawford maintained that Cody, while drunk, had stabbed and shot him in the leg. But the Nevada newspapers reported that Crawford had accidentally shot himself by firing his revolver when it was still in his holster. Whatever the truth, Crawford was wounded both physically and emotionally, and this incident ended their long friendship.

Crawford had a wife and three children, but he didn't see them often. He was too busy traveling around the frontier scouting for various generals, giving dramatic readings, performing in Buffalo Bill's Wild West Show. When he wasn't in the Black Hills, which seemed to be his home base, he was prospecting in the Klondike, reading his poetry in San Francisco, performing in his own plays in Chicago. At one time he was post trader and contractor at Fort Craig, NM, and he sent for his wife and children in Pennsylvania to join him there briefly.

Captain Jack spent the last ten years of his life touring the east on the Chautauqua and Lyceum circuits. He died in New York in 1917 and is buried in a Brooklyn cemetery, far from the Black Hills and the west he loved so well.

It was in 1886 that he had published a book of his poetry entitled **The Poet Scout.** In the preface he wrote that "I have no thought of grasping literary or poetical distinction. They are the crude, unpolished offspring of my idle hours—wandering thoughts which came to me on the lonely trail and in the bivouac and camp."

The greatest influence on his life was his mother, "one of God's good angels," who made him promise on her death bed that he would never drink liquor. And Captain Jack kept that promise.

Mother's Prayers

Oh, my brother, do not drink it,
Think of all your mother said;
While upon her death-bed laying,
Or perhaps she is not dead;
Don't you kill her, then, I pray you,
She has got enough of cares,
Sign the pledge, and God will help you,
If you think of mother's prayers. (last verse)

According to Leigh Irvine, Crawford's biographer, Captain Jack's reading of this one brought Wild Bill Hickok to tears. And Wild Bill said, "God bless you, Jack; you strike a tender spot, old boy, when you talk mother that way."

Wild Bill and Captain Jack were good friends, and Captain Jack gave readings to raise money to improve Wild Bill's grave. He wrote several poems in tribute to the Kansas marshal and scout while sitting on his graves in Deadwood, first in the original boot hill, and later in Mount Moriah cemetery.

An Epitaph on Wild Bill

Sleep on, brave heart, in peaceful slumber,
Bravest scout in all the West;
Lightning eyes and voice of thunder,
Closed and hushed in quiet rest.
Peace and rest at last is given;
May we meet again in heaven.
Rest in peace.

When Captain Jack was on a dangerous scouting expedition and received a letter from his wife, he was inspired to write this poem:

Little Ones Praying at Home

So tonight I am happy in Old Mexico,
While I sit in the moonlight alone;
For surely 'tis pleasant to feel and to know
There are little ones praying at home. (chorus)

In July, 1876, Buffalo Bill Cody sent Captain Jack a telegram: "Have you heard about the death of our brave Custer?" In response, Captain Jack wrote a 72-line poem which was hailed as a masterpiece. Author and educator Annie Tallent called it a "specimen of real Black Hills literature."

The Death of Custer

Did I hear the news from Custer?
Well, I reckon I did, old pard.
It came like a streak o' lightning.
And you bet, it hit me hard.
I ain't no hand to blubber,
And the briny ain't run for years,
But chalk me down for a lubber
If I didn't shed regular tears. (first verse)

The poet predicted the future in the last lines of this poem:

Spring in the Black Hills

Farmers will come with their ploughs and their harrows,
The bright golden grain will be waving ere long;
While civilization will bury the arrows,
And the red man will sing his last sad death song.

Here is Captain Jack Crawford's final verse in his book, **The Poet Scout:**

Dear reader, farewell, the affliction is o'er—
Your powers of endurance astound me;
With my horse I am off for the trail once more,
Where the wandering muse first found me.

POTATO CREEK JOHNNY— THE BIGGEST LITTLE PROSPECTOR

"Throw up your hands!" ordered Potato Creek Johnny, pointing a gun-shaped nugget at Goldbug Nelson, his mining partner. Goldbug wasn't scared, only flabbergasted at the size of the large gold piece. That memorable event took place in May, 1929.

Johnny repeated over and over how he found the biggie, every gold miner's dream, in the sparkling waters of Potato Creek, a tributary of

Spearfish Creek, not far from Spearfish Canyon, the entire region one of the most beautiful in the Black Hills.

Potato Creek Johnny showing off his big nugget which he found in Potato Creek near Spearfish Canyon. His watch chain is linked with nuggets he found in the streams of the northern Black Hills. *Photo credit—Centennial Archives, Deadwood.*

Of course, the nugget actually resembled a human leg more than it did a toy gun, and it wasn't the biggest nugget ever found in the Black Hills, as it was publicized. Just one of the biggest. Johnny sold it to W. E. Adams of Deadwood for $250. On the fluctuating gold market of the 1970's and '80's, its value has reached $3,000. An exact replica of Johnny's nugget is displayed in the Adams Museum in Deadwood.

Johnny didn't get rich but he certainly became famous; tourists and reporters often visited his homemade log cabin in the tall pines along Potato Creek. Here, before he became a celebrity, he had lived quietly for over thirty years with only squirrels, chipmunks, and birds for companionship. However, he was not a hermit and frequently played the fiddle at country dances in the Spearfish Canyon area. He loved company and enjoyed showing visitors his two brick hearths, one on top of another, where he baked biscuits and rattlesnake steaks. Always hospitable, he offered people the use of his rusty tin cup hanging on a bush for drinking spring water, from what he called "The Last Chance Saloon."

Both old and new friends decided he looked just the way a prospector should look with a long scraggly beard and hair, crinkly eyes, and grimy clothes. Johnny was only four feet, three inches tall, but he made up for his elfin size with his quaint personality, charming everyone with his Welsh accent and tall tales. He often complained that "so many amachoors have riled up the streams and don't know to get the gold out that placer mining has gone to hell."

After the sensational nugget discovery, Johnny stayed in Deadwood during the summer months in the 1930's and 1940's. The Deadwood Chamber of Commerce knew genuine gold when they saw it, and they hired Potato Creek Johnny to show the tourists how to pan gold in the nearby streams. He kept up a running monologue describing how a vicious humming bird who couldn't hold her liquor attacked him and his burro until they jumped into the creek and hid under water. And when he and the frightened burro surfaced, Johnny's pockets were full of fish.

Potato Creek Johnny panning gold in Potato Creek; he lived in a rustic cabin beside this beautiful stream. In Deadwood, he enjoyed showing tourists how to pan gold while telling tall tales of his adventures and quaffing the many drinks they bought him. *Photo credit—South Dakota State Historical Society.*

Johnny liked to repeat a popular saying of early day poker games, "I've got the Deadwood on you," which meant that "you haven't got a chance."

Nobody had a chance competing with Johnny in attention-getting. The Deadwood Chamber of Commerce took him to Chicago where the entrepreneurs set up a gold-panning situation with water in the lobbies of the big hotels. Johnny amazed the city slickers with his specialty and doubtlessly convinced many in his audience to visit the fabled Black Hills.

For many years, Potato Creek Johnny was the main attraction in the annual "Days of '76" parade in Deadwood. He pushed a small wheelbarrow, threw pennies at the kids, walked on his hands, and sometimes built a campfire in the middle of the street. When he got too old and tottery to walk, he rode a big saddle horse with stirrups set up high for his short little legs. How the crowd loved being able to see the little elf better while exchanging waves. Unfortunately, both local friends and tourists often bought him too many drinks. One year the little man rode his big parade horse right into the Old Style Saloon No. 10 in Deadwood—to the delight of the customers.

Potato Creek Johnny for years was a star attraction in the "Days of '76" parade in Deadwood. He danced jigs, pushed a wheelbarrow, walked on his hands, rode a big horse, threw pennies at the kids, and often built a campfire in the middle of the street. He died at age 77 in 1942. *Photo credit —Centennial Archives, Deadwood.*

Potato Creek Johnny, the good-will ambassador for the Black Hills, "crossed the Great Divide" at age 77, in February, 1942.

He is buried in Mount Moriah cemetery in Deadwood beside Wild Bill Hickok and Calamity Jane. This cluster of three notable graves is the most popular tourist attraction in Deadwood. Wild Bill and Calamity Jane may be the most famous—or infamous—characters in the Black Hills, but Johnny was the best-loved.

At a ceremony held at the Deadwood Rodeo Grounds during the "Days of '76" the year that Potato Creek Johnny died, a prayerful verse was read to honor his memory:

> Johnny, old pard, we hope you
> Have found that claim,
> And that long-lost gold mine in the sky.

What old prospector could ask for more?

Alice and Joseph Gossage, after they retired from many years of publishing the **Rapid City Journal**. The devoted couple is sitting in front of the fireplace made from stones from the Black Hills and from their travels. Fireplace now in Minnelusa Museum, Rapid City. *Photo credit—Minnelusa Historical Museum, Rapid City.*

ALICE GOSSAGE—INSPIRING LADY

"Glory Hallelujah! Hooray for the Black Hills!" wrote an enthusiastic Alice Bower in her diary when she was day-dreaming about moving west to live in the exciting mountains of western South Dakota. She also hoped to marry a Republican who was a newspaper man. Eventually all her wishes were realized: she married Joseph Gossage, a Republican who was publisher and editor of the **Black Hills Journal;** and she did move to the Black Hills and live happily ever after.

Following her marriage in 1882, which turned out to be as idyllic as a romantic girl could wish, she lived and worked the rest of her life in Rapid City, SD, where she became affectionately known as "A.G." in her role as editor and full-time partner with her husband on the daily newspaper, the **Rapid City Journal.** In addition to her newspaper career, she also devoted her talents and energies into becoming an outstanding civic leader in the community.

But before Alice Gossage became known as the leading lady of Rapid City and made her mark as a newspaper woman, she lived in Vermillion in the southeastern corner of the state with her parents, Calvin and Kezia Bower. Alice, the oldest of eight children, worked hard cooking and cleaning and sewing, being a second mother to her younger siblings in a poor but talented family. She recorded in her diary about the terrible flood in Vermillion, SD, in 1881 when "the mighty, rushing, rolling Missouri is upon us" and how the Bower house floated away, down the rampaging river, "the worst sight I ever saw."

A precocious Alice, when she was only fourteen, received a teaching certificate and began teaching country school for $38 a month. One day she had to whip an obstreperous boy named Carl Gunderson into shape. Fifty years later, he was elected Governor of South Dakota, and Carl Gunderson was always proud of having had Alice Gossage for his teacher and appreciated the political support of the **Rapid City Journal.**

Young Alice must certainly have had the proverbial printer's ink coursing in her veins because she was determined to learn how to set type; and despite her father's objections to what he thought was an unlady-like profession, she worked in several newspaper offices as a typesetter.

A proud aunt in Rapid City told publisher Joe Gossage about her gifted niece, and he immediately wrote Alice offering her a job. Thus began a lengthy and romantic courtship by mail. The two exchanged innumerable letters describing their appearances, their likes and dislikes, and revealing their attitudes toward religion and politics. When they exchanged photographs, she sent him one taken two years before when she was seventeen and better looking, she said. Alice cautioned him not to write back and "tell me how beautiful I am and all that for I know better and I don't want you to tell me what isn't true."

When she received his picture, she wrote back that she was suprised he was so young and good-looking because he sounded like an "elderly businessman." Actually, he was twenty-four years old.

Gossage decided he had to meet this candid young lady who wrote such clever, interesting letters, even confessing that she had a temper and "I am ambitious and will not give up."

He made the long trip to Vermillion to visit her, and they liked each other even better in person than through their letters. Alice had been engaged twice before, but she had broken off both engagements, once because she discovered the young man was addicted to the bottle. Joe Gossage did not drink. The two fell in love; he bought her an engagement ring; and their engagement was heartily endorsed by the entire Bower family.

On Gossage's second trip to Vermillion, in June, 1882, the young couple was married in the Bower family home. Alice sewed her own wedding dress and also the dresses worn by her mother and five sisters at the wedding. She and Joseph came by stagecoach and train to Rapid City and moved into the new house he had built for her with a bay window in the parlor. Later, he bought musical Alice a piano which was transported on the Sidney stage.

Despite Alice's intense happiness with her husband, she greatly missed her big family, and they missed her. Everyone was delighted in 1885 when her father took up a claim in Custer County on Battle Creek where the parents and seven children lived in three rooms for two years.

The entire Bower family loved to make music. Eventually, Calvin Bower mortgaged his cattle to buy them band instruments. And thus began the Bower Family Band which became famous making one-night stands throughout the southern Black Hills, playing and marching for Fourth of July celebrations and other occasions in Hermosa, Custer, and Keystone. The Bowers performed at Rapid City on July 4, 1886, to celebrate the coming of the railroad.

President Calvin Coolidge in 1927 visiting Alice Gossage and her Congregational Sunday School pupils on Flower Festival Day. *Photo credit—Minnelusa Historical Museum, Rapid City.*

Alice, the oldest Bower, did not play with the band. Laura, the youngest, began playing the baritone horn at age four. When Laura grew up, she wrote a delightful book, **The Family Band,** in which she quoted extensively from Alice's diaries.

Alice came as a bride to Rapid City when it was a hay camp for the long bull trains heading north to the gold fields. The settlement was mainly just a scattering of log cabins, and Alice immediately determined to improve the primitive conditions and promote civilizing influences like schools, churches, and worthy organizations.

She loved working in the offices of the **Rapid City Journal** where she started out folding papers, setting type, proofreading; soon she was reporting, writing, editing, and thus becoming a true partner with her beloved husband Joe. The Gossages had strong opinions which they injected into their reporting of the news. A cardinal rule was not to publish the name of a juvenile offender, but woe to an official in the city government who needed chastising.

Alice was a short, stocky woman and her clothes were often dowdy. Instead of worrying about dressing stylishly, she was much more concerned with providing clothing for the poor. She wrote the "Sunshine Column" in the **Journal** in which she requested help from the community: clothes, blankets, and food for needy families. She stored the donations in the Journal building and then distributed them to poverty-stricken families whose homes she visited. Many times she took neglected children, white and Indian, into her home where she saw to it that they had baths, clean clothes, and a bowl of hot soup.

In her Congregational Sunday School class which she taught for forty years, she presented the children with packets of flower seeds and explained how they should plant them to beautify their yards. When the flowers bloomed, it was time for a blossom display and prizes for the most beautiful. The project grew and adults took part until Alice Gossage's Flower Reception became an annual affair.

The Bower Family Band played throughout the southern Black Hills. Alice, who did not play in the band, is holding the music. Laura, the youngest, grew up to write a delightful book, **The Family Band,** and quoted extensively from Alice's diaries. *Photo credit—Kelvin Van Nuys.*

Ruby Lee, author and long-time Rapid Citian, remembers with gratitude and love how Alice Gossage took her in when she was a runaway seventh grader from Battle Creek, sick with pneumonia, and desperate for the ways and means to acquire more schooling.

Young Ruby, with her parents' permission, lived with the Gossages for two years, earning her board and room while going happily to school. Ruby recalled: "She taught me so much. All she had to do was look hard at me, and I would do anything in the world to please her. She didn't even get angry the time I used up all the bread starter and instead of baking seven loaves of bread, I ended up with fourteen. Mrs. Gossage just laughed—of course she gave most of it away. She was a wonderful woman. She helped so many young people finish their schooling. No wonder everyone called her 'Mother of Rapid City' even though she had no children of her own."

Mrs. Gossage, in addition to her Sunday School work and concern for providing educational opportunities, also served on the library board. She campaigned for prohibition, woman suffrage, and was active in the Women's Christian Temperance Union. A highlight of her later life was being able to attend a world convention of the WCTU in Geneva, Switzerland.

As the years went on and Joe Gossage's health declined, A.G. (as she signed her columns) took over more and more responsibilities in the newspaper office. In 1925, the Gossages sold the controlling interest in the **Journal** and retired.

Alice Gossage continued to write her column, "Tales of the Hills, a History of Early Days." She wrote about riding the stagecoach, ferrying across the Missouri River, fighting droughts and floods and blizzards. She wrote character sketches about Lame Johnny, Doc Peirce, Captain Jack Crawford. She described the wonders of the Rockerville Flume and recorded the legend of the grape design in Black Hills Gold Jewelry. No wonder A.G.'s column was so popular.

Joseph Gossage died in 1927. Alice Gossage, age 68, died in June, 1929. The mayor of Rapid City proclaimed that all businesses be closed for A.G.'s funeral. He said: "For nearly half a century she has been closely identified with every religious, social, philanthropic, and commercial interest and activity in Rapid City. She has spent her life in performing acts of kindness, charity, and services for humanity."

Eventually, in 1937, on the 76th anniversary of Alice Gossage's birth, Rapid City dedicated a handsome shaft with a sundial on its top to honor her memory. From the memorial site at the highest point on Skyline Drive, the monument overlooked Rapid City to the east, Cowboy Hill to the north, Rapid Valley to the southwest, the Harney range to the west.

Surely a fitting memorial to the enthusiastic girl who had exclaimed "Glory Hallelujah! Hooray for the Black Hills!" and then spent the rest of her life proving she meant it.

Note: The Gossage Memorial has been moved to the grounds of the Minnelusa Historical Museum in Rapid City.

DORA DuFRAN— BROTHEL MADAM AND HUMANITARIAN

Dora DuFran, at various times, was a notorious madam of brothels in Deadwood, Lead, Belle Fourche, and Rapid City—all communities in the Black Hills of South Dakota where settlement was not begun until the Black Hills Gold Rush of 1874-1879.

Dora DuFran was born in England at an uncertain date (her tombstone says 1873) and eventually came with her parents to Nebraska. About 1886, she arrived in Rapid City as Amy Helen Dorothy Bolshow. Early in life when she was reported to be a good-looking girl, she began working as a dance hall floozy entertaining cowboys from the West River ranching country and miners from the booming gold and silver mines of the Black Hills.

She moved to Deadwood, then married Joseph DuFran, a personable gentleman gambler, and together they joined the Deadwood sporting fraternity by opening a brothel; in addition to sex, the "resort" also offered gambling, dancing, and drinking.

Dora DuFran, a notorious madam of brothels in Deadwood, Lead, Belle Fourche, and Rapid City. A humanitarian, she is also remembered for her kindness to the destitute. *Photo credit—Dr. Leland Michael.*

After her husband died, Dora DuFran managed a famous brothel in Coney Island in Rapid City during the 1920's and 1930's. An oft-repeated story relates how a flood marooned many prominent Rapid City businessmen at Dora's ramshackle resort on Coney Island. Their wives heard the shocking news, the only bridge went out, and the angry wives confronted their husbands with rolling pins and umbrellas when the culprits came floundering out of the receding waters to take their punishment.

Dora lived in a big, multi-purpose house on Coney Island where she performed abortions and delivered illegitimate babies for destitute mothers. Her housekeeper was widowed Mrs. Lavange Michael who with her three children lived with Dora. The Michael family remembers grandmotherly Dora with great affection for her generosity and kindness to them.

Dora DuFran and her pet monkey at her big, multi-purpose brothel on Coney Island, Rapid City. Dora loved children and pets. *Photo credit—Dr. Leland Michael.*

Dora DuFran was a confidante and occasional employer of Calamity Jane, about whom she wrote a booklet entitled, **Low Down on Calamity Jane,** published in 1932. Calling herself D. Dee, the mysterious authoress never revealed her identity or the fact that she was a madam and Calamity an occasional prostitute. Although DuFran made some historical errors, her booklet presents an accurate picture of Calamity's personality by one who actually knew her. She provides many colorful sidelights from Calamity's life as a howling drunk, a scout, a bullwhacker, and a ministering angel to the sick and dying.

In the booklet, DuFran writes at length about the infamous Gem Theater in Deadwood, but she does not say whether she was ever associated with this den of iniquity which combined the usual gambling, drinking, dancing, and prostitution with its bawdy stage shows. She described how the Gem band played every night from the balcony "when the ladies of the night came forth to drink, dance, and hustle." The girls received ten cents for every dance, twenty cents for every bottle of beer sold, and one dollar for every bottle of wine. The author does not specify how much these soiled doves were paid for their work behind the small curtained rooms lining both sides of the theater.

Like many women involved with the sporting fraternity, Dora DuFran was a scarlet woman with a heart of gold. When Dora, a huge woman, died of heart failure in 1934, the **Rapid City Journal** eulogized her

The Gem Theater, Deadwood, the most infamous den of iniquity in Sin City. Dora, under a pseudonym, wrote about the Gem's activities in her book, **Low Down on Calamity Jane.** *Photo credit—South Dakota State Historical Society.*

humanitarianism, philanthropy, and free nursing services to the poverty-stricken, under the banner headline, "Dora DuFran Served Suffering Humanity."

This controversial woman is buried in an imposing lot in Mount Moriah cemetery in Deadwood, and on each corner of the lot is an urn adored with a grinning gargoyle. She rests beside her husband Joseph and her pet parrot who was buried in a tiny wooden casket under a small tombstone marked "Fred." Just across the flagstone walk is the grave of her friend Calamity Jane. Engraved on Dora's tombstone in addition to her name, dates of birth and death, and "age 60" is the inscription: "Mother—Gone But Not Forgotten."

The ornate DuFran lot in Mount Moriah cemetery, Deadwood, where Dora is buried beside her husband Joseph and Fred, her pet parrot. All have individual markers. *Photo credit—Al Gunther.*

A GALLERY OF DEADWOOD DICKS

Deadwood Dick was the title five or possibly six characters who lived in Deadwood assumed—or tried to assume—during their lifetimes. Historians have generally credited—or blamed—the sensational western novelist Edward Wheeler for stimulating Black Hillers to yearn after this sobriquet. Beginning no earlier than 1877 and continuing through the 1890's, Wheeler became the published author of about sixty little pocket-size books featuring the adventures of an imaginary Deadwood Dick on the frontier.

Yet, oddly enough, the first documented impersonator who called himself Deadwood Dick did so before Wheeler's books were published. He was Nat Love, a black cowboy, who, in July, 1876, claimed in his spurious autobiography that he was awarded the title, "Deadwood Dick" because he had won top prizes in riding and marksmanship at the first Fourth of July celebration in the gold camp.

The name "Deadwood Dick" must have had a charismatic ring to it because later in that memorable year of 1876, another man came along who wanted to be called that. He was Banjo Dick Brown who was married to singer Fannie Garretson, and they both entertained the rowdy gold miners at the Melodeon saloon in Deadwood. This banjo player was said to have

Deadwood Dick, The Prince of the Road or **The Black Rider of the Black Hills,** was originally a fictional character created by Edward K. Wheeler who wrote exciting frontier tales in the late 1800's. *Photo credit—Fielder Collection, Devereaux Library, South Dakota School of Mines and Technology.*

Nat Love, a black cowboy in Deadwood, 1876, was the first person to call himself "Deadwood Dick." He claimed the title because he won top prizes in riding and marksmanship at the first Fourth of July celebration in the gold camp. *Photo credit—South Dakota State Historical Society.*

used the words "Deadwood Dick" many times in the dramatic lyrics of every tune he strummed on the banjo in the burlesque house. But he never made extravagant claims about himself.

Who knows? Maybe author Wheeler visited Deadwood, did some saloon research or read about the colorful activities in the **Black Hills Pioneer**, the first newspaper, and was struck with the drawing power of the name "Deadwood Dick," which after all was not such an unusual moniker for the west at that time.

By the 1890's, Wheeler's Deadwood Dick books, as part of Beadle's Dime and a Half series, had bombarded the reading public, avid for any believe-it-or-not plots about the Wild West. Three more Deadwood-ites were supposed to have aspired to being called by the magic name: a stagecoach driver, a stagecoach guard of the bullion, and an obscure gold-seeker. None could ever convince people he was worthy of being called by the famous nickname—even though their first names were all Dick.

Meanwhile, Edward Wheeler, who sometimes wrote under the psuedonym of Ned Buntline, was going great guns churning out adventures with a western background. The public was delighted with this escape fiction and accepted it as an accurate portrayal of the Wild West, especially because real people like Calamity Jane and Captain Jack Crawford mingled with fictitious ones. Deadwood Dick was characterized as a handsome Robin Hood who robbed stagecoaches to help the poor and rescued fair ladies in distress, all the while maintaining his image of the gallant but lawless hero.

Even the titles of the Deadwood Dick series stirred the imagination of the gullible public: *Deadwood Dick Trapped, Deadwood Dick As Detective, Deadwood Dick's Doom, The Buffalo Demon, The Phantom Miner,* and *Deadwood Dick, the Prince of the Road.*

Here is a typical paragraph from *The Double Daggers* or *Deadwood Dick's Defiance:*

"All of the road agents were slaughtered without quarter—all except Deadwood Dick. He, on his big black stallion, was seen to ride straight up the mountain side, where none could follow. Nor did bullets seem to check his progress. So much again, for the notorious youth, who is making for himself a name, as a daring road rider second to none in the world."

By the time the fifth or sixth candidate for the Deadwood Dick role appeared on the scene, everybody had read or heard about Wheeler's superman of the old west.

The last and most successful Deadwood Dick was Richard Clark, who took on the role in the 1920's. A Black Hills pioneer of 1876, Clark had lived a varied but obscure life as a ferryboater, a mail carrier, a shotgun messenger on stagecoaches, a miner, a handyman, and a railroad worker.

The best-known and last Deadwood Dick was Richard Clark. The Deadwood Chamber of Commerce persuaded him to play the part in the "Days of '76" parade. Clark played the role to perfection for the rest of his life. Tourists believed he was the genuine character with countless heroic adventures. *Photo credit—South Dakota State Historical Society.*

Then, in the 1920's, the Deadwood Chamber of Commerce persuaded him, because he looked the part, to be Deadwood Dick in the "Days of '76" parade. After he clumsily fell off a prancing horse in the parade, he was assigned every year to march along carrying a rifle and a shovel for "giving the men he killed a Christian burial." Dressed in buckskins and a cowboy hat, he let his hair and moustache grow long enough until he looked like an aging but dignified hero. He never told lies about his exploits because most of the time he refused to talk; he answered all innocent questions about his exotic life with an enigmatic stare. His charmed audiences gazed into his melodramatic eyes and imagined chivalrous romances and stagecoach holdups and murders and dare-devil deeds.

Richard Clark apparently loved playing the role of Deadwood Dick, for he kept it up for years. When he wasn't performing for the tourists, he was a genuine recluse who lived alone in a log cabin and shunned conversation. However, he made such a hit that the Deadwood Chamber of Commerce convinced him to accompany a delegation to Washington to encourage President Calvin Coolidge to spend the summer of 1927 in the Black Hills. Which Coolidge did. There is no record of whether Silent Cal and Deadwood Dick exchanged meaningful long silences.

Richard Clark died in 1930 at age 85. In an elaborate ceremony, usually reserved for an illustrious pioneer, he was buried in a lonely grave on Sunrise Mountain just northwest of Deadwood. Newspapers throughout the country carried obituaries about his amazing adventures and accomplishments, some with tongue in cheek. Richard Clark had played his part well. He had earned the right to cross "The Great Divide" as the legendary Deadwood Dick.

POKER ALICE—LUCKY GAMBLER

Poker Alice Tubbs smoked big black cigars. Of course, she had other claims to fame: she was a professional gambler, a brothel madam, a crack shot, and a murderer. And once she broke the casino bank at Silver City, NM. Oh yes, she had three husbands and seven kids.

That's just a bare listing suggesting the varied roles she played in life. No wonder she ranks not far behind Wild Bill Hickok and Calamity Jane as a famous personality enlivening Black Hills history. Although she contributed nothing constructive to society, she has been romanticized along with other notorious characters whose lives have been publicized to improve the tourist trade, a major industry in the Black Hills.

Consider the contrasts between Poker Alice and her lady doctor. Poker Alice was reported to have been a patient of the first lady doctor in the Black Hills, Flora Hayward Stanford. In the late 19th century, Dr. Stanford practiced medicine in both Deadwood, SD, and Sundance, WY, traveling by horseback and buggy over the wilderness trails to visit her patients in the best humanitarian traditions of the country doctor. She never got rich, and she died from overwork at age 62.

Poker Alice Tubbs with her trademark. She was a professional gambler, a brothel madam, a crack shot, and a murderer. Deadwood is proud to claim her but Sturgis, SD, where she lived, isn't so sure. *Photo credit—Centennial Archives, Deadwood.*

Mention Dr. Flora Stanford to a Black Hills history buff—and you will most likely draw a blank. Drop Poker Alice's name and the listener's eyes will light up like a jackpot on a slot machine.

Why is it that the shady characters who lived dangerously on the fringes of society are more interesting than the admirable lady pioneers?

Dr. Flora Stanford and her daughter in front of Deadwood home. Dr. Stanford, the first woman physician in the Black Hills, was Poker Alice's doctor. Why is it that disreputable Poker Alice is better known than her admirable lady doctor who is buried in a lost grave in Mount Moriah cemetery? *Photo credit—Centennial Archives, Deadwood.*

Poker Alice was born in England about 1851, and with her parents immigrated to America where she grew into a beautiful young lady. She married her first husband Frank Duffield, a mining engineer and gambler in Colorado gold camps. After he was killed in a mining accident, Alice became the merry widow. She took up gambling full-time, attracting customers with her glamorous appearance, and not even smiling while she raked in the chips for the house. When Alice was in the chips, she took off for New York to replenish her wardrobe of fancy low-cut gowns and ostrich plumes. An attractive dealer was always a come-on in the gambling business.

Not until the 1890's did Poker Alice astonish Deadwood with her gambling skills. She married a Sturgis man named Warren Tubbs who painted houses during the day and gambled at night. Poker Alice, far luckier than he, often told him to leave the wheeling and dealing to her.

She and Tubbs had seven children, but mother Alice wasn't the type to stay at home in Sturgis nursing babies, cooking, and bringing her husband his slippers. Somehow the family survived, but when the children were grown, they disappeared; reportedly, she occasionally visited them but never let them return home for a visit.

For many years, Poker Alice with an impassive expression expertly dealt poker and faro games in the gambling dives of Deadwood. When she lost she said, "God-damn me!" When she won, she silently raked in the

Poker Alice playing poker at the Bodega in Deadwood, 1927. Standing on her left is Fred Borsch Sr. Seated is bearded Grasshopper Jim who once lived in a cave beside Bear Butte. Can you believe Poker Alice was described as glamorous in her youth and wore fancy low-cut gowns? *Photo credit—Centennial Archives.*

chips. Legend says that she won more than $250,000 gambling in Deadwood, Sturgis, and other Black Hills towns. How she spent her winnings is a mystery. Even after her beauty faded and she became a rough-talking heavy drinker, gambling customers continued to get a kick out of her company while placing their bets.

One memorable time in a Deadwood saloon she took time out from card-dealing to shoot a man in the hand who was holding a knife over her husband Warren Tubbs. She wouldn't stand for male shenanigans.

The historic year when Poker Alice took up cigar-smoking is lost in the smoky mists of history, probably after she was getting fat and began wearing her favorite costume consisting of an old army shirt and a wool skirt. But the big black cigar, which she called jack-ass rope, became her trademark or talisman.

When Warren Tubbs contracted tuberculosis, Alice gave up her lucrative gambling career and moved with him to a little ranch on the Moreau River, 100 miles from Sturgis, where she tried to nurse him back to health. In later years, she confessed that she welcomed the peace and quiet on the plains. Warren Tubbs died in the winter of 1910. With true pioneer courage, in below-zero weather, Alice brought his body in a horse-drawn wagon to Sturgis for burial.

After Tubbs' death, Poker Alice went back to work. She set up a sporting house and bootlegging establishment in Sturgis, frequented by soldiers from nearby Fort Meade. During a drunken brawl which became a shootout, Alice shot and killed one soldier and wounded several others. She was tried for murder, but the jury acquitted her on self-defense. Eventually, she was forced to close what was called her "disorderly house."

An amusing folk tale about Poker Alice is how a nervous Sturgis banker loaned her several thousand dollars to make improvements on her sporting house and to enable her to travel to big cities for the recruitment of fresh prostitutes. She signed the note that she would repay the loan over several years time. When in a few months, she paid it all back with interest, the banker was overwhelmed with gratitude. Curious, he asked Alice if she had made a big killing at the poker table.

Chewing on her unlit cigar, she drawled, "No such luck. Happened like this. I was a-counting on the Grand Army of the Republic holding an Encampment at Sturgis, and I figgered on the Elks Convention. But I was damn surprised and happy with them men attending the Lutheran Conference." (substitute any Christian denomination)

Alice, always the good business woman, married a deserving man named Huckert for her third husband; the story goes that she owed him a thousand dollars and marriage was the easiest way to pay off the debt. He died shortly after their marriage, and she took back the name of Tubbs, her second husband and father of her children.

After a hard life of booze and gambling and sporting houses, Poker Alice had a gall bladder operation from which she never recovered. She let her last cigar go out and cashed in her chips, aged about 77. She is buried in St. Aloysius Cemetery in Sturgis. Engraved on her tombstone are these words: "Poker Alice—Alice Huckert Tubbs."

Poker Alice's one-time physician, Dr. Flora Stanford, is buried in a lost grave in Mount Moriah cemetery, Deadwood, SD.

Tourists often make pilgrimages to Poker Alice's final resting place, perhaps hoping while they bow their heads in reverent silence that they might hear a deep voice from the grave saying, "Place your bets, gentlemen."

DR. VALENTINE McGILLYCUDDY—UNSUNG HERO OF THE BLACK HILLS

A well-qualified candidate for the unsung hero title of the Black Hills is Dr. Valentine T. McGillycuddy, the first white man to climb Harney Peak to the actual summit.

McGillycuddy's accomplishments far exceeded mountain climbing; he was a physician, topographer, surveyor, Indian agent, member of the State Constitutional Convention, President of the South Dakota School of Mines in Rapid City, SD, and mayor of Rapid City. A controversial benevolent despot of the Pine Ridge Reservation, he was also a tolerant friend of Calamity Jane's, a powerful foe of Red Cloud's, and a compassionate doctor to the dying Crazy Horse.

Dr. Valentine T. McGillycuddy, the first white man to climb Harney Peak to the actual summit. He was also physician, topographer, surveyor, Indian agent, member of State Constitutional Convention, president of South Dakota School of Mines, and mayor of Rapid City. *Photo credit—South Dakota State Historical Society.*

Yet, McGillycuddy (sometimes spelled M'Gillycuddy) is relatively unknown compared to Wild Bill Hickok who ranks as the number one hero of the Black Hills even though he did nothing for them except to get himself assassinated in a Deadwood saloon and thus became a valuable commercial property. Such are the incongruities of fame and immortality when gunslingers and prostitutes are glorified as the pioneers who matter most in Black Hills history.

Valentine Trant O'Connell McGillycuddy was born to Irish immigrants in Racine, WI, in 1840 on Valentine's Day. At age twenty, he graduated from the Detroit Medical School which was connected to a Marine Hospital.

After practicing medicine for a year and teaching at the medical college, he got a job with the geodetic survey working on Lake Michigan. He had some background in engineering and liked working outdoors.

McGillycuddy was a skinny six-footer with incredible energy and capacity for hard work. When the lanky young man with the quick speech and crooked smile was 24, he accepted a position with the International Survey of the Boundary between the United States and Canada surveying the 49th parallel. He loved working in the wilderness even though herds of buffalo made the earth tremble so violently that the surveying instruments wavered erratically. McGillycuddy met his first Indian chief, Sitting Bull, the Hunkpapa medicine man, and presented him with a gift of tobacco.

When the field work was finished, the surveying party came down the Missouri River by boat, celebrated at Bismarck, then boarded the Northern Pacific train for Washington, D.C. and the long, tedious job of making boundary maps. On the train McGillycuddy met General George Custer who was also on his way to Washington to report on the success of the Black Hills Expedition of 1874. History does not record whether Custer showed the surveyor a gold nugget from French Creek.

Dr. V. T. McGillycuddy, topographer for the Jenney-Newton Expedition which explored the Black Hills in 1875. He is holding a sextant, an instrument for measuring altitudes. *Photo credit—South Dakota State Historical Society.*

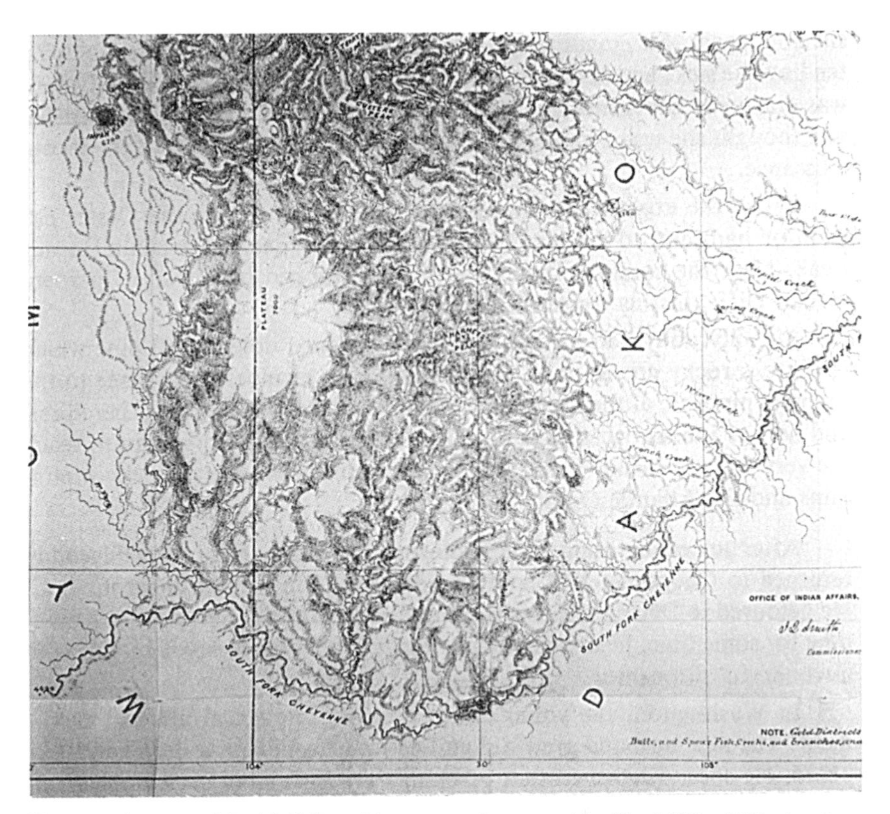

Close-up of section of the McGillycuddy topographic map of the Black Hills, 1875, showing south fork of the Cheyenne, French Creek, Spring Creek, Rapid Creek, and Harney Peak. The topographer traversed the district by numerous intersecting routes, sketching and observing the country as he went. *Photo credit—From* **The Mineral Wealth, Climate and Rainfall and Natural Resources of the Black Hills of Dakota** *by Walter P. Jenney, Fielder Collection, Devereaux Library, South Dakota School of Mines and Technology.*

But no matter. McGillycuddy had a look at the gold for himself the following year, in 1875, when he became topographer for the Jenney-Newton Expedition. The government assigned this group to check up on the glowing Custer reports of "gold at the roots of the grass" and to study the geology and topography of the Black Hills. Gold-seekers were already slipping into the Hills, and the Sioux were incensed at the continual invasions, whether by expeditions or by the prospectors.

At Fort Laramie, WY, where the Jenney-Newton Expedition was organized with the Dodge military command as escort, the young doctor met a girl named Calamity Jane who entertained him with fantastic stories of her life. Although she begged the officers for permission to accompany the all-male expedition, they refused. But Calamity Jane was determined and sneaked into the group dressed like a man. Every day when the officers recognized her, they banished her back to the fort, and every morning there she was again. She made herself useful mending clothes for the soldiers, tending the sick, and shooting deer for the mess. Obviously, Calamity Jane was crazy for adventure and had no morals, but McGillycuddy liked her and thought she was a valuable though unauthorized member of the reconnaissance.

When the expedition camped on French Creek where the Custer Expedition had camped the year before, a contingent decided to climb Harney Peak. Near the summit, the climbers were stopped by a wall of perpendicular cliffs, just as Custer had been.

McGillycuddy had an idea: the men chopped down a tall pine which fell into a rocky crevice, and they were able to clamber up the tree to the topmost pinnacle of the mountain. McGillycuddy's long legs got there first, and he was jubilant to realize that he must be the first white man to reach the very top of Harney Peak, the highest point between the Rocky Mountains and the Atlantic Ocean.

After an exhilerating time exploring the Black Hills, McGillycuddy returned to Cheyenne, WY, and boarded the train for Washington, D.C. He detoured to Detroit where he accomplished something he had been planning for some time: he married Fanny Hoyt, a pretty, blue-eyed blonde with a wonderful disposition.

In Washington, the young couple enjoyed the social life and excitement. The new husband grew a dignified moustache and a neat Van Dyke beard. He soon discovered that perching on a high stool drawing maps of his travels in the wilderness was not as thrilling as being there.

When General George Crook offered him a position as field surgeon with his army out west, McGillycuddy was overjoyed and Fanny urged him to go. Good sport that she was, Fanny went back to Detroit to wait for his return. She was learning quickly how to be a "good soldier" wife to her adventurous husband whom she always called "the Doctor."

Back to Cheyenne again where he met two well-known frontier characters, Wild Bill Hickok and Buffalo Bill Cody, who warned him not to start off alone in Indian country to find Crook's army.

During the late 1800's, when the increasing conflicts of the opposing red and white cultures held the center stage of American expansion, the paths of the main characters in the historic drama inevitably crossed. Their fates in real life were interwoven much as a novelist might structure a network of plots and sub-plots in a work of fiction. Increasingly, McGillycuddy's life was dominated by the entire spectrum of philosophies, attitudes, and actions involving Indian and white relationships. Could the problems ever be solved, he wondered.

Thus far, young McGillycuddy, who was rapidly becoming a professional frontiersman, had already met Sitting Bull, Custer, Calamity Jane,

Wild Bill Hickok, and Buffalo Bill Cody—a galaxy of star performers on the western scene. He had yet to meet Crazy Horse or Red Cloud.

Before McGillycuddy was reunited with Fanny, he became field surgeon for the casualties in the Battle of the Rosebud where a young warrior named Crazy Horse and his braves had out-maneuvered and out-fought Crook's armies; he had been in charge of the wounded train on the famous "horse-meat" march after the Battle of Slim Buttes north of the Black Hills when the men were forced to eat their starving horses to keep from starving themselves; he had been cursed by troopers for giving medical aid to a dying Sioux chief whom two squaws had carried into camp; he had danced the schottische with a boozy Calamity Jane at a wild Deadwood celebration for Crook's bedraggled armies.

Dr. V. T. McGillycuddy, Field Surgeon with General Crook's Third Cavalry. On hunger march after the Battle of Slim Buttes north of the Black Hills. Several troopers had cursed Dr. McGillycuddy for giving medical aid to a dying Sioux chief whom two squaws had carried into camp. *Photo credit—South Dakota State Historical Society.*

McGillycuddy's next assignment was assistant post surgeon at Fort Robinson, NE. The young couple were happy to be together again, and Fanny accompanied him on his rounds taking care of patients, both white and Indian. When he gave medical treatment to Crazy Horse's wife who had tuberculosis, he actually met Crazy Horse for the first time although the Doctor had observed the Chief's leadership at the Rosebud. The two became friends and had many conversations through interpreters. Crazy Horse related his version of the Battle of the Little Big Horn, not taking enough credit for himself in the stunning Sioux and Cheyenne victory.

In September, 1877, when Crazy Horse was tricked into surrendering at Fort Robinson, then bayoneted by a white guard, it was McGillycuddy who stayed with him, gave him morphine, and insisted that the Chief be allowed to die in the adjutant's office instead of in the guard house.

After a long death-watch by Crazy Horse's family and friends, the Doctor at last gave the Indian sign that Crazy Horse was dead. Touch the

Cloud, Crazy Horse's uncle who was seven feet tall, pointed to the body, "That is the lodge of Crazy Horse." Then the tall Indian drew himself up to his impressive height and pointed upward, "The Chief has gone above."

That night, Touch the Cloud slept outside McGillycuddy's door to guard him from harm; the white doctor who had taken care of the dying Crazy Horse was henceforth known as Tasunka Witko Kola, "Crazy Horse's friend." That was McGillycuddy's first Indian name. He would acquire another.

The Indian victories over the best military forces the white could muster availed them nothing. After the Custer battle, the hostiles scattered; Sitting Bull eventually fled to Canada, and the Sioux supremacy of the plains was broken. The agency Indians signed away the Black Hills over which so much blood had been spilled. During 1877-1878, the United States armies were rounding up bands of Indians to confine them to miserable reservations where they were often starved and threatened into submission.

During this period on the frontier, McGillycuddy was preparing to go to Omaha, NE, to take the examination to become a regular army surgeon. But he became so incensed by the terrible conditions at Fort Robinson that he went to Washington instead to report to the authorities on the inhuman treatment of Indians.

Carl Schurz, the Secretary of the Interior, asked to meet this fiery young doctor from the border country who was brave enough to tell the truth about injustices.

McGillycuddy asked many questions of Schurz: Now that the Indians were subjugated, what were the government's plans on helping them adjust to a new life? Should they be treated worse than animals and kept under constant military surveillance? Should the military and the Indian agents be allowed to exploit them and fill their own pockets with government moneys?

Secretary Schurz was greatly impressed with the concern of the young doctor and with his ideas on how to handle the new wards of the nation.

Eventually, Dr. Valentine T. McGillycuddy was offered the agent's job at Pine Ridge Reservation, Indian Territory in Dakota. With Fanny's blessing, he accepted. She had earned a good reputation, "a wife who goes everywhere with her husband."

Challenging was the word. In 1879, Pine Ridge (formerly the Red Cloud Agency) was the largest reservation in the country at the time, 4,000 square miles, four times as large as Rhode Island, ranging along the border between Dakota and Nebraska, 150 miles from the nearest railroad, and located on the god-forsaken plains in the long shadow of the Black Hills. And 8,000 Indians had been herded there, many of the braves fresh from the warpath.

Dr. Valentine T. McGillycuddy was a self-confident young man of thirty with hypnotic eyes and an authoritative manner that commanded respect. He had definite ideas on how best to deal with the dejected and angry Indians, who had been stripped of their nomadic life style, their weapons, and most of their horses. They huddled in huts and ragged tents crowding around the agency, dreaming of past glories and dreading their future. There was nothing to look forward to except their rations—if they got them.

The first thing McGillycuddy did was to hold a big council with all the Indians. Red Cloud, the arrogant reigning chief, presided and passed the peace pipe to the new agent, whom the Indians called "Father."

Red Cloud, powerful chief of the Oglala Sioux, in 1868 forced the U.S. government to abandon the forts on the Bozeman Trail in Montana. Red Cloud and McGillycuddy maintained a long feud during McGillycuddy's seven years as agent at Pine Ridge Reservation 100 miles southeast of Rapid City. *Photo credit—South Dakota State Historical Society. Photo by Bell.*

Through an interpreter, Red Cloud spoke: "I am Red Cloud, the great Chief of the Oglalas. When Red Cloud speaks, everyone listens. I have not asked you white men to come here." However, he did encourage the assemblage to listen to what the young man had to say.

McGillycuddy unrolled a map, and through an interpreter, he explained the extent of the Pine Ridge territory which belonged to the Indians. He pointed out that there was plenty of room for the Indians to spread out instead of living so close to the agency and promised that those who lived the farthest away would receive more rations. He suggested that there was enough land for all the men to begin farming or ranching and to learn to live independently.

Red Cloud, 57 years old, was as tall as the "Father" and almost twice his age. In response to the "Father," Red Cloud delivered his famous pronoucement, "Father, the Great Spirit did not make us to work. He made us to hunt and fish. . . . The white man can work if he wants to but the Great Spirit did not make us to work. The white man owes us a living for the lands he has taken from us."

During this get-acquainted parley, the new agent said one thing at least that the Indians liked: he promised to get rid of the army troops stationed on the reservation. He also said he was going to organize an Indian police force to handle their own problems. Everyone approved of that plan—except Red Cloud, who knew his power as head chief was being threatened.

Red Cloud was indeed a powerful chief who had led a fierce war against the white man's expansion in 1866-1868. Incredibly, he had forced the government to close the hated Bozeman trail in Montana and abandon three forts. Red Cloud had many followers who thought as he did and wanted no part of becoming an imitation white man even though their old life was gone forever.

Fortunately for McGillycuddy, there was another and larger faction at Pine Ridge led by Young Man Afraid (Young Man of Whose Horse They Are Afraid) who was at least willing to try the alien ways the "Father" suggested.

The position of the agent was that of an absolute dictator. The territorial government of Dakota had no jurisdiction over the Indian land, and the agent was responsible, through the Indian Bureau, only to the "Great Father" in Washington.

McGillycuddy started immediately to implement his long-range program. Upon Young Man Afraid's recommendation, he appointed a strapping Indian who had a reputation for bravery in battle to head the Indian police of fifty carefully selected young braves. His name was Sword (Man Who Carries the Sword), and he and the agent developed a good working relationship. The agent outfitted them with old Civil War uniforms and rifles which they were cautioned not to use except in dire circumstances. The Indian Police became a proud, effective organization and followed the "Father's" orders, often infringing on tribal customs while enforcing the law and agency rules for reservation life.

The Indian Police also disciplined the white men who were horse thieves and illegal liquor dealers hanging around the reservation. It was McGillycuddy's order that brought about the arrest of Lame Johnny, the notorious horse thief who had stolen horses from Pine Ridge.

This benevolent despot signed all his orders "McGillycuddy—Agent." Years later, this was the title of a biography written by Julia, his second wife, which details his experiences at Pine Ridge and his happy marriage with Fanny.

McGillycuddy was especially proud to build a boarding school for Indian children with large schoolrooms and small clean beds. The kitchen range could bake 100 loaves of bread at a time. The bathrooms were equipped with bathtubs and hot and cold water.

On the opening day everything was in perfect readiness for the 200 frightened children who were brought in. The white teachers had an efficient assembly line set up in the bathrooms and laundry room. First, the teachers cut off each child's long, lice-covered braids, then came the bath,

A Day School at Pine Ridge Reservation. On the opening day of McGillycuddy's first boarding school for Indians, the white teachers cut each child's long braids. This terrified the children and their parents who rushed madly out of the brand new schoolhouse, screaming "They are cutting the hair!" *Photo credit—South Dakota State Historical Society.*

followed by a head-washing. Hundreds of squaws and bucks had gathered suspiciously at the strange new building to see what was going on, and many adults and children were trying to peer through the windows. One child peeping through a window saw the white lady wielding big shears on his friend; the window-peeper yelled in fright: "They are cutting the hair!" That cry started a mass exodus. The children ran out of the building; the mothers and fathers followed in a mad flight as though pursued by an evil spirit. Even the commands of the "Father" could not stop the fleeing throng. The excited teachers felt bad that their first attempt at civilizing the Sioux had not been successful. But the students came back; including Red Cloud's daughter; and school on the reservation began, much to "Father's" satisfaction.

Fanny kept busy in her garden and tended a flock of chickens and turkeys, while Louise, the mulatto maid, did the cooking and housework. The Indians called Fanny "Mother" and followed her around as did the pet buffalo calves and sand-hill crane they had given her.

Visitors were always amazed at the McGillycuddy home with a Brussels carpet on the floor and a coffin-shaped music box that played six numbers, including "I Dreamt I Dwelt in Marble Halls." The Doctor was fond of music, everything from classical to the tom-tom of an Indian drum. In the bedroom, the bed was suspended from the ceiling by huge iron hooks and decorated lavishly with satin and lace. Their house was definitely a contrast to the bleak surroundings.

McGillycuddy's life at Pine Ridge did not run smoothly; there were too many problems to solve and too many obstacles to overcome before the agent's plans for teaching the Indians how to work according to the white man's standards could be realized. Still there was remarkable progress. Many Indians worked hard learning how to build and live in houses, how to cultivate the field, how to raise cattle, how to freight the agency supplies.

Tall McGillycuddy with Pine Ridge Indians. He insisted that the Indians learn how to work according to white man's standards. Red Cloud insisted that Indians were not made to work but to hunt and fish. *Photo credit—South Dakota State Historical Society.*

Red Cloud opposed the agent every step of the way, sending endless complaints to Washington, accusing him of stealing rations and of commiting every conceivable crime. Red Cloud accused the agent of exceeding his authority—and he undoubtedly did. The agent had himself appointed United States Court Commissioner which empowered him to hold jurisdiction over accused criminals on the reservation. An unpopular order signed "McGillycuddy—Agent" was banning unauthorized guns for both races; and he had fifty loyal Indian police to back him up.

The notorious Indian Ring encouraged Red Cloud in his attacks against McGillycuddy. The Indian Ring was a group of politicians who made vast sums from swindling both the government and the Indians out of their appropriations and agency supplies on many reservations.

Red Cloud, aided and abetted by the Indian Ring, went by train to Washington at least fifteen times, sometimes wearing white men's clothes, to bring charges against the Pine Ridge agent. One time the agent, along with Young Man Afraid, had to testify in his own defense. No one ever proved that McGillycuddy was anything except scrupulously honest, dictatorial, and high-handed. In spite of negative publicity, Pine Ridge maintained its reputation as being a well-run and progressive agency with a

"Father" who was always supremely confident that he knew what was best for his children.

Apparently both McGillycuddy and Red Cloud secretly enjoyed their long-standing feud. Sometimes Red Cloud would come to the agency office and the two would have a friendly chat, each having learned to converse some in the other's language. Perhaps they discussed Red Cloud's nice house which at first he refused to live in. On these occasions, they would share a drink together from the doctor's whiskey bottle for medicinal purposes which had a special lock on it. Of course, drinking anywhere else on the reservation was illegal.

Despite a few peaceful interludes, the show-down between the two adversaries eventually came.

Red Cloud, plotting a rebellion, had been sending threats to the agent that he and his wife must leave in three days or they would be killed. The agent called a council of chiefs and sent orders for Red Cloud to appear. When he didn't come, the agent sent the Indian Police to persuade the old painted warrior.

In the council room, McGillycuddy read a telegram from President Rutherford B. Hayes, the "Great Father" in Washington, that the agent had the authority to arrest Red Cloud if necessary. The agent said: "Red Cloud, stand up!" He repeated the words until the chief did as he was ordered. It was a dramatic moment with the two towering personalities staring into each other's eyes, the room packed with friends and enemies of both men, and the Indian police armed with carbines in the center of the room.

The agent said: "Red Cloud, you have been mean and insolent. You have defied your agent and insulted the Great Father. You are no longer fit to be chief. Therefore, I remove you as chief. You are no longer head chief of the Oglalas."

According to Julia McGillycuddy, Red Cloud cried out in rage and sprang toward the agent with a knife, but a warrior named Little Wound stopped Red Cloud, saving McGillycuddy's life and probably preventing a bloody battle.

The audience yelled and shouted in both consternation and approval at the climax of this power struggle. McGillycuddy raised his hand and said, "The Great Father whose words I speak is to be listened to and not argued with. Clear the council room."

The howling mob left the room, followed by the police. Red Cloud's power was broken, and he never again caused serious trouble for the agent.

After Grover Cleveland, a Democrat, became the "Great Father" in 1885, the spoils system went into effect. Eventually, government officials ordered McGillycuddy to get rid of his efficient clerk and to accept a newly appointed Democrat as clerk at Pine Ridge.

The agent, who said he was tired of "government buncome and red tape" refused to comply with the order, knowing he would be dismissed. And he was. Hundreds of people, both red and white, protested his dismissal, attesting to his "effective, intelligent and just administation."

With conflicting feelings, the McGillycuddys, in 1886, left Pine Ridge and their exciting life with the Indians which had been both rewarding and frustrating and sometimes dangerous. Escorted by the Indian police, they rode in a wagon pulled by oxen over the road he himself had ordered built. The wagon train was loaded with their household possessions, and trailing along behind were two buffalo who also moved to Rapid City, SD, about 100 miles northwest of the agency.

Dr. V. T. McGillycuddy and Fanny, his beloved first wife. They were childless. She had the reputation for being a wife who went everywhere with her husband. Fanny always called him "the Doctor." *Photo credit—Clara Lobdell.*

In Rapid City, the McGillycuddys built a large house with fancy Victorian architecture, a red sandstone base topped with an olive-green roof. The Doctor said he liked color; he was used to painted Indians and the red sandstone harmonized with the landscape and matched the color of the race track surrounding the Black Hills.

Dr. McGillycuddy and dog in front of the ornate Victorian house he and Fanny built in Rapid City —to the amazement of the natives. The base was red sandstone and the top was olive green. The Doctor said he liked color. *Photo credit—Minnelusa Historical Museum, Rapid City.*

Dr. McGillycuddy said his new life was so different from his agency life that he felt like a different person. He became president of the Lakota Bank; the Governor appointed him Surgeon-General. He was also elected to the state constitutional convention; and in that capacity served on a joint committee to settle the affairs of North and South Dakota when they became states in 1889. He also found time to organize a hydroelectric power company in Rapid City and undertook supervision of its construction which enabled him to work outside again and to experiment with static electricity.

ARTHUR C. MELLETTE,

Governor of the Territory of Dakota.

To all to whom these Presents shall come, Greeting:

KNOW YE, That reposing special trust and confidence in the PATRIOTISM AND ABILITY OF V. T. McGillycuddy I, Arthur C. Mellette, Governor of the Territory of Dakota, by virtue of the authority vested in me by the laws of said Territory do hereby APPOINT AND COMMISSION HIM, the said V. T. McGillycuddy Surgeon General on the Staff of Commander in Chief with rank of Colonel, and do authorize, empower and require him to EXECUTE AND FULFILL the duties of said office, with all the rights, authorities, privileges and emoluments thereunto appertaining during the pleasure of the Governor.

In Witness Whereof, I have hereunto set my hand and caused to be affixed the Great Seal of the Territory of Dakota, the day of July in the year of our Lord, one thousand eight hundred and eighty-nine.

BY THE GOVERNOR.

Secretary of Dakota Territory

GOVERNOR.

Certificate signed by Arthur C. Mellette, Governor of Dakota Territory in 1889, appointing "V. T. McGillycuddy Surgeon General on the Staff of Commander in Chief with rank of Colonel." Mellette, who was both Governor of Dakota Territory and of the new state of South Dakota in 1889, asked ex-agent McGillycuddy to visit Pine Ridge and report on the Ghost Dance and Messiah Craze. *Photo credit—Document on loan from Minnelusa Historical Museum to Devereaux Library, South Dakota School of Mines and Technology.*

In 1890, after McGillycuddy had been away from Pine Ridge for four years, the Indians throughout the west became involved in the Messiah Craze and the Ghost Dance which they believed would bring back the buffalo, make the white men disappear, and allow the Indians to resume their old free life. They awaited the appearance of the Messiah to liberate them from their unhappy existence on reservations.

The new agent at Pine Ridge, whom his charges called "Man Afraid of Indians" feared the Ghost Dancers on the reservation were preparing for an

The Indians in camp at Pine Ridge. In 1890, the Indians throughout the west became involved in the Ghost Dance and Messiah Craze which they believed would bring back the buffalo, make the white man disappear, and allow Indians to resume their old free life. Ex-agent McGillycuddy saw no reason to fear the Ghost Dance—unlike many inexperienced white leaders. *Photo credit—South Dakota State Historical Society.*

uprising. He requested army troops to be stationed at the agency to protect him and to prevent trouble.

Governor Arthur Mellette asked ex-agent McGillycuddy to go to Pine Ridge and assess the situation.

When McGillycuddy arrived at Pine Ridge, the Indians requested permission from the new agent for their old "Father" to council with them. The former agent explained at the meeting that he no longer had any authority at Pine Ridge and could make no promises but that he would try to help them any way he could. The Indians did not understand why the soldiers were there—he had never had any.

At last, Red Cloud, his old adversary, rose to his feet. He pointed to McGillycuddy: "That is Wasicu Wakan. For seven winters he was our Father. He said to me, 'Some day you will say that my way was best for the Indian.' I will tell him now that he spoke the truth. He was a young man with an old man's head on his shoulders and he never sent for soldiers." Red Cloud explained that he had not wanted McGillycuddy to come to the agency and that there had been much bad feeling between them.

McGillycuddy was pleased that Red Cloud had mellowed and had actually paid him a compliment.

The ex-agent warned the military officers and the inexperienced agent not to ban the ghost dance and that there was no harm in letting the Indians practice their new religion. When no Messiah appeared as expected, he felt sure the frenzy would pass. Further, he strongly recommended that the troops leave Pine Ridge and remove the two howitzer cannons which were aimed at the Indian camp. They could only cause trouble.

As it turned out, McGillycuddy was right.

The Indians wanted to council with him again, but the new authorities would not allow it. Sadly, the ex-agent returned to Rapid City worrying about what could happen.

In the meantime, Sitting Bull up at Standing Rock reservation had been arrested for ghost dancing and had been shot down while resisting arrest. The rest of Sitting Bull's band under Big Foot fled through winter snows to the Badlands where they planned to continue ghost dancing. However, they decided to continue their long march on to Pine Ridge reservation. Soldiers intercepted the Indians; and under a flag of truce, Big Foot surrendered. The Indians, as instructed by the military, set up camp under guard at Wounded Knee.

The next day, on December 29, 1890, the Seventh Cavalry joined the troops guarding Big Foot and placed four artillery pieces on a hill overlooking the encampment. The soldiers ordered the Indians to surrender their weapons. While the soldiers were searching the tepees, a shot rang out, a shot that no one ever knew who had fired. Then the shooting began. Some of the soldiers in the Seventh Cavalry yelled, "Remember Custer and the Little Big Horn!" and mowed down men, women, and children until at least 150 Sioux people and 31 soldiers lay dead in the blood-stained snow.

The wounded from both sides were taken to Pine Ridge. Because of the bad weather, the frozen bodies of the Indian dead were not buried for several days. Then they were all dumped into big trenches.

When McGillycuddy heard about the massacre, he immediately rode out to Pine Ridge. He was sickened to hear of the bloodshed and the un-

After the Battle of Wounded Knee, December, 1890. The Seventh Cavalry mowed down 150 Indian men, women and children. Then the frozen bodies were all dumped into huge trenches. State Historian Doane Robinson believed "that had Dr. McGillycuddy been at the helm there would have been no bloodshed, no soldiers, and the Messiah War would have been wholly averted." *Photo credit—South Dakota State Historical Society.*

necessary tragedy. The Doctor went to the Episcopal church where 33 Indians were willing to accept the services of a doctor. While working to save lives with his skillful hands and his medical kit, he kept looking for old Indian friends. He found American Horse who explained to those who did not know the Doctor: "This is Wasicu Wakan who was our 'Father.' "

After the debacle, McGillycuddy was asked many times who was responsible for the Wounded Knee Massacre or what was called the Messiah War. His answer was: "Whoever fired the first shot. After that, nothing short of the Almighty could have stopped the killing."

Doane Robinson, State Historian of South Dakota, later wrote: "It may be safely assumed that had Dr. McGillycuddy been at the helm there would have been no bloodshed, no soldiers, and the Messiah war would have been wholly averted."

During their life in Rapid City, the McGillycuddys enjoyed living in their picturesque house and taking part in the social life and the development of Rapid City. Indians from Pine Ridge frequently visited them and kept them informed of what was going on at the reservation.

Throughout his life, McGillycuddy held many responsible positions. He was President of the South Dakota School of Mines at Rapid City from

STATE OF SOUTH DAKOTA.

BOARD OF REGENTS. Department of Education.

CERTIFICATE OF APPOINTMENT.

KNOW YE, That reposing special trust and confidence in the integrity and ability of V. T. McGillycuddy

The Regents of Education, of the State of South Dakota, by virtue of authority vested in them do hereby appoint the said [illegible] member of the Board of Trustees of the School of Mines for the term ending March 26th 1898 [illegible] with authority to execute and fulfill the duties of said office with all the rights and privileges thereunto appertaining.

In Witness, The Regents of Education have caused these presents to be signed by their President, and attested by their Secretary, this [illegible] day of [illegible] 189[illegible]

[illegible] Secretary [illegible] President

The Certificate of Appointment from the Board of Regents, Department of Education of State of South Dakota to V. T. McGillycuddy appointing him on the Board of Trustees for the School of Mines, 1895. McGillycuddy was President of the School of Mines from 1892-1897 when the college expanded and added much-needed engineering equipment. *Photo credit —Copy of document on long-term loan from Minnelusa Historical Museum to Devereaux Library, South Dakota School of Mines and Technology.*

1892-1897, and under his leadership the school expanded and added much-needed engineering equipment. He was elected Mayor of Rapid City in 1897 and served for two years.

The life of the McGillycuddys in Rapid City was eventful if not exciting, and they became mildly affluent, at least financially better off than when they had lived on an Indian agent's salary of $2,500 a year.

Fanny gained weight alarmingly and after she had a stroke, the Doctor nursed her back to comparative health. Then she had a second stroke and died in 1897.

After Fanny's death, the Doctor was lonely and bereft. It was no fun living in the big house without her. He was only 47 years old when he became a widower. He decided to leave all the memories and move to San Francisco.

In California, he eventually married Julia Blanchard, the daughter of a licensed trader who had grown up at Pine Ridge. They had a daughter named Valentine.

During World War I, Dr. McGillycuddy enlisted as a surgeon offering to go anywhere his services might be needed. Even though the authorities thought he was too old for active service, the 68-year-old doctor traveled to many western mining towns and Alaska to fight the influenza epidemic with all the vigor he had always mustered to combat enemies wherever he found them.

Dr. V. T. McGillycuddy in his mature years. After his first wife Fanny died in 1897 he moved to California. Here he married Julia Blanchard whom he had known as a little girl at Pine Ridge. She wrote a colorful biography, **McGillycuddy—Agent**. They had one daughter named Valentine. *Photo credit—South Dakota State Historical Society.*

His second wife Julia in the preface to her biography of **McGillycuddy—Agent** explains how she gathered information from his archives and from listening to him tell the story of his life, as she had requested him to do. He rejected a fictionized account and did not want her to deviate from the facts. He ordered her to write exact history, which she has done as objectively as a loving wife can, in writing about her husband. Her accounts of the events in his life are, in general, supported by historical accounts. She confessed that when she was a little girl, she had asked Fanny if she thought the Doctor would marry her when Fanny died. And he did—even though Julia was very much younger than he.

Julia reported that in his last years when McGillycuddy reviewed his life, that of all his varied experiences, Pine Ridge was uppermost in his mind. He understood more clearly how the Indians felt about being forced to learn the white man's ways of work, a poor substitute for hunting buffalo and fishing as Red Cloud had said the Indians were born to do. He regretted how arbitrarily he had treated Red Cloud, and he believed that under different circumstances and without the "influence of squaw men, the Indian Ring, and Eastern sentimentalists" that the two strong-willed leaders could have been friends.

Dr. Valentine T. McGillycuddy died at age 90 in San Francisco. The next day, June 7, 1939, the flag at Pine Ridge, SD, flew at half mast. Even those Indians who hadn't known him had heard the legend.

On October 17, 1940, sixty-five years and eighty days from the day the young topographer was the first white man to set foot on Harney Peak, his ashes were buried on this highest peak overlooking the panorama of the Black Hills and the high plains sweeping down to Pine Ridge.

Trant McGillycuddy of Rapid City, a nephew of the famous pioneer, carried the ashes up the rugged trail, accompanied by Rapid City civic leaders, old friends, historians, United States Forest Service officials, and an American Legion Color Guard.

At the ceremonies on Harney Peak, Thomas Lone Eagle, speaking Lakota, paid tribute to a man he said was one of the greatest friends the Sioux ever had.

Then a small box with the ashes was mortared into the stone stairway of the lookout tower. On the brass plate is this inscription:

Valentine T. McGillycuddy—Wasicu Wakan*
1849-1939

*Holy White Man

THE END

Aerial view of Harney Peak and the Needles. McGillycuddy's ashes are buried in the lookout tower on Harney Peak which he was the first white man to climb. The high plains in the distance sweep down to Pine Ridge. *Photo credit—Rushmore Photo.*

BIBLIOGRAPHY

Andreas, A. T. **Andreas' Historical Atlas of Dakota.** Chicago: Donnelly & Sons, 1884.

Andrist, Ralph K. **The Long Death** The Last Days of the Plains Indians. New York: The Macmillan Company, 1964.

Aplan, James O. "In Search of the Poet Scout," (unpublished). Aplan Collection, Midland, South Dakota.

Belle Fourche, South Dakota, **Belle Fourche Bee,** Files.

Bennett, Estelline. **Old Deadwood Days.** New York: Charles Scribner's Sons, 1935.

Bonham, Barbara. **The Battle of Wounded Knee.** Chicago: Reilly & Lee Books, a Division of the Henry Regnery Company, 1970.

Borglum, Lincoln. **My Father's Mountain.** Rapid City, SD: Fenwyn Press, 1966.

Bourke, John. **On the Border With Crook.** New York: Charles Scribner's Sons, 1891.

Bronson, William and Watkins, T. H. **Homestake The Centennial History of America's Greatest Gold Mine,** San Fancisco: Homestake Mining Company, 1977.

Brown, Dee. **Bury My Heart at Wounded Knee.** New York: Holt, Rinehart & Winston, 1971.

Brown, Dee. **The Gentle Tamers.** Lincoln: University of Nebraska Press, 1958.

Brown, Jesse, and A. M. Willard. **The Black Hills Trails.** Rapid City: Rapid City Journal Company, 1924.

Brown, Joseph Epes. **The Sacred Pipe—Black Elk's Account of the Seven Rites of the Oglala Sioux.** Norman: University of Oklahoma Press, 1953.

Brown, Mable, ed. "A Dark Day at Cambria," **Bits and Pieces,** IV ( ), Newcastle, Wyoming.

Brown, Mable, ed. "Bits About Old Cambria," **Bits and Pieces,** I (Sept. 1965), Newcastle, Wyoming.

Canary, Martha Jane. **Life and Adventures of Calamity Jane** by Herself. Privately printed, about 1896.

Case, Lee. **Lee's Official Guide Book to the Black Hills and the Badlands.** Sturgis, SD: The Black Hills and Badlands Association, 1952.

Case, Leland D. **Preacher Smith—Martyr.** Mitchell, SD: Friends of the Middle Border, 1929.

Casey, Robert J. **The Black Hills and Their Incredible Characters.** New York: The Bobbs-Merrill Company, 1949.

Catlin, George. **Letters and Notes on the North American Indians.** New York: Clarkston N. Potter, Inc., 1975.

Clark, Badger. **Sun and Saddle Leather.** Boston: The Gorham Press, 1922.

Clark, Badger. **When Hot Springs Was a Pup.** Hermosa, SD: Lame Johnny Press, 1976.

Clark, Ella E. **Indian Legends from the Northern Rockies.** Norman: University of Oklahoma Press, 1966.

Clowser, Don. **Deadwood—The Historic City.** Rapid City: Fenwyn Press Books, 1969.

Conn, Herb and Jan. **The Jewel Cave Adventure.** Teaneck, N.J.: Zephyrus Press, 1977.

Crawford, Captain Jack. **The Poet Scout.** New York: Funk and Wagnalls, 1886.

Curley, Edwin. **Curley's Guide to the Black Hills.** Facsimile, Mitchell, SD: Dakota Wesleyan Press, 1973.

Custer, Elizabeth B. **Boots and Saddles.** New York: Harper & Row, 1885.

Custer, Elizabeth B. **Following the Guidon.** New York: Harper & Brothers, 1890.

Custer, General George A. **My Life on the Plains.** Lincoln: University of Nebraska Press, 1971.

Deadwood, South Dakota, **Black Hills Daily Times,** Files.

Deadwood, South Dakota, **Black Hills Pioneer,** Files.

Deadwood, South Dakota, **Deadwood Pioneer-Times,** Files.

Deloria, Ella C. **Speaking of Indians.** Vermillion, SD: Dakota Press, 1979.

DeWall, Robb, ed. **Crazy Horse—Storytelling in Stone.** Crazy Horse: The Black Hills, South Dakota. (no date)

Dodge, Richard Irving. **The Black Hills.** Minneapolis: Ross & Haines, 1965.

DuFran, Dora. **Low Down on Calamity Jane.** Helen Rezatto, ed. Stickney, SD: Argus Printers, 1981.

Eastman, Mary. **Dacotah or Life and Legends of the Sioux Around Fort Snelling.** Minneapolis: Ross & Haines, 1962.

Fall River County History. Book Committee, Fall River County Historical Society, Fall River, SD.

Fielder, Mildred. **Deadwood Dick.** Lead, SD: Bonanza Trails, 1974.

Fielder, Mildred. **A Guide to Black Hills Ghost Mines.** Aberdeen, SD: North Plains Press, 1972.

Fielder, Mildred. **Poker Alice.** Deadwood, SD: Centennial Distributors, 1978.

Fielder, Mildred. **Silver is the Fortune.** Aberdeen, SD: North Plains Press, 1978.

Fielder, Mildred. **Sioux Indian Leaders.** Seattle: Superior Publishing Company, 1975.

Fite, Gilbert. **Mount Rushmore.** Norman: University of Oklahoma Press, 1952.

Fite, Gilbert. **Peter Norbeck: Prairie Statesman.** Columbia: University of Missouri, 1948.

Froiland, Sven G. **Natural History of the Black Hills.** Sioux Falls, SD: Augustana College.

Gage, William C. Illustrated Guide to the Black Hills and Picturesque **Souvenir of Hot Springs, South Dakota.** Published by Hot Springs Commercial Club, 1901. Published by Evans Plunge, 1978.

Galvin, Seth. Memoirs (unpublished), Galena, South Dakota.

Goodson, Rose Mary. **The Rushmore Story—Why the Mountain Memorial.** Stickney, SD: Argus Printers, 1979.

Graham, W. A. ed. **The Custer Myth.** Harrisburg, PA: Bonanza Books, The Telegraph Press, 1953.

Grinnell, George Bird. **By Cheyenne Campfires.** London and New Haven: Yale University Press, 1926.

Hagedorn, Hermann, ed. **The Theodore Roosevelt Treasury**—A Self-Portrait from His Writings. New York: G. P. Putnam's Sons, 1957.

Hasselstrom, Linda. "On the Trail of Lame Johnny," **Black Hills Monthly,** June, 1981.

Heiderstadt, Dorothy. **Frontier Leaders and Pioneers.** New York: David McKay, 1962.

Holiday Greetings from Rapid City, South Dakota in the Black Hills. Rapid City: Rapid City Journal, 1919-1920.

Holley, Frances Chamberlain. **Once Their Home.** Chicago: Donahue and Hennery, 1892.

Hot Springs, South Dakota, **Hot Springs Star,** Files.

Hughes, Richard B. **Pioneer Years in the Black Hills.** Glendale, CA: Arthur H. Clark Company, 1957.

Hunt, N. Jane, ed. **Brevet's South Dakota Historical Markers.** Sioux Falls, SD: Brevet Press, 1974.

Hyde, George E. **A Sioux Chronicle.** Norman: University of Oklahoma Press, 1956.

Hyde, George E. **Spotted Tail's Folk**—A History of the Brule Sioux. Norman: University of Oklahoma Press, 1961.

Jackson, Donald. **Custer's Gold.** Lincoln: University of Nebraska Press, by Yale University, 1966.

Jennewein, J. Leonard. **Black Hills Book Trails.** Huron, SD: Dakota Books, 1953.

Jennewein, J. Leonard. **Calamity Jane of the Western Trails.** Huron, SD: Dakota Books, 1953.

Jewel Cave National Monument, South Dakota, National Park Service, U.S. Department of Interior, 1981.

Judd, Mary Catherine. **Wigwam Stories** Told by North American Indians. Boston: Ginn & Company, Athenaem Press, 1904.

Judson, Katherine Berry, **Myths and Legends of the Great Plains.** Chicago: A. C. McClurg & Company, 1913.

Kellar, Kenneth. **Seth Bullock—Frontier Marshal.** Aberdeen, SD: North Plains Press, 1972.

Kingsbury, George. **History of Dakota Territory.** IV, Chicago: S. J. Clark Company, 1915.

Klock, Irma. **All Roads Lead to Deadwood.** Aberdeen, SD: North Plains Press, 1979.

Klock, Irma. **Black Hills Outlaws, Lawmen and Others.** Deadwood, SD: Dakota Graphics, 1981.

Klock, Irma. **Black Hills Ladies: The Frail and the Fair.** Deadwood, SD: Dakota Graphics, 1980.

Klock, Irma. **Yesterday's Gold Camps and Mines in the Northern Black Hills.** Lead, SD: Seaton Publishing Company, 1975.

Krause, Herbert, and Gary D. Olson. **Custer's Prelude to Glory.** Sioux Falls, SD: Brevet Press, 1974.

LaPointe, James. **Legends of the Lakota.** San Francisco: The Indian Historian Press, 1976.

Lee, Bob, ed. **Gold—Gals—Guns—Guts.** Deadwood-Lead '76 Centennial Inc., 1976.

Leedy, Carl. **Golden Days of the Black Hills.** Rapid City, SD: Holmgrens, Inc., 1967.

Linde, Martha. **Rushmore's Golden Valleys.** Custer, SD, 1976.

Lobdell, Clara B. "His Wife Goes Everywhere With Him," (unpublished paper), Rapid City, South Dakota.

McClintock, John S. **Pioneer Days in the Black Hills.** New York: J. J. Little & Ives, 1939.

McGillycuddy, Julia. **McGillycuddy—Agent.** Stanford, CA: Stanford University Press, 1941.

McLaughlin, James. **My Friend the Indian.** Boston & New York: Houghton-Mifflin, Riverside Press, Cambridge, 1910.

Margret, Helen. **Father DeSmet.** Milwaukee: Bruce Publishing Company, 1940.

Marquis, Thomas B. **Cheyenne and Sioux—The Reminiscences of Four Indians and a White Soldier.** Monograph No. 3. Stockton, CA: University of Pacific, Pacific Center for Western Historical Studies, 1973.

Mattison, Ray H. **Devils Tower National Monument—A History.** Published by Devils Tower National History Association, 1973.

Memorial Biographical Record, The Black Hills Region. Chicago: George A. Ogle & Company, 1889.

Minnelusa Museum, Rapid City, South Dakota. C. Irwin Leedy Historical Collection.

Mooney, James. **The Ghost-Dance Religion.** Phoenix Books, Chicago: University of Chicago Press, 1965.

Morgan, Dale. **Jedediah Smith.** Indianapolis—New York: Bobbs-Merrill Company, 1953.

Mount Rushmore National Memorial. Published by Mount Rushmore National Memorial Society of the Black Hills. (no date)

Neihardt, John G. **Black Elk Speaks.** New York: Pocket Books, 1959.

Nelson, Bruce. **Land of the Dacotahs.** Minneapolis: University of Minnesota Press, 1946.

Newton, Henry and Walter P. Jenney. **Report on the Geology and Resources of the Black Hills of Dakota.** Washington, D.C.: Government Printing Office, 1888.

Odell, Thomas E. **Mato Paha—The Story of Bear Butte.** Ann Arbor, MI: Edwards Brothers, Inc. Lithoprinters, 1942.

O'Harra, Cleophas C. **Custer Expedition Number, The Black Hills Engineer.** Rapid City: South Dakota School of Mines, November, 1929.

O'Harra, Cleophas C. and Joseph P. Connolly. **The Geology, Mineralogy, and Scenic Features of Custer State Park, South Dakota.** Bulletin No. 14, Departments of Geology and Mineralogy. Rapid City: South Dakota School of Mines, 1926.

O'Harra, Cleophas C. **O'Harra's Handbook of the Black Hills.** Rapid City, SD: Black Hills Handbook Company, 1913.

Olson, James C. **Red Cloud and the Sioux Problem.** Lincoln: University of Nebraska Press, 1965.

One Feather, Vivian, Principal Investigator Research Project, 1972. Oglala Sioux Culture Center, Red Cloud Indian School, Inc. Pine Ridge, SD, in cooperation with Black Hills State College, Spearfish, SD.

Owen, Luella Agnes. **Cave Regions of the Ozarks and Black Hills.** Cincinnati: Editor Publishing Company, 1898.

Paige, Harry W. **Songs of the Teton Sioux.** Los Angeles: Westernlore Press, 1970.

Parker, Watson. **Deadwood The Golden Years.** Lincoln: University of Nebraska Press, 1981.

Parker, Watson and Hugh K. Lambert. **Black Hills Ghost Towns.** Sage Books, Chicago: The Swallow Press, 1974.

Parker, Watson. **Gold in the Black Hills.** Norman: University of Oklahoma Press, 1966.

Peattie, Roderick, ed. **The Black Hills.** New York: Vanguard Press, 1952.

Peirce, Ellis T. "Odd Characters and Incidents of the Black Hills," **History of South Dakota,** I: Chapter LXXXV. Aberdeen, SD: B. F. Bowen Company, 1904.

Penfield, Thomas. **Treasure Guide Series.** Conroe, TX: True Treasure Publications, 1971.

Powell, J. W., Director. **Fourth Annual Report of Bureau of Ethnology to the Secretary of the Smithsonian Institute, 1882-1883.** Washington D. C.: Government Printing Office, 1886.

Price, S. Goodale. **Ghosts of Golconda.** Deadwood, SD: Western Publishers, 1952.

Price, S. Goodale. **The Black Hills—Land of Legend.** Los Angeles: DeVorss & Company, Publishers, 1935.

Progulske, Donald R. **Yellow Ore, Yellow Hair, Yellow Pine.** A Photographic Study of a Century of Forest Ecology. Bulletin 616, Brookings, SD: Agricultural Experiment Station, South Dakota State University, 1974.

Rapid City, South Dakota, **Rapid City Journal,** Files.

Rapid City Public Library, South Dakota. Rapid City Scrapbooks (unpublished).

Record Book of the Deadwood Cemetery Association, 1878-1979. (unpublished), City Finance Office, Deadwood, South Dakota.

Reese, Montana Lisle, Supervisor for South Dakota Writer's Project. **Legends of the Mighty Sioux.** Sioux Falls, SD: Fantab, Inc., 1960.

Rezatto, Helen. **Mount Moriah, "Kill a Man—Start a Cemetery."** Aberdeen, SD: North Plains Press, 1980.

Robinson, Charles S. **Geology of Devils Tower.** Casper, WY: Mountain States Lithographing, (no date).

Robinson, Doane. **A History of the Dakota or Sioux Indians.** Minneapolis: Ross & Haines, 1904, 1967.

Rosen, Reverend Peter. **Pa-Ha-Sa-Pah or The Black Hills of South Dakota.** St. Louis: Nixon-Jones Printing Company, 1895.

Rowe, Ealsa L. **Rapid City in Retrospect—The Settlement That Knew It Was a City.** Rapid City, SD: Fenske Printing Inc., 1982.

Sandoz, Mari. **The Battle of the Little Big Horn.** Philadelphia—New York: J. B. Lippincott Company, 1966.

Sandoz, Mari. **Cheyenne Autumn.** New York: McGraw-Hill Book Company, Inc., 1953.

Sandoz, Mari. **Crazy Horse—The Strange Man of the Oglalas.** New York: Hastings House, 1942.

Schaefer, Jack. **Heroes Without Glory.** Boston: Houghton-Mifflin Company, 1965.

Senn, Edward L. **Deadwood Dick and Calamity Jane.** Deadwood, SD: The Author, 1939.

Senn, Edward L. **Preacher Smith—Martyr of the Cross.** Deadwood, SD: The Author, 1939.

Senn, Edward L. **Wild Bill Hickok—Prince of Pistoleers.** Deadwood, SD: The Author, 1939.

Seymour, Flora Warren. **Indian Agents of the Old Frontier.** London—New York: D. Appleton-Century Company, 1941.

Sneve, Virginia Driving Hawk. **The Dakota's Heritage.** Webster, SD: Reporter and Farmer, 1973.

A South Dakota Guide. Compiled by the Works Progress Administration. Pierre, SD: State Publishing Company, 1938.

South Dakota Historical Collections. II, VI, XIV. Compiled by the State Historical Society. Aberdeen, SD: News Printing Company, 1904, 1912.

Spearfish, South Dakota, **Queen City Mail,** Files.

Spring, Agnes Wright. **The Cheyenne and Black Hills Stage and Express Routes.** Lincoln: University of Nebraska Press, 1948.

Standing Bear, Luther. **My People The Sioux.** Cambridge, MA: Houghton-Mifflin, the Riverside Press, 1928.
Stevens, James. **Paul Bunyan.** Garden City, NY: Garden City Publishing Company by Alfred A. Knopf, 1925.
Stine, Lawrence. **A History of Theater and Theatrical Activities in Deadwood, South Dakota, 1876-1890.** A Thesis for the University of Iowa, February, 1956.
Sulentic, Joe. **Deadwood Gulch—The Last Chinatown.** Deadwood, SD, 1975.
Sundstrom, Jessie Y., ed. **Custer County History to 1976.** Compiled by Custer County Historical Society. Rapid City: Rapid City Printing, 1975.
Tallent, Annie D. **The Black Hills or The Last Hunting Grounds of the Dakotahs.** Second Edition, Sioux Falls, SD: Brevet Press, 1974.
Thompson, Frank. **The Thoen Stone**—A Saga of the Black Hills. Detroit: Harlo Press, 1966.
Van Nuys, Laura Bower. **The Family Band.** Lincoln: University of Nebraska Press, 1961.
Wind Cave National Park, South Dakota, National Park Service, U.S. Department of the Interior. (no date)
Wenzlaff, Gustav Gottlieb. **Sketches and Legends of the West.** Pierre, SD: Capital Supply, 1912.
Wheeler, Edward. **The Minor Sport.** New York: Beadle and Adams Pocket Library, 1895.

INDEX

(Listings omitted because of their frequent use are Deadwood, Deadwood Gulch, Sioux Indians, and the Great Spirit.)